DISCOVERING THE AMERICAN PAST

DISCOVERING THE AMERICAN PAST

A LOOK AT THE EVIDENCE

FOURTH EDITION

∽ VOLUME I: TO 1877 ∾

William Bruce Wheeler
University of Tennessee

Susan D. Becker
University of Tennessee

HOUGHTON MIFFLIN COMPANY   Boston   New York

Executive Editor: Patricia A. Coryell
Assistant Editor: Keith Mahoney
Senior Project Editor: Christina M. Horn
Senior Production/Design Coordinator: Jennifer Waddell
Manufacturing Manager: Florence Cadran
Marketing Manager: Sandra McGuire

Cover Design: Len Massiglia
Cover Image: *New York, From Brooklyn Heights.* Engraving by William James Bennett after watercolor by John William Hill, 1836. Miriam and Ira D. Wallach Division of Art, Prints Collection, The New York Public Library—Astor, Lenox and Tiden Foundations.

Printed in the U.S.A.

Library of Congress Catalog Card Number: 97-72559

ISBN: 0-395-87187-5

3 4 5 6 7 8 9-QF-01 00 99 98

CONTENTS

∽ **CHAPTER SIX** ∽

Assessing Historical Alternatives:
The Removal of the Cherokees, 1838–1839   114

∽ **CHAPTER SEVEN** ∽

Away from Home:
The Working Girls of Lowell   139

∽ CHAPTER EIGHT ∽

The "Peculiar Institution": Slaves Tell Their Own Story

Reminiscences and narratives from former slaves
Slave songs
*Excerpts from autobiographies of Frederick Douglass
 and Linda Brent (Harriet Jacobs)*

∽ CHAPTER NINE ∽

The Compromise of 1850: The Rhetoric of the Slavery Question

*Excerpts from four speeches given in the U.S. Senate
 regarding slavery and the Union*

PREFACE

Of all the books published on American history in 1997, one of the most interesting and controversial was Annette Gordon-Reed's *Thomas Jefferson and Sally Hemings: An American Controversy* (Charlottesville: University Press of Virginia, 1997). In the book, Gordon-Reed did not really attempt to answer the long-debated question of whether Thomas Jefferson did or did not have an extended, intimate relationship with Sally Hemings, one of his slaves. Instead, Gordon-Reed concentrated her attention on how a number of earlier historians who had examined this issue had—intentionally or unintentionally—distorted, misused, or occasionally even ignored key pieces of evidence. Gordon-Reed is an attorney and associate professor of law at New York University Law School. How, she asked, can we trust historians' accounts of the past unless we can see how they are using—or misusing—evidence?

Similarly, in the complex world in which we live, how can we rely on statements made by a president of the United States, any other world leader, the chairman of the Federal Reserve Board, a member of Congress, a radio talk show host, or a professor unless we are able to examine and analyze the available evidence to understand how it is being used? How can we ourselves learn to use evidence intelligently when we write a report, make a public address, or participate in a debate? The subject of this volume is American history, but the important skills of examination, analysis, and proper use of evidence are important to every person in every vocation.

In *Discovering the American Past: A Look at the Evidence,* we show students the importance of acquiring and sharpening these skills. Moreover, as they acquire or hone these skills, students generally discover that they enjoy "doing history," welcome the opportunity to become active learners, retain more historical knowledge, and are eager to solve a series of historical problems themselves rather than simply being told about the past. Unlike a source reader, this book prompts students actually to *analyze* a wide variety of authentic primary-source material, make inferences, and draw conclusions based on the available evidence, much in the same way that historians do.

As in previous editions, we try to expose students to the broad scope of the American experience by providing a mixture of types of historical problems and a balance among political, social, diplomatic, economic, intellectual, and cultural history. This wide variety of historical topics and events engages students' interest and rounds out their view of American history.

FORMAT OF THE BOOK

Historians are fully aware that everything that is preserved from the past can be used as evidence to solve historical problems. In that spirit, we have included as many different *types* of historical evidence as we could. Almost every chapter gives students the opportunity to work with a different type of evidence: works of art, first-person accounts, trial transcripts, statistics, maps, letters, charts, biographical sketches, court decisions, music lyrics, prescriptive literature, newspaper accounts, congressional debates, speeches, diaries, proclamations and laws, political cartoons, photographs, architectural plans, advertisements, posters, film reviews, fiction, memoirs, and oral interviews. In this book, then, we have created a kind of historical sampler that we believe will help students learn the methods and skills historians use, as well as help them learn historical content.

Each type of historical evidence is combined with an introduction to the appropriate methodology in an effort to teach students a wide variety of research skills. As much as possible, we have tried to let the evidence speak for itself and have avoided leading students to one particular interpretation or another. This approach is effective in many different classroom situations, including seminars, small classes, discussion sections, and large lecture classes. Indeed, we have found that the previous editions of *Discovering the American Past* have proven themselves equally stimulating and effective in very large classes as well as very small ones. An Instructor's Resource Manual that accompanies the book offers numerous suggestions on how *Discovering the American Past* can be used effectively in large classroom situations.

Each chapter is divided into six parts: The Problem, Background, The Method, The Evidence, Questions to Consider, and Epilogue. Each of the parts relates to or builds upon the others, creating a uniquely integrated chapter structure that helps guide the reader through the analytical process. "The Problem" section begins with a brief discussion of the central issues of the chapter and then states the questions students will explore. A "Background" section follows, designed to help students understand the historical context of the problem. The section called "The Method" gives students suggestions for studying and analyzing the evidence. "The Evidence" section is the heart of the chapter, providing a variety of primary source material on the particular historical event or issue described in the chapter's "Problem" section. The section called "Questions to Consider" focuses students' attention on specific evidence and on linkages among different evidence material. The "Epilogue" section gives the aftermath or the historical outcome of the evidence—what happened to the people involved, who won the election, the results of a debate, and so on.

CHANGES IN THE FOURTH EDITION

In response to student and faculty reactions, we have made significant alterations in the content of this edition. There are six new chapters, three in Volume I and three in Volume II.

In Volume I, Chapter 6 focuses on the removal of the Cherokees, using contemporary letters, speeches, essays, a message to Congress, and a petition to assess the historical alternatives that were available to President Andrew Jackson. Chapter 9 examines the rhetoric of the slavery question through a close analysis of excerpts from the U.S. Senate debates on the Compromise of 1850. The final new chapter in the first volume, Chapter 11, considers the difficult question of why President Andrew Johnson allowed so many former Confederates to vote while at the same time opposing suffrage for freedmen. A variety of sources, including letters, proclamations, and interviews, helps students to explain why Johnson acted in the way he did.

The three new chapters in Volume II begin with Chapter 8 and the controversial events surrounding the USS *Greer* and the coming of World War II. In this chapter, students are asked to determine what actually happened in the North Atlantic on that day and then to analyze President Franklin Roosevelt's actions in relation to public opinion. To answer these questions, students need to sort through and arrange evidence consisting of public opinion polls, news reports, and speeches. Our new focus in the postwar period is on African American civil rights and *Brown v. Board of Education of Topeka, Kansas* (1954). Through *amicus curiae* briefs, oral arguments of attorneys for both sides, and excerpts from the U.S. Supreme Court decision, students are asked to explain the reasoning that led to the reversal of the "separate but equal" doctrine in education. Lastly, Chapter 11 requires students to understand recent major demographic trends and to consider the changing meanings of the American ideal of equality as illustrated in a variety of evidence. Because of its diverse population and recent referendum on state affirmative action legislation, California provides a kind of "test case" that students can use to analyze current events.

INSTRUCTOR'S RESOURCE MANUAL

An Instructor's Resource Manual suggests ways that might be useful in guiding students through the evidence, provides answers to questions students often ask, and offers a variety of methods in which the students' learning may be evaluated. The manual also clarifies our teaching and learning objectives for each chapter. Indeed, many useful ideas have come from instructors who have used the first three editions of this book. For this edition, we have also updated the bibliographic suggestions for further reading in each chapter.

ACKNOWLEDGMENTS

We would like to thank all the students and instructors who have helped us in developing and refining our ideas. In addition to our colleagues across the United States, we would like to thank especially our colleagues at the University of Tennessee who offered suggestions and read chapter drafts. Stephen Ash, John R. Finger, Charles W. Johnson, and Jonathan G. Utley were particularly helpful. Jennifer Breeden, Penny Hamilton, and Kim Harrison helped in preparing the manuscript. At Houghton Mifflin, we are indebted to Keith Mahoney and Christina Horn for their editorial assistance. Finally, colleagues at other institutions who reviewed chapter drafts made significant contributions to this edition, and we would like to thank them for their generosity, both in time and in helpful ideas and specific suggestions:

Harriet Hyman Alonso, *Fitchburg State College*
Elizabeth Ansnes, *San Jose State University*
Regina Lee Blaszczyk, *Boston University*
Bill Cecil-Fronsman, *Washburn University*
Jonathan M. Chu, *University of Massachusetts—Boston*

Claudia Clark, *Central Michigan University*

Bruce Cohen, *Worcester State College*

Kari Frederickson, *University of Central Florida*

Connie Jones, *Tidewater Community College*

Gaylen Lewis, *Bakersfield College*

Dane Morrison, *Salem State College*

Robert C. Pierce, *Foothill College*

Kim Risedorph, *Nebraska Wesleyan University*

Susan Sessions Rugh, *Brigham Young University*

Margaret A. Spratt, *California University of Pennsylvania*

Lillian Taiz, *California State University, Los Angeles*

William Tanner, *Humboldt State University*

Tom Taylor, *Wittenberg University*

Bruce Way, *Tiffin University*

Lynn Y. Weiner, *Roosevelt University*

As with our three previous editions, we dedicate these volumes to all our colleagues who seek to offer a challenging and stimulating academic experience to their students, and to those students themselves, who make all our work worthwhile.

W. B. W.
S. D. B.

CHAPTER 1

FIRST ENCOUNTERS:
THE CONFRONTATION BETWEEN
CORTÉS AND MONTEZUMA
(1519–1521)

⧫ THE PROBLEM ⧫

In 1492, Christopher Columbus became the first European to meet Indians[1] and record his observations. In the next few years, Europeans became increasingly fascinated with the New World and its inhabitants. Explorers' accounts were published and widely circulated, as were artistic renderings of the Indians by European artists, many of whom had never traveled to the New World or met a single Indian.

In turn, Native Americans doubtless recorded their own impressions of Europeans. Since most Indian cultures had not developed forms of writing, these impressions were preserved orally, largely through stories and songs. In central Mexico, however, the Aztecs and other peoples did record their observations of Europeans in writing and art. And although the Spanish *conquistadores* (conquerors) attempted to destroy all such records, a few of the written and artistic renderings did survive to tell the Indians' side of the story of the first encounters.[2]

1. Although Europeans quickly realized that the name Columbus conferred on Native Americans was inaccurate, the word *Indian* continued to be used. Alternative names have never replaced it.

2. The major repositories for these written and artistic works are museums in Paris, Florence, and Mexico City.

CHAPTER 1

FIRST
ENCOUNTERS:
THE
CONFRONTATION
BETWEEN
CORTÉS AND
MONTEZUMA
(1519–1521)

There is little doubt that the impressions created by these written and artistic works fostered perceptions that made Indian-white relations confusing, difficult, and ultimately tragic. The European hunger for land and treasure may have made the tragedies that followed almost inevitable, and yet Europeans' early perceptions of Indians were an important factor in how explorers and early colonists dealt with Native American peoples and, in the end, subdued them. At the same time, the early impressions that Indians gained of Europeans (whether passed down orally or by other means) offered to many Native Americans a clear message concerning how they should respond to white encroachment.

In this chapter, you will be concentrating on the conquest of Mexico by Hernando Cortés, which took place between 1519 and 1521. In many ways, that confrontation was typical of the "first encounters" between Europeans and Native Americans. You will be examining and analyzing two separate sets of evidence: (1) selections written by Cortés to King Charles V of Spain, together with some artistic representations of Native Americans by European artists, and (2) selected written and artistic impressions of Cortés and his *conquistadores* by Aztecs and other Native Americans of central Mexico created within a few years of the events they described. Your task is twofold. First, you must use written and artistic accounts to determine the impressions that each side created of the other. Second, you must reach some conclusions about how those impressions (whether totally accurate or inaccurate) might have influenced how Europeans and early colonists dealt with Native Americans and how Native Americans dealt with them.

Before you begin, we would like to issue a note of caution. When dealing with the evidence provided by European conquerors such as Cortés or by European artists, you will *not* be trying to determine what the Native Americans the Europeans encountered were really like, but only what Cortés and selected European artists perceived them to be like. To find out what the diverse peoples collectively known as Indians were really like, you would have to consult the works of archaeologists, cultural anthropologists, and cultural geographers. And yet, if we want to determine how Europeans perceived Indians, Cortés's letters and selected European works of art can provide excellent clues.

This chapter also will give you a revealing look at how historical evidence is created and how the availability—and unavailability—of that evidence influences the ways in which a past event or person is depicted by historians. For example, Cortés and his soldiers attempted to destroy as many of the Native American historical records as they could, for obvious reasons. But some pieces of that evidence survived. Without those pieces of evidence, historians' accounts of the "first encounters" very likely would be dramatically different.

☙ BACKGROUND ❧

By the time Europeans first encountered the various peoples they collectively called Indians, Native Americans had inhabited the Western Hemisphere for approximately 20,000 to 40,000 years.[3] Although there is considerable disagreement about when these people first appeared in the Americas, it is reasonable to assume that they first migrated to the Western Hemisphere sometime in the middle of the Pleistocene Age. During that period (roughly from 75,000 to 8000 B.C.), huge glaciers covered a large portion of North America, the ice cap extending southward to the approximate present border of the United States and Canada. These glaciers, which in some places were more than 9,000 feet thick, interrupted the water cycle because moisture falling as rain or snow was caught by the glaciers and frozen and was thus prevented from draining back into the seas or evaporating into the atmosphere.

This process lowered ocean levels 250 to 300 feet, exposing a natural land bridge spanning the Bering Strait (between present-day Alaska and the former Soviet Union)[4] across which people from Asia could easily migrate,

probably in search of game. It is almost certain that various peoples from Asia did exactly that and then followed an ice-free corridor along the base of the Rocky Mountains southward into the more temperate areas of the American Southwest (which, because of the glaciers, were wetter, cooler, and contained large lakes and forests) and then either eastward into other areas of North America or even farther southward into Central and South America. These migrations took thousands of years, and some Indian peoples were still moving when Europeans first encountered them.

About 8000 B.C., the glacial cap began to retreat fairly rapidly, raising ocean levels to approximately their present-day levels and cutting off further migration from Asia, thus isolating America's first human inhabitants from other peoples for thousands of years. This isolation was almost surely the cause of the inhabitants' extraordinarily high susceptibility to the diseases that Europeans later brought with them, such as measles, tuberculosis, and smallpox, to which the peoples of other continents had built up natural resistance. The glacial retreat also caused large portions of the American Southwest to become hot and arid, thus scattering Indian peoples in almost all directions. Nevertheless, for thousands of years a strong oral tradition enabled Indians to preserve stories of their origins and subsequent isolation. Almost all Indian peoples retained accounts of a long migration from the west and a flood.

3. Other estimates run as high as 70,000 years. Whatever the case, it is almost certain that Indians were not native to the Western Hemisphere because no subhuman remains have ever been found.

4. Today the Bering Strait is only 180 feet deep. Thus a lowering of ocean levels 250 to 300 feet would have exposed a considerable land bridge between Asia and North America.

CHAPTER 1

FIRST
ENCOUNTERS:
THE
CONFRONTATION
BETWEEN
CORTÉS AND
MONTEZUMA
(1519–1521)

The original inhabitants of the Western Hemisphere obtained their food principally by hunting and gathering, killing mammoths, huge bison, deer, elk, antelope, camels, horses, and other game with stone weapons and picking wild fruits and grasses. Beginning about 5000 B.C., however, Indians in present-day Mexico began practicing agriculture. By the time Europeans arrived, most Indians were domesticating plants and raising crops, although their levels of agricultural sophistication were extremely diverse.

The development of agriculture (which occurred about the same time in Europe and the Americas) profoundly affected Indian life. Those peoples who adopted agriculture abandoned their nomadic ways and lived in settled villages (some of the Central American ones became magnificent cities). This more sedentary life permitted them to erect permanent housing, create and preserve pottery and art, and establish more complex political and social institutions. Agriculture also led to a sexual division of labor, with women planting, raising, and harvesting crops and men hunting to supplement their villages' diets with game. With more and better food, most likely Indian populations grew more rapidly, thus furthering the need for more complex political and social structures. The development of agriculture also affected these peoples' religious beliefs and ceremonies, increasing the homage to sun and rain gods who could bring forth good harvests. Contact with other Indian peoples led to trading, a practice with which Indians were quite familiar by the time of European intrusion.

Those Indian cultures that made the transition from food gathering to food producing often attained an impressive degree of economic, political, social, and technological sophistication. In Central America, the Mayas of present-day Mexico and Guatemala built great cities, fashioned elaborate gold and silver jewelry, devised a form of writing, were proficient in mathematics and astronomy, and constructed a calendar that could predict solar eclipses and was more accurate than any system in use in Europe at the time. The conquerors of the Mayas, the Aztecs, built on the achievements of their predecessors, extending their political and economic power chiefly by subjugating other Indian peoples. By the time Cortés and his army of 400 men, 16 horses, and a few cannon landed at Vera Cruz in 1519, the Aztecs had constructed the magnificent city of Tenochtitlán (the site of present-day Mexico City), which rivaled European cities in both size (approximately 300,000 people) and splendor.

Tenochtitlán contained magnificent pyramids and public buildings, a fresh water supply brought to the city by complex engineering, causeways that connected the island city to other islands and the mainland, numerous skilled craftsmen, and even a compulsory education system for all male children (no state in the United States would have such a system for more than 300 years). Raw materials and treasure flowed into Tenochtitlán from all over the Aztec empire, which stretched from the Pacific Ocean to the Gulf of Mexico and from central Mexico to present-day Guatemala. Little wonder that the *conquistadores* with Hernando Cortés were awed and enchanted when they saw it.

In many ways, Cortés was the typical Spanish *conquistador*. Born in 1485 to a respected but poor family (his father had been a career military officer but never rose above the rank of captain), Cortés spent two unsuccessful years studying for the law. Abandoning that goal, he became a soldier and was determined to gain fame and fortune through a military career. In 1504 (when he was but nineteen years old), he boarded a ship bound for the Spanish possessions in the New World. After fourteen years of military service, Cortés finally got his big break in 1518, when he was chosen to command a new armada whose purpose was to conquer Mexico. Earlier, unsuccessful expeditions had given some indications of gold in Mexico, and Cortés was sent to find it (as well as to try to locate members of the earlier expeditions who might still be alive). Since Cortés himself financed a good portion of the new armada (he had to borrow money to do so), he had the opportunity to realize his dreams of wealth if his men found treasure. When Cortés landed at Vera Cruz, he was thirty-four years old.

❦ THE METHOD ❦

In this chapter, you will be working with two distinct types of evidence: (1) written accounts and (2) artistic representations. In addition, the evidence has been divided into two sets: (1) Hernando Cortés's and European artists' perceptions of Indians and (2) Indians' written and artistic accounts of Cortés's invasion of the Aztec capital, Tenochtitlán (1519–1521). As noted previously, Cortés's account comes from letters he wrote to the Spanish king soon after the events he described took place. As for the European artists, some of them undoubtedly used their active imaginations to construct their images of Indians, whereas others relied on explorers' accounts or word-of-mouth reports from those who had seen Native Americans whom the explorers had brought to Europe.

The Indians' accounts of Europeans pose something of a problem. We cannot be sure that all (or any) of the written or artistic representations were done by eyewitnesses to the events they describe. We do know, however, that most of the written selections were completed by 1528 (only seven years after Cortés's conquest of Tenochtitlán) and that all the written and artistic representations were created within the normal lifetimes of eyewitnesses. Therefore, if the writers and artists themselves were not eyewitnesses, they doubtless knew of eyewitnesses who could have reported to them what they saw. Thanks to Roman Catholic missionaries who saved

CHAPTER 1

FIRST
ENCOUNTERS:
THE
CONFRONTATION
BETWEEN
CORTÉS AND
MONTEZUMA
(1519–1521)

these accounts from the *conquistadores,* we have what we can assume are firsthand reactions by Native Americans to European intruders.

Even so, the Native American accounts of Cortés's conquest pose some problems for historians. In addition to the nightmare that Native American place and people names present to non-Indians who attempt to pronounce them, it is not always clear in these accounts precisely what is being described. For example, remember that the Native Americans at first believed that Cortés and his party were some form of gods ("As for their food, it is like human food"), which explains their sacrifices before Cortés, their offering of gifts, and their preparations to "celebrate their god's fiesta." Precisely when they abandoned this notion is unclear, for at the same time that they were conducting their celebration, they simultaneously posted guards at the Eagle Gate. It will take some care and thought to determine exactly what was taking place.

Also, occasionally historical evidence can be contradictory. For instance, Cortés claimed that he attacked the Aztecs only after learning that they were plotting to kill him and his men. Yet the Native American account suggests that no such plot existed and that Cortés's attack was unprovoked. Can you determine from the accounts which explanation is the more nearly correct? Read carefully through both Cortés's and the Native American accounts, and you will see that determining what actually happened is not so difficult as it first appears to be. Also, you will see that both Cortés and the Native American

chroniclers occasionally describe the same events, which can make for some fascinating comparisons.

The two types of evidence in this chapter (written accounts and artistic representations) must be dealt with differently. As you read the written accounts (whether by Cortés or by Native Americans), think of some adjectives that, after reading these accounts, Europeans who read Cortés's letters (some of which were published and widely distributed) might have used to describe Indians. For the Native American written accounts, imagine what adjectives Native Americans who shared the accounts might have used to describe Europeans. How do those adjectives present a collective image of Indians? Of Europeans? How do the stories each author tells reinforce that image? As you read each written account, make a list of adjectives for each set of evidence, then combine them to form a collective image. Be willing to read between the lines. Sometimes, for example, Cortés may simply have been trying to explain a specific incident or practice of the Indians. Yet, intentionally or unintentionally, he was creating an image in the minds of readers. Be equally cautious and sensitive when reading the Indians' written accounts.

The second type of evidence, artistic representations, is quite different from the written accounts. If you think of art as words made into pictures, you will see that you can approach this type of evidence as you did the written accounts. Study each picture carefully, looking especially for how Native Americans or Europeans are portrayed. How are they portrayed physically? How is their supposed nature or character portrayed in their behavior in the works of art? Again, as with the written accounts, create a list of adjectives and deduce the images Europeans would have had of Indians and the images Indians would have had of Europeans. As you analyze the evidence in this chapter, keep two central questions in mind: (1) What images do the written and artistic accounts create of Native Americans and of Europeans? (2) How might those images (or impressions) have influenced how European explorers and early colonists dealt with Native Americans and how Native Americans dealt with them?

 THE EVIDENCE

EUROPEAN ACCOUNTS

Source 1 from Francis Augustus MacNutt, *Fernando Cortés: His Five Letters of Relation to the Emperor Charles V* (Cleveland: Arthur H. Clark Co., 1908), Vol. I, pp. 161–166, 211–216.

1. Selections from Cortés's First Letter to Charles I of Spain, July 10, 1519.

. . . According to our judgment, it is credible that there is everything in this country which existed in that from whence Solomon is said to have brought the gold for the Temple, but, as we have been here so short a time, we have not been able to see more than the distance of five leagues inland, and about ten or twelve leagues of the coast length on each side, which we have explored since we landed; although from the sea it must be more, and we saw much more while sailing.

The people who inhabit this country, from the Island of Cozumel, and the Cape of Yucatan to the place where we now are, are a people of middle size, with bodies and features well proportioned, except that in each province their customs differ, some piercing the ears, and putting large and ugly objects in them, and others piercing the nostrils down to the mouth, and putting in large round stones like mirrors, and others piercing their under lips down as far as their gums, and hanging from them large round stones, or pieces of gold, so weighty that they pull down the nether lip, and make it appear very deformed. The clothing which they wear is like long veils, very curiously worked. The men wear breech-cloths about their bodies, and large mantles, very thin, and painted in the style of Moorish draperies. The women of the ordinary people wear, from their waists to their feet, clothes also very much painted, some covering their breasts and leaving the rest of

CHAPTER 1

FIRST
ENCOUNTERS:
THE
CONFRONTATION
BETWEEN
CORTÉS AND
MONTEZUMA
(1519–1521)

the body uncovered. The superior women, however, wear very thin shirts of cotton, worked and made in the style of *rochets* [blouses with long, straight sleeves]. Their food is maize and grain, as in the other Islands, and *potuyuca,* as they eat it in the Island of Cuba, and they eat it broiled, since they do not make bread of it; and they have their fishing, and hunting, and they roast many chickens, like those of the Tierra Firma, which are as large as peacocks.[5]

There are some large towns well laid out, the houses being of stone, and mortar when they have it. The apartments are small, low, and in the Moorish style, and, when they cannot find stone, they make them of adobes, whitewashing them, and the roof is of straw. Some of the houses of the principal people are very cool, and have many apartments, for we have seen more than five courts in one house, and the apartments very well distributed, each principal department of service being separate. Within them they have their wells and reservoirs for water, and rooms for the slaves and dependents, of whom they have many. Each of these chiefs has at the entrance of his house, but outside of it, a large court-yard, and in some there are two and three and four very high buildings, with steps leading up to them, and they are very well built; and in them they have their mosques and prayer places, and very broad galleries on all sides, and there they keep the idols which they worship, some being of stone, some of gold, and some of wood, and they honour and serve them in such wise, and with so many ceremonies, that much paper would be required to give Your Royal Highnesses an entire and exact description of all of them. These houses and mosques,[6] wherever they exist, are the largest and best built in the town, and they keep them very well adorned, decorated with feather-work and well-woven stuffs, and with all manner of ornaments. Every day, before they undertake any work, they burn incense in the said mosques, and sometimes they sacrifice their own persons, some cutting their tongues and others their ears, and some hacking the body with knives; and they offer up to their idols all the blood which flows, sprinkling it on all sides of those mosques, at other times throwing it up towards the heavens, and practising many other kinds of ceremonies, so that they undertake nothing without first offering sacrifice there.

They have another custom, horrible, and abominable, and deserving punishment, and which we have never before seen in any other place, and it is this, that, as often as they have anything to ask of their idols, in order that their petition may be more acceptable, they take many boys or girls, and

5. These were turkeys, which were unknown in Europe.
6. Temples.

even grown men and women, and in the presence of those idols they open their breasts, while they are alive, and take out the hearts and entrails, and burn the said entrails and hearts before the idols, offering that smoke in sacrifice to them. Some of us who have seen this say that it is the most terrible and frightful thing to behold that has ever been seen. So frequently, and so often do these Indians do this, according to our information, and partly by what we have seen in the short time we are in this country, that no year passes in which they do not kill and sacrifice fifty souls in each mosque; and this is practised, and held as customary, from the Isle of Cozumel to the country in which we are now settled. Your Majesties may rest assured that, according to the size of the land, which to us seems very considerable, and the many mosques which they have, there is no year, as far as we have until now discovered and seen, when they do not kill and sacrifice in this manner some three or four thousand souls. Now let Your Royal Highnesses consider if they ought not to prevent so great an evil and crime, and certainly God, Our Lord, will be well pleased, if, through the command of Your Royal Highnesses, these peoples should be initiated and instructed in our Very Holy Catholic Faith, and the devotion, faith, and hope, which they have in their idols, be transferred to the Divine Omnipotence of God; because it is certain, that, if they served God with the same faith, and fervour, and diligence, they would surely work miracles.

It should be believed, that it is not without cause that God, Our Lord, has permitted that these parts should be discovered in the name of Your Royal Highnesses, so that this fruit and merit before God should be enjoyed by Your Majesties, of having instructed these barbarian people, and brought them through your commands to the True Faith. As far as we are able to know them, we believe that, if there were interpreters and persons who could make them understand the truth of the Faith, and their error, many, and perhaps all, would shortly quit the errors which they hold, and come to the true knowledge; because they live civilly and reasonably, better than any of the other peoples found in these parts.

To endeavour to give to Your Majesties all the particulars about this country and its people, might occasion some errors in the account, because much of it we have not seen, and only know it through information given us by the natives; therefore we do not undertake to give more than what may be accepted by Your Highnesses as true. Your Majesties may, if you deem proper, give this account as true to Our Very Holy Father, in order that diligence and good system may be used in effecting the conversion of these people, because it is hoped that great fruit and much good may be obtained; also that His Holiness may approve and allow that the wicked and rebellious, being first admonished, may be punished and chastised as

CHAPTER 1

FIRST
ENCOUNTERS:
THE
CONFRONTATION
BETWEEN
CORTÉS AND
MONTEZUMA
(1519–1521)

enemies of Our Holy Catholic Faith, which will be an occasion of punishment and fear to those who may be reluctant in receiving knowledge of the Truth; thereby, that the great evils and injuries they practise in the service of the Devil, will be forsaken. Because, besides what we have just related to Your Majesties about the men, and women, and children, whom they kill and offer in their sacrifices, we have learned, and been positively informed, that they are all sodomites,[7] and given to that abominable sin. In all this, we beseech Your Majesties to order such measures taken as are most profitable to the service of God, and to that of Your Royal Highnesses, and so that we who are here in your service may also be favoured and recompensed. . . .

. . . Along the road we encountered many signs, such as the natives of this province had foretold us, for we found the high road blocked up, and another opened, and some pits, although not many, and some of the city streets were closed, and many stones were piled on the house tops. They thus obliged us to be cautious, and on our guard.

I found there certain messengers from Montezuma, who came to speak with those others who were with me, but to me they said nothing, because, in order to inform their master, they had come to learn what those who were with me had done and agreed with me. These latter messengers departed, therefore, as soon as they had spoken with the first, and even the chief of those who had formerly been with me also left.

During the three days which I remained there I was ill provided for, and every day was worse, and the lords and chiefs of the city came rarely to see and speak to me. I was somewhat perplexed by this, but the interpreter whom I have, an Indian woman of this country whom I obtained in Putunchan, the great river I have already mentioned in the first letter to Your Majesty, was told by another woman native of this city, that many of Montezuma's people had gathered close by, and that those of the city had sent away their wives, and children, and all their goods, intending to fall upon us and kill us all; and that, if she wished to escape, she should go with her, as she would hide her. The female interpreter told it to that Geronimo de Aguilar, the interpreter whom I obtained in Yucatan, and of whom I have written to Your Highness, who reported it to me. I captured one of the natives of the said city, who was walking about there, and took him secretly apart so that no one saw it, and questioned him; and he confirmed all that the Indian woman and the natives of Tascaltecal had told me. As well on account of this information as from the signs I had observed, I determined

7. People who practice anal or oral copulation with members of the opposite (or same) gender or who have sex with animals.

to anticipate them, rather than be surprised, so I had some of the lords of the city called, saying that I wished to speak with them, and I shut them in a chamber by themselves. In the meantime I had our people prepared, so that, at the firing of a musket, they should fall on a crowd of Indians who were near to our quarters, and many others who were inside them. It was done in this wise, that, after I had taken these lords, and left them bound in the chamber, I mounted a horse, and ordered the musket to be fired, and we did such execution that, in two hours, more than three thousand persons had perished.

In order that Your Majesty may see how well prepared they were, before I went out of our quarters, they had occupied all the streets, and stationed all their men, but, as we took them by surprise, they were easily overcome, especially as the chiefs were wanting, for I had already taken them prisoners. I ordered fire to be set to some towers and strong houses, where they defended themselves, and assaulted us; and thus I scoured the city fighting during five hours, leaving our dwelling place which was very strong, well guarded, until I had forced all the people out of the city at various points, in which those five thousand natives of Tascaltecal and the four hundred of Cempoal gave me good assistance. . . .

CHAPTER 1

FIRST
ENCOUNTERS:
THE
CONFRONTATION
BETWEEN
CORTÉS AND
MONTEZUMA
(1519–1521)

Sources 2 through 5 from Hugh Honor, *The European Vision of America* (Cleveland: Cleveland Museum of Art, 1975), plates 3, 8, 64, 65. Source 2 photo: The British Library.

2. German Woodcut, 1509.

3. Portuguese Oil on Panel, 1550.

4. German Engraving, 1590.

CHAPTER 1

FIRST
ENCOUNTERS:
THE
CONFRONTATION
BETWEEN
CORTÉS AND
MONTEZUMA
(1519–1521)

Source 5: Library of Congress/Rare Book Division.

5. German Engraving, 1591.

Sources 6 and 7 from Stefan Lorant, ed., *The New World: The First Pictures of America* (New York: Duell, Sloan & Pearce, 1946), pp. 51, 119. Photos: Metropolitan Museum of Art.

6. German Engraving, 1591.

7. German Engraving, 1591.

Sources 8 and 9 from Honor, *The European Vision of America,* plates 85, 91. Photos: New York Historical Society.

8. French Engraving, 1575.

CHAPTER 1

FIRST
ENCOUNTERS:
THE
CONFRONTATION
BETWEEN
CORTÉS AND
MONTEZUMA
(1519–1521)

9. French Engraving, 1579–1600.

AMERICA,

NATIVE AMERICAN ACCOUNTS

Source 10 from Miguel Leon-Portilla, ed., *The Broken Spears: The Aztec Account of the Conquest of Mexico,* trans. Lysander Kemp (Boston: Beacon Press, 1962), pp. viii–ix, 30, 92–93, 128–144.

10. Cortés's Conquest of Tenochtitlán.

Year 1-Canestalk. The Spaniards came to the palace at Tlayacac. When the Captain[8] arrived at the palace, Motecuhzoma[9] sent the Cuetlaxteca[10] to greet him and to bring him two suns as gifts. One of these suns was made of the yellow metal, the other of the white.[11] The Cuetlaxteca also brought him a mirror to be hung on his person, a gold collar, a great gold pitcher, fans and ornaments of quetzal feathers[12] and a shield inlaid with mother-of-pearl.

The envoys made sacrifices in front of the Captain. At this, he grew very angry. When they offered him blood in an "eagle dish," he shouted at the man who offered it and struck him with his sword. The envoys departed at once. . . .

When the sacrifice was finished, the messengers reported to the king. They told him how they had made the journey, and what they had seen, and what food the strangers ate. Motecuhzoma was astonished and terrified by their report, and the description of the strangers' food astonished him above all else.

He was also terrified to learn how the cannon roared, how its noise resounded, how it caused one to faint and grow deaf. The messengers told him: "A thing like a ball of stone comes out of its entrails: it comes out shooting sparks and raining fire. The smoke that comes out with it has a pestilent odor, like that of rotten mud. This odor penetrates even to the brain and causes the greatest discomfort. If the cannon is aimed against a mountain, the mountain splits and cracks open. If it is aimed against a tree, it shatters the tree into splinters. This is a most unnatural sight, as if the tree had exploded from within."

The messengers also said: "Their trappings and arms are all made of iron. They dress in iron and wear iron casques[13] on their heads. Their swords are iron; their bows are iron; their shields are iron; their spears are iron.

8. Cortés.
9. Montezuma.
10. The Cuetlaxteca were an Indian people allied with the Aztecs.
11. Gold and silver.
12. Quetzal: A type of bird native to Central America; the male has tail feathers up to 2 feet in length.
13. Helmets.

CHAPT

FIRST
ENCOL
THE
CONFF
BETWF
CORTÉ
MONTI
(1519–1

CHAPTER 1

FIRST
ENCOUNTERS:
THE
CONFRONTATION
BETWEEN
CORTÉS AND
MONTEZUMA
(1519–1521)

The illness was so dreadful that no one could walk or move. The sick were so utterly helpless that they could only lie on their beds like corpses, unable to move their limbs or even their heads. They could not lie face down or roll from one side to the other. If they did move their bodies, they screamed with pain.

A great many died from this plague, and many others died of hunger. They could not get up to search for food, and everyone else was too sick to care for them, so they starved to death in their beds.[17]

Some people came down with a milder form of the disease; they suffered less than the others and made a good recovery. But they could not escape entirely. Their looks were ravaged, for wherever a sore broke out, it gouged an ugly pockmark in the skin. And a few of the survivors were left completely blind. . . .

[*Here the account describes Cortés's siege of Tenochtitlán, a siege that was successful due in part to bickering among the Aztecs themselves (in which several leaders were put to death), in part to the panic caused by Cortés's cannon, and in part to a number of nearby Indian peoples whom the Aztecs had dominated turning on their former masters and supporting the Spanish. Of course, the devastating smallpox epidemic and general starvation due to the siege also played important roles.*]

Broken spears lie in the roads;
we have torn our hair in our grief.
The houses are roofless now, and their walls
are red with blood.

Worms are swarming in the streets and plazas,
and the walls are splattered with gore.
The water has turned red, as if it were dyed,
and when we drink it,
it has the taste of brine.

We have pounded our hands in despair
against the adobe walls,
for our inheritance, our city, is lost and dead.
The shields of our warriors were its defense,
but they could not save it.

We have chewed dry twigs and salt grasses;
we have filled our mouths with dust and bits of adobe;
we have eaten lizards, rats and worms. . . .

---

17. The epidemic probably was smallpox.

Cuauhtemoc was taken to Cortes along with three other princes. The Captain was accompanied by Pedro de Alvarado and La Malinche.

When the princes were made captives, the people began to leave, searching for a place to stay. Everyone was in tatters, and the women's thighs were almost naked. The Christians searched all the refugees. They even opened the women's skirts and blouses and felt everywhere: their ears, their breasts, their hair. Our people scattered in all directions. They went to neighboring villages and huddled in corners in the houses of strangers.

The city was conquered in the year 3-House. The date on which we departed was the day 1-Serpent in the ninth month. . . .

[*The account next describes Cortés's torture of the remaining Aztec leaders in an attempt to find where the Aztecs' treasures were hidden.*]

When the envoys from Tlatelolco had departed, the leaders of Tenochtitlan were brought before the Captain, who wished to make them talk. This was when Cuauhtemoc's feet were burned. They brought him in at daybreak and tied him to a stake.

They found the gold in Cuitlahuactonco, in the house of a chief named Itzpotonqui. As soon as they had seized it, they brought our princes—all of them bound—to Coyoacan.

About this same time, the priest in charge of the temple of Huitzilopochtli was put to death. The Spaniards had tried to learn from him where the god's finery and that of the high priests was kept. Later they were informed that it was being guarded by certain chiefs in Cuauhchichilco and Xaltocan. They seized it and then hanged two of the chiefs in the middle of the Mazatlan road. . . .

They hanged Macuilxochitl, the king of Huitzilopochco, in Coyoacan. They also hanged Pizotzin, the king of Culhuacan. And they fed the Keeper of the Black House, along with several others, to their dogs.

And three wise men of Ehecatl, from Tezcoco, were devoured by the dogs. They had come only to surrender; no one brought them or sent them there. They arrived bearing their painted sheets of paper. There were four of them, and only one escaped; the other three were overtaken, there in Coyoacan. . . .

CHAPTER 1

FIRST
ENCOUNTERS:
THE
CONFRONTATION
BETWEEN
CORTÉS AND
MONTEZUMA
(1519–1521)

Sources 11 through 14 are present-day adaptations of Aztec artistic works that were created not long after the events they depict took place. The modern adaptations can be found in Leon-Portilla, *The Broken Spears,* pp. 21, 82, 75, 143. Illustrations by Alberto Beltran.

11. Native Americans Greet Cortés and His Men.

12. Spanish Response to Native American Greeting.

13. The Massacre at the Fiesta.

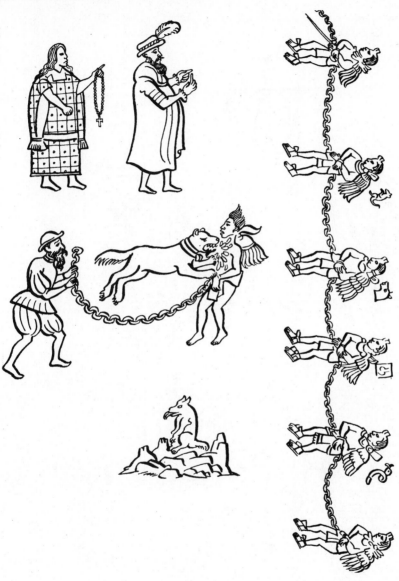

CHAPTER 1

FIRST
ENCOUNTERS:
THE
CONFRONTATION
BETWEEN
CORTÉS AND
MONTEZUMA
(1519–1521)

14. Fate of the Wise Men of Ehecatl.

∽ QUESTIONS TO CONSIDER ∾

As you read Cortés's account (Source 1), it helps to look for five factors:

1. Physical appearance (bodies, hair, clothing, jewelry, and so on). This description can provide important clues about Cortés's attitude toward the Indians he confronted.
2. Nature or character (childlike, bellicose, cunning, honest, intellectual, lazy, and so on). Be sure to note the examples Cortés used to provide his analysis of the Indians' nature or character.
3. Political, social, and religious practices (behavior of women, ceremonies, eating habits, government, and so on). Descriptions of these practices can provide excellent insight into the explorer's general perception of the Indians he encountered. Be especially sensitive to Cortés's use of descriptive adjectives.
4. Overall impression of the Indians. What was Cortés's collective image or impression?
5. What did Cortés think should be done with the Indians?

Once you have analyzed Cortés's account using points 1 through 4, you should be able to explain how, based on his overall impression of the Indians, he thought the Indians should be dealt with (point 5). Sometimes Cortés comes right out and tells you, but in other cases you will have to use a little imagination. Ask yourself the following question: If I had been living in Spain in 1522 and read Cortés's account, what would my perception of

Native Americans have been? Based on that perception, how would I have thought those peoples should be dealt with?

You can handle the artistic representations (Sources 2 through 9) in the same way. Each artist tried to convey his notion of the Indians' nature or character. Some of these impressions are obvious, but others are less so. Think of the art as words made into pictures. How are the Indians portrayed? What are they doing? How are they dealing with Europeans? On the basis of these artistic representations, decide how the various artists believed Indians should be dealt with. For example, the Indian woman with child in Source 4 depicts Native Americans in a particular way. What is it? On the basis of this depiction, what would you say was the artist's perception of Indians? Moreover, how would that perception have affected the artist's—and viewer's—opinion of how Indians should be treated? Follow these steps for all the artistic representations.

Finally, put together the two types of evidence. Is there more than one "image" of Native Americans? How might each perception have affected the ways Europeans and early colonists dealt with Indians?

On the surface, the Native Americans' perception of Europeans was one-dimensional and is easily discovered: the Aztec writers and artists portrayed Cortés and his men as brutal and sadistic murderers who were driven mad by their lust for gold. Closer examination of the early sec-

CHAPTER 1

FIRST
ENCOUNTERS:
THE
CONFRONTATION
BETWEEN
CORTÉS AND
MONTEZUMA
(1519–1521)

tion of the written account (Source 10) and of one of the artistic representations (Source 11), however, reveals other perceptions as well. In the written account, when Montezuma's envoys reported back to him, how did they describe the Europeans (you may use points 1 through 4 above)? What was Montezuma's reaction to the report? The other written and artistic accounts are quite direct, and you should have no difficulty discovering the Indians' overall perception of Europeans. You will, however, have to infer from the accounts how Indians believed Europeans should be dealt with in the future, since none of the written or artistic accounts deals with that question.

⬥ EPILOGUE ⬥

In many respects, the encounter between Cortés and the native peoples of Mexico was typical of many first encounters between Europeans and Native Americans. For one thing, the Indian peoples were terribly vulnerable to the numerous diseases that Europeans unwittingly brought with them. Whether warlike or peaceful, millions of Native Americans fell victim to smallpox, measles, and other diseases against which they had no resistance. Whole villages were wiped out and whole nations decimated as (in the words of one Roman Catholic priest who traveled with Cortés) "they died in heaps."

In addition, Indians were no match for European military technology and modes of warfare. Although many Indian peoples were skillful and courageous warriors, their weaponry was no equal to the European broadsword, pike, musket, or cannon. Moreover, battles between Indian peoples could best be described as skirmishes, in which few lives were lost and several prisoners taken. The Indians could not imagine wholesale slaughtering of their enemies, a practice some Europeans found acceptable as a means of acquiring gold and land. By no means passive peoples in what ultimately would become a contest for a hemisphere, Indians nevertheless had not developed the military technology and tactics to hold Europeans permanently at bay.

Nor were the Indians themselves united against their European intruders. All the explorers and early settlers were able to pit one Indian people against another, thus dividing the opposition and in the end conquering them all. In this practice Cortés was particularly adept; he found a number of villages ready to revolt against Montezuma and used those schisms to his advantage. Brief attempts at Indian unity against European intruders generally proved temporary and therefore unsuccessful.

Sometimes the Native Americans' initial misperceptions of Europeans worked to their own disadvantage. As we have seen, some Central American Indians, including the mighty Aztecs, thought Cortés's men were the "white gods" from the east whom prophets predicted would appear. Cortés's actions quickly disabused them of this notion, but by then much damage had been done. In a somewhat similar vein, Indians of the Powhatan Confederacy in Virginia at first thought the Europeans were indolent because they could not grow their own food. Like the Aztecs' misperception, this mistaken image was soon shattered. In sum, Native Americans' perceptions of Europeans often worked against any notions that they were a threat—until it was too late.

Finally, once Europeans had established footholds in the New World, the Indians often undercut their own positions. For one thing, they rarely were able to unite against the Europeans, fractured as they so often were by intertribal conflicts and jealousies. Therefore, Europeans often were able to enlist Indian allies to fight against those Native Americans who opposed them. Also, after the Indians came to recognize the value of European manufactured goods, they increasingly engaged in wholesale hunting and trapping of animals with the skins and furs Europeans wanted in exchange for those goods. Before the arrival of Europeans, Native Americans saw themselves as part of a complete ecosystem that could sustain all life so long as it was kept in balance. In contrast, Europeans saw the environment as a series of commodities to be exploited, a perception that Indians who desired European goods were quickly forced to adopt. Thus not only did the Indians lose their economic and cultural independence, but they also nearly eliminated certain animal species that had sustained them for so long. An ecological disaster was in the making, driven by the European view of the environment as something to conquer and exploit.

For a number of reasons, Native Americans were extremely vulnerable to the European "invasion" of America. At the same time, however, a major biological "event" was in process that would change life in both the Old World and the New. Called by historians the Columbian exchange, the process involved the transplantation to the New World (sometimes accidentally) of various plants (cabbages, radishes, bananas, wheat, onions, sugar cane), animals (horses, pigs, cattle, sheep, cats), and diseases. At the same time, Europeans returned home with maize, peanuts, squash, sweet potatoes, pumpkins, pineapples, tomatoes, and cocoa. Less beneficial was the possible transportation from the New World to the Old of venereal syphilis. Indeed, some five hundred years later, the Columbian exchange is still going on. In the Great Smoky Mountains of North Carolina and Tennessee, wild boars (imported from Germany in the nineteenth century for sportsmen) threaten the plants, grasses, and small animals of the region. The zebra mussel, released by accident into the Great Lakes in ballast water from Eastern Europe, has spread into the Illinois, Mississippi, Ohio, and Tennessee rivers. An Asian variety of the gypsy moth is chewing its way through the forests of the Pacific Northwest. A recent survey in Olympic National Park has identified 169 species of plants and animals not indigenous to the Western Hemisphere. In the South, the kudzu vine (imported from Japan to combat erosion) was dubbed by the *Los Angeles Times* (July 21, 1992) "the national plant of Dixie." Whether

CHAPTER 1

FIRST
ENCOUNTERS:
THE
CONFRONTATION
BETWEEN
CORTÉS AND
MONTEZUMA
(1519–1521)

purposeful or by accident, whether beneficial or detrimental, the Columbian exchange continues.

Because Europeans ultimately were victorious in their "invasion" of the Western Hemisphere, it is their images of Native Americans that for the most part have survived. Christopher Columbus, who recorded the Europeans' first encounter, depicted Native Americans as innocent, naive children. But he also wrote, "I could conquer the whole of them with fifty men, and govern them as I pleased." For his part, Amerigo Vespucci was less kind, depicting Native Americans as barbarous because "they have no regular time for their meals . . . [and] in making water they are dirty and without shame, for while talking with us they do such things." By placing this badge of inferiority on Indian peoples, most Europeans could justify a number of ways Indians could be dealt with (avoidance, conquest, "civilizing," trading, removal, extermination). Ultimately for the Indian peoples, all methods proved disastrous. Although different European peoples (Spanish, French, English) often treated Indians differently, in the end the results were the same.

Hernando Cortés returned to Spain in 1528 a fabulously wealthy man. But the ultimate *conquistador* lost most of his fortune in ill-fated expeditions and died in modest circumstances in 1547. In his will, he recognized the four children he had fathered by Native American women while in Mexico (Cortés was married at the time) and worried about the morality of what he had done. In 1562, his body was taken to Mexico to be reburied, but for Hernando Cortés's remains, there would be no rest. In 1794, they were moved again, this time to the chapel of a Mexican hospital that he had endowed. In 1823, Cortés's remains disappeared for good, perhaps as the result of an effort to protect them from politically oriented grave robbers after Mexico declared its independence from Spain. (Rumors abound that they were secretly carried back across the Atlantic, this time to Italy.) The ultimate *conquistador* has vanished, but his legacy lives on.

CHAPTER 2

THE THREAT OF ANNE HUTCHINSON

∽ THE PROBLEM ∽

In the cold, early spring of 1638, Anne Hutchinson and her children left Massachusetts to join her husband and their many friends who had moved to an island in Narragansett Bay near what is now Rhode Island. Just a year before, in 1637, Hutchinson and her family had been highly respected, prominent members of a Puritan church in Boston. But then she was put on trial and sentenced to banishment from the Massachusetts Bay colony and excommunication from her church—next to death, the worst punishment that could befall a Puritan in the New World.

What had Anne Hutchinson done? Why was she such a threat to the Massachusetts Bay colony? You will be reading the transcript of her trial in 1637 to find the answers to these questions.

∽ BACKGROUND ∽

The English men and women who came to the New World in the seventeenth and early eighteenth centuries did so for a variety of reasons. Many who arrived at Jamestown colony were motivated by the promise of wealth; at one point, Virginians grew tobacco in the streets and even threatened their own existence by favoring tobacco (a crop they could sell) over food crops. In contrast, the majority of the early settlers of Pennsylvania were Friends (Quakers) in search of religious freedom. In short, the American colonies represented for thousands of English men and women a chance to make significant changes in their lives.

Such was the case with the Puritans who settled and dominated the colony of Massachusetts Bay, founded in 1630. Although technically still members of the Church of England, the Puritans were convinced that many of that church's beliefs and practices were wrong and that the Church of England needed to be thoroughly purified (hence their name). Puritans were convinced that the Church of England, which had broken away from the Roman Catholic church and the pope during the reign of Henry VIII, was still encumbered with unnecessary ceremony, rituals, and hierarchy—things they called "popery." Popery, the Puritans believed, actually obstructed the ties between God and human beings, and therefore should be eliminated.

Believing it impossible to effect their reforms in England, many Puritans sought "voluntary banishment," as one of them called it, to the New World. Fired by the sense that God was using them to revolutionize human history, more than one thousand men, women, and children arrived during the first decades of the founding of New England to form their model community based on the laws of God and following his commandments. "We shall be as a city upon a hill," exulted Puritan leader and colonial governor John Winthrop, "the eyes of all people are upon us."

There were at least five central characteristics of American Puritanism. First, the idea that Massachusetts Bay should be a "city upon a hill" implied that the New World experiment was a kind of holy mission. Its success could be a very important

stimulus to religious reformers back home in England. Failure of the mission, however, would be a disaster. The Massachusetts settlers thus carried with them a double responsibility: to create a successful, orderly, Godly community in the New World and to serve as a perfect, shining example to the rest of the Protestant world, especially to England.

Belief in a "covenant of grace" was a second important aspect of the New England Way. American Puritans did not believe that human salvation could be earned by individual effort, such as going to church, leading a good life, or helping one's neighbors. The Puritans call the idea that one could *earn* salvation a "covenant of works," a notion they believed was absolutely wrong. They insisted that salvation came only as a free gift from God (a "covenant of grace"), and those few who received it were the true "saints," full members of the church.

Yet there was a paradox at the heart of this distinction between the covenant of grace and the covenant of works. Puritans believed that God expected everyone to lead a good life and behave themselves. Those who were not yet saved would be preparing for the possibility of God's grace, while those who were already saints would naturally live according to God's laws. Some ministers, like John Cotton, deemphasized the idea of preparation, maintaining that God's grace could be granted instantaneously to anyone. Other ministers put more emphasis on preparing to receive God's grace.

The third significant characteristic of Puritanism was the belief that the community, as well as the individual, entered into a contract, or covenant, with God. Seeing themselves as the modern version of the ancient Israelites, Puritans believed that God had made a specific contract with the Puritans of New England. As Winthrop explained, "Thus stands the cause between God and us: we are entered into covenant with Him. . . . The God of Israel is among us." To Puritans, the covenant meant that the entire community must follow God's laws as interpreted by Puritan leaders. If they did, God would reward them; if not, the community would be punished. Therefore, community solidarity was essential, and individual desires and thoughts had to be subjugated to those of the community.

Thus, although Puritans sought religious freedom for themselves, they were not really willing to grant it to others. Dissent and discord, they reasoned, would lead to the breakdown of community cohesion, the inevitable violation of the covenant, and the punishment of the community in the same way God had punished the ancient Israelites when they had broken their covenant. Non-Puritans who migrated to the Massachusetts Bay colony were required to attend the Puritan church, although they could not become members and hence could not vote in either church or civil elections. Those who refused to abide by these rules were banished from the colony. Moreover, those Puritans who were not saints also had to obey these regulations and similarly could not be church members or vote.

Thus, there was a hierarchy of authority in Massachusetts that controlled both the colony's church and the government. Within this hierarchy, the ministers played a very important role. Expected to be highly educated and articulate, the ministers of each Puritan church were to be the teachers and leaders of their respective congregations. Of course, the civil officials of Massachusetts Bay, such as the governor and his council, were good Puritans and full members of their churches. Their job was to ensure that the laws and practices of civil government were in accord with the requirements of living in a Godly community. Civil authorities, then, were expected to support the religious authorities, and vice versa.

Finally, New England Puritans placed more emphasis than English Puritans on the importance of having a conversion experience—an experience when you knew that you had been "saved." Young adults and adults prayed, tried to live according to biblical precepts, and often kept diaries in which they reflected on their shortcomings and "sinfulness." Only a conversion experience would admit a person into full church membership. To become a saint, one had to be examined by a church committee and demonstrate that he or she had experienced the presence of God and the Holy Spirit. There was no agreement among the ministers about the exact nature of this revelation, although people sometimes reported a physical sensation. For most, it simply meant that individuals would recognize the Holy Spirit moving within themselves. Some ministers urged their congregations not to fear, and even to seek out, more direct contact with God. This was far more controversial, as you will see in Anne Hutchinson's trial.

In fact, there was a good deal of dissension in Massachusetts Bay colony. Religious squabbles were common, often arising between saints over biblical interpretation, the theological correctness of one minister or another, or the behavior of certain fellow colonists. Indeed, to a limited extent, Puritans actually welcomed these disputes because they seemed to demonstrate that religion was still a vital part of the colonists' lives. As John Winthrop said, "The business of religion is the business of the Puritans." Participants of weeknight gatherings at various church members' homes often engaged in these religious debates, tolerated by both the ministers and the colony's civil leaders as long as the squabbles did not get out of control.

By the mid-1630s, however, one of the disputes had grown to such an extent that it threatened the religious and secular unity of the colony. Some Puritans in both England and Massachusetts Bay had begun to espouse an extreme version of the covenant of grace: They believed that, having been assured of salvation, an individual was virtually freed from the man-made laws of both church and state, taking commands only from God, who communicated his wishes to the saints. Called Antinomians (from *anti,* "against," and *nomos,* "law"), these Puritan extremists attacked what one of them called the "deadness" of religious services and charged that several ministers were preaching the covenant of works. This charge was extremely offensive to these ministers, who did not at all believe they were

teaching salvation through good behavior but rather preparation for the possibility of God's grace. Carried to its logical extension, of course, Antinomianism threatened to overthrow the authority of the ministers and even the power of the colonial government itself. Growing in number and intensity, the Antinomians in 1636 were able to elect one of their followers to replace Winthrop as colonial governor, although Winthrop managed to return to office the next year.

Into this highly charged atmosphere stepped Anne Hutchinson, age forty-three, who had arrived in Massachusetts Bay in 1634 and soon became embroiled in the Antinomian controversy, or, as other Puritans called it, the "Antinomian heresy." The daughter of a clergyman who had been imprisoned twice for his religious unorthodoxy, Anne had married prosperous businessman William Hutchinson in 1612, when she was twenty-one years old. Before arriving in Massachusetts Bay, she had given birth to fourteen children, eleven of whom were alive in 1634.

In a society that emphasized the greater good of the community rather than the concept of individual happiness, relationships between men and women were complementary and complex. New England "goodwives," as married women were called, performed a variety of tasks essential to their families and communities. Spiritually, they were equal to their husbands in the eyes of God, but economically and politically, wives were expected to help with and supplement their husbands' public activities. In other words, both men and women had rights and responsibilities with respect to each other, their children, their neighbors, their communities, and their church. In carrying out these responsibilities, male and female roles sometimes overlapped, but more often they were divided into public (male) and private (female) spheres.

As in any other society, there were some unhappy marriages, cases of domestic violence and desertion, and even what we would call divorce. But the shared ideals and sense of mission of so many of the immigrants ensured that such dysfunctional relationships were relatively uncommon. Although building a new society in a wilderness was a difficult and dangerous undertaking, most women fulfilled their roles willingly and competently.

Anne Hutchinson's many duties at home did not prevent her from remaining very active in the church. Extremely interested in religion and theological questions, she was particularly influenced by John Cotton, a Puritan minister who had been forced to flee from England to Massachusetts Bay in 1633 because of his religious ideas. Upon arrival in the colony, Cotton said he was shocked by the extent to which colonists had been "lulled into security" by their growing belief that they could earn salvation through good works. Attacking this in sermons and in letters to other clergymen, Cotton helped fuel the Antinomian cause as well as Anne Hutchinson's religious ardor.

At first the Hutchinsons were seen as welcome additions to the community, largely because of William's prosperity and Anne's expertise in herbal medicines, nursing the sick, and midwifery. Soon, however, Anne Hutchinson began to drift into religious issues.

She began to hold weeknight meetings in her home, at first to expand upon the previous Sunday's sermons and later to expound her own religious notions—ideas very close to those of the Antinomians. In November 1637, Anne's brother-in-law (John Wheelwright, another Puritan minister) was banished from the colony because of his radical sermons, and Anne was brought to trial before the General Court of Massachusetts Bay. With Governor Winthrop presiding, the court met to decide the fate of Anne Hutchinson. Privately, Winthrop called Hutchinson a person of "nimble wit and active spirit and a very voluble [fluent] tongue." Winthrop himself, however, believed that women should be submissive and supportive, like his wife and sister, and there was ample support for his position in the Bible.[1] No matter what he thought of Hutchinson's abilities, publicly the governor was determined to be rid of her.

Why were Winthrop and other orthodox Puritans so opposed to Hutchinson? What crime had she committed? Some of Wheelwright's followers had been punished for having signed a petition supporting him, but Hutchinson had not signed the petition. Many other Puritans had held religious discussions in their homes, and more than a few had opposed the views of their ministers. Technically, Hutchinson had broken no law. Why, then, was she considered such a threat that she was brought to trial and ultimately banished from the colony?

1. Genesis 1:28–3:24; the First Letter of Paul to the Corinthians 11:1–16; the Letter of Paul to the Ephesians, Chapters 5 and 6, all verses.

⬭ THE METHOD ⬭

For two days, Anne Hutchinson stood before the General Court, presided over by the unsympathetic Governor John Winthrop. Fortunately, a fairly complete transcript of the proceedings has been preserved. In that transcript are the clues that you as the historian-detective will need to answer the questions previously posed. Although spelling and punctuation have been modernized in most cases, the portions of the transcript you are about to read are reproduced verbatim. At first, some of the seventeenth-century phraseology might seem a bit strange. As are most spoken languages, English is constantly changing (think of how much English has changed since Chaucer's day). Yet if you read slowly and carefully, the transcript should give you no problem.

Before you begin studying the transcript, keep in mind two additional instructions:

1. Be careful not to lose sight of the central question: Why was Anne Hutchinson such a threat to Massa-chusetts Bay colony? The transcript raises several other questions, some of them so interesting that they might pull you off the main track. As you read through the transcript, make a list of the various ways you think Hutchinson might have threatened Massachusetts Bay.

2. Be willing to read between the lines. As you read each statement, ask yourself what is being said. Then try to deduce what is actually meant by what is being said. Sometimes people say exactly what they mean, but often they do not. They might intentionally or unintentionally disguise the real meaning of what they are saying, but the real meaning can usually be found. In conversation with a person face to face, voice inflection, body language, and other visual clues often provide the real meaning to what is being said. In this case, where personal observation is impossible, you must use both logic and imagination to read between the lines.

⬭ THE EVIDENCE ⬭

Source 1 from an excerpt of the examination from Thomas Hutchinson (Anne's great-grandson), *The History of the Colony and Province of Massachusetts-Bay,* ed. Lawrence Shaw Mayo (Cambridge, Mass.: Harvard University Press, 1936), Vol. II, pp. 366–391.

1. The Examination of Mrs. Anne Hutchinson at the Court of Newton, November 1637.[2]

CHARACTERS

Mrs. Anne Hutchinson, the accused

General Court, consisting of the governor, deputy governor, assistants, and deputies

Governor, John Winthrop, chair of the court

Deputy Governor, Thomas Dudley

Assistants, Mr. Bradstreet, Mr. Nowel, Mr. Endicott, Mr. Harlakenden, Mr. Stoughton

Deputies, Mr. Coggeshall, Mr. Bartholomew, Mr. Jennison, Mr. Coddington, Mr. Colborn

Clergymen and Ruling Elders:

  Mr. Peters, minister in Salem

  Mr. Leveret, a ruling elder in a Boston church

  Mr. Cotton, minister in Boston

  Mr. Wilson, minister in Boston, who supposedly made notes of a previous meeting between Anne Hutchinson, Cotton, and the other ministers

  Mr. Sims, minister in Charlestown

MR. WINTHROP, GOVERNOR. Mrs. Hutchinson, you are called here as one of those that have troubled the peace of the commonwealth and the churches here; you are known to be a woman that hath had a great share in the promoting and divulging of those opinions that are causes of this trouble, and to be nearly joined not only in affinity and affection with some of those the court had taken notice of and passed censure upon, but you have spoken divers things as we have been informed very prejudicial to the honour of the churches and ministers thereof, and you have maintained a meeting and an assembly in your house that hath been condemned by the general assembly as a thing not tolerable nor comely in the sight of God nor fitting for your sex, and notwithstanding that was cried down you have continued the same. Therefore we have thought good to send for you to understand how things are, that if you be in an erroneous way we may reduce you so that you may become a profitable member here among us. Otherwise if you be obstinate in your course that then the court may take such course that you

---

2. Normally the trial would have been held in Boston, but Anne Hutchinson had numerous supporters in that city, so the proceedings were moved to the small town of Newton, where she had few allies.

may trouble us no further. Therefore I would intreat you to express whether you do assent and hold in practice to those opinions and factions that have been handled in court already, that is to say, whether you do not justify Mr. Wheelwright's sermon and the petition.

MRS. HUTCHINSON. I am called here to answer before you but I hear no things laid to my charge.

GOV. I have told you some already and more I can tell you.

MRS. H. Name one, Sir.

GOV. Have I not named some already?

MRS. H. What have I said or done?

[*Here, in a portion of the transcript not reproduced, Winthrop accused Hutchinson of harboring and giving comfort to a faction that was dangerous to the colony.*]

MRS. H. Must not I then entertain the saints because I must keep my conscience?

GOV. Say that one brother should commit felony or treason and come to his brother's house. If he knows him guilty and conceals him he is guilty of the same. It is his conscience to entertain him, but if his conscience comes into act in giving countenance and entertainment to him that hath broken the law he is guilty too. So if you do countenance those that are transgressors of the law you are in the same fact.

MRS. H. What law do they transgress?

GOV. The law of God and of the state.

MRS. H. In what particular?

GOV. Why in this among the rest, whereas the Lord doth say honour thy father and thy mother.[3]

MRS. H. Ey, Sir, in the Lord.

GOV. This honour you have broke in giving countenance to them.

MRS. H. In entertaining those did I entertain them against any act (for there is the thing) or what God hath appointed?

GOV. You knew that Mr. Wheelwright did preach this sermon and those that countenance him in this do break a law?

MRS. H. What law have I broken?

GOV. Why the fifth commandment.[4]

MRS. H. I deny that for he [Wheelwright] saith in the Lord.

GOV. You have joined with them in the faction.

MRS. H. In what faction have I joined with them?

3. Exodus 20:12. Anne Hutchinson's natural father was in England and her natural mother was dead. To what, then, was Winthrop referring?
4. "Honour thy father and thy mother: that thy days may be long upon the land which the Lord thy God giveth thee." Exodus 20:12.

GOV. In presenting the petition.

MRS. H. Suppose I had set my hand to the petition. What then?

GOV. You saw that case tried before.

MRS. H. But I had not my hand to the petition.

GOV. You have councelled them.

MRS. H. Wherein?

GOV. Why in entertaining them.

MRS. H. What breach of law is that, Sir?

GOV. Why dishonouring of parents.

MRS. H. But put the case, Sir, that I do fear the Lord and my parents. May not I entertain them that fear the Lord because my parents will not give me leave?

GOV. If they be the fathers of the commonwealth, and they of another religion, if you entertain them then you dishonour your parents and are justly punishable.

MRS. H. If I entertain them, as they have dishonoured their parents I do.

GOV. No but you by countenancing them above others put honour upon them.

MRS. H. I may put honour upon them as the children of God and as they do honour the Lord.

GOV. We do not mean to discourse with those of your sex but only this: you do adhere unto them and do endeavour to set forward this faction and so you do dishonour us.

MRS. H. I do acknowledge no such thing. Neither do I think that I ever put any dishonour upon you.

GOV. Why do you keep such a meeting at your house as you do every week upon a set day? . . .

MRS. H. It is lawful for me so to do, as it is all your practices, and can you find a warrant for yourself and condemn me for the same thing? The ground of my taking it up was, when I first came to this land because I did not go to such meetings as those were, it was presently reported that I did not allow of such meetings but held them unlawful and therefore in that regard they said I was proud and did despise all ordinances. Upon that a friend came unto me and told me of it and I to prevent such aspersions took it up, but it was in practice before I came. Therefore I was not the first.

GOV. For this, that you appeal to our practice you need no confutation. If your meeting had answered to the former it had not been offensive, but I will say that there was no meeting of women alone, but your meeting is of another sort for there are sometimes men among you.

MRS. H. There was never any man with us.

GOV. Well, admit there was no man at your meeting and that you was sorry for it, there is no warrant for your doings, and by what warrant do you continue such a course?

MRS. H. I conceive there lies a clear rule in Titus[5] that the elder women should instruct the younger and then I must have a time wherein I must do it.

GOV. All this I grant you, I grant you a time for it, but what is this to the purpose that you Mrs. Hutchinson must call a company together from their callings to come to be taught of you?

MRS. H. Will it please you to answer me this and to give me a rule for then I will willingly submit to any truth. If any come to my house to be instructed in the ways of God what rule have I to put them away?

GOV. But suppose that a hundred men come unto you to be instructed. Will you forbear to instruct them?

MRS. H. As far as I conceive I cross a rule in it.

GOV. Very well and do you not so here?

MRS. H. No, Sir, for my ground is they are men.

GOV. Men and women all is one for that, but suppose that a man should come and say, "Mrs. Hutchinson, I hear that you are a woman that God hath given his grace unto and you have knowledge in the word of God. I pray instruct me a little." Ought you not to instruct this man?

MRS. H. I think I may. Do you think it is not lawful for me to teach women and why do you call me to teach the court?

GOV. We do not call you to teach the court but to lay open yourself.

[*In this portion of the transcript not reproduced, Hutchinson and Winthrop continued to wrangle over specifically what law she had broken.*]

GOV. Your course is not to be suffered for. Besides that we find such a course as this to be greatly prejudicial to the state. Besides the occasion that it is to seduce many honest persons that are called to those meetings and your opinions being known to be different from the word of God may seduce many simple souls that resort unto you. Besides that the occasion which hath come of late hath come from none but such as have frequented your meetings, so that now they are flown off from magistrates and ministers and since they have come to you. And besides that it will not well stand with the commonwealth that families should be neglected for so many neighbours and dames and so much time spent. We see no rule of God for this. We see not that any should have

5. A reference to The Epistle of Paul to Titus in the Bible, probably the section stating that older women "may teach the young women to be sober, to love their husbands, to love their children," etc.

authority to set up any other exercises besides what authority hath already set up and so what hurt comes of this you will be guilty of and we for suffering you.

MRS. H. Sir, I do not believe that to be so.

GOV. Well, we see how it is. We must therefore put it away from you or restrain you from maintaining this course.

MRS. H. If you have a rule for it from God's word you may.

GOV. We are judges, and not you ours and we must compel you to it.

[Here followed a discussion of whether men as well as women attended Hutchinson's meetings. In response to one question, Hutchinson denied that women ever taught at men's meetings.]

DEPUTY GOVERNOR. I would go a little higher with Mrs. Hutchinson. About three years ago we were all in peace. Mrs. Hutchinson from that time she came hath made a disturbance, and some that came over with her in the ship did inform me what she was as soon as she was landed. I being then in place dealt with the pastor and teacher of Boston and desired them to enquire of her, and then I was satisfied that she held nothing different from us. But within half a year after, she had vented divers of her strange opinions and had made parties in the country, and at length it comes that Mr. Cotton and Mr. Vane[6] were of her judgment, but Mr. Cotton had cleared himself that he was not of that mind. But now it appears by this woman's meeting that Mrs. Hutchinson hath so forestalled the minds of many by their resort to her meeting that now she hath a potent party in the country. Now if all these things have endangered us as from that foundation and if she in particular hath disparaged all our ministers in the land that they have preached a covenant of works,[7] and only Mr. Cotton a covenant of grace,[8] why this is not to be suffered, and therefore being driven to the foundation and it being found that Mrs. Hutchinson is she that hath depraved all the ministers and hath been the cause of what is falled out, why we must take away the foundation and the building will fall.

MRS. H. I pray, Sir, prove it that I said they preached nothing but a covenant of works.

DEP. GOV. Nothing but a covenant of works. Why a Jesuit[9] may preach truth sometimes.

6. Henry Vane, an ally of the Antinomians, was elected governor of Massachusetts Bay colony in 1636 and lost that office to Winthrop in 1637.

7. For an explanation of the covenant of works, see the "Background" section.

8. For an explanation of the covenant of grace, see the "Background" section.

9. The Society of Jesus (Jesuits) is a Roman Catholic order that places special emphasis on missionary work. The Jesuits were known at this time for combating Protestantism and were particularly detested by many Protestants, including the Puritans.

MRS. H. Did I ever say they preached a covenant of works then?

DEP. GOV. If they do not preach a covenant of grace clearly, then they preach a covenant of works.

MRS. H. No, Sir. One may preach a covenant of grace more clearly than another, so I said.

DEP. GOV. We are not upon that now but upon position.

MRS. H. Prove this then Sir that you say I said.

DEP. GOV. When they do preach a covenant of works do they preach truth?

MRS. H. Yes, Sir. But when they preach a covenant of works for salvation, that is not truth.

DEP. GOV. I do but ask you this: when the ministers do preach a covenant of works do they preach a way of salvation?

MRS. H. I did not come hither to answer to questions of that sort.

DEP. GOV. Because you will deny the thing.

MRS. H. Ey, but that is to be proved first.

DEP. GOV. I will make it plain that you did say that the ministers did preach a covenant of works.

MRS. H. I deny that.

DEP. GOV. And that you said they were not able ministers of the New Testament, but Mr. Cotton only.

MRS. H. If ever I spake that I proved it by God's word.

COURT. Very well, very well.

MRS. H. If one shall come unto me in private, and desire me seriously to tell then what I thought of such an one, I must either speak false or true in my answer.

[*In this lengthy section, Hutchinson was accused of having gone to a meeting of ministers and accusing them all—except John Cotton—of preaching a covenant of works rather than a covenant of grace. The accusation, if proved, would have been an extremely serious one. Several of the ministers testified that Hutchinson had made this accusation.*]

DEP. GOV. I called these witnesses and you deny them. You see they have proved this and you deny this, but it is clear. You said they preached a covenant of works and that they were not able ministers of the New Testament; now there are two other things that you did affirm which were that the scriptures in the letter of them held forth nothing but a covenant of works and likewise that those that were under a covenant of works cannot be saved.

MRS. H. Prove that I said so.

GOV. Did you say so?

MRS. H. No, Sir. It is your conclusion.

DEP. GOV. What do I do charging of you if you deny what is so fully proved?

GOV. Here are six undeniable ministers who say it is true and yet you deny that you did say that they did preach a covenant of works and that they were not able ministers of the gospel, and it appears plainly that you have spoken it, and whereas you say that it was drawn from you in a way of friendship, you did profess then that it was out of conscience that you spake and said, "The fear of man is a snare. Wherefore shall I be afraid, I will speak plainly and freely."

MRS. H. That I absolutely deny, for the first question was thus answered by me to them: They thought that I did conceive there was a difference between them and Mr. Cotton. At the first I was somewhat reserved. Then said Mr. Peters, "I pray answer the question directly as fully and as plainly as you desire we should tell you our minds. Mrs. Hutchinson we come for plain dealing and telling you our hearts." Then I said I would deal as plainly as I could, and whereas they say I said they were under a covenant of works and in the state of the apostles why these two speeches cross one another. I might say they might preach a covenant of works as did the apostles, but to preach a covenant of works and to be under a covenant of works is another business.

DEP. GOV. There have been six witnesses to prove this and yet you deny it.

MRS. H. I deny that these were the first words that were spoken.

GOV. You make the case worse, for you clearly shew that the ground of your opening your mind was not to satisfy them but to satisfy your own conscience.

[*There was a brief argument here about what Hutchinson actually said at the gathering of ministers, after which the court adjourned for the day.*]

The next morning

GOV. We proceeded the last night as far as we could in hearing of this cause of Mrs. Hutchinson. There were divers things laid to her charge: her ordinary meetings about religious exercises, her speeches in derogation of the ministers among us, and the weakening of the hands and hearts of the people towards them. Here was sufficient proof made of that which she was accused of in that point concerning the ministers and their ministry, as that they did preach a covenant of works when others did preach a covenant of grace, and that they were not able ministers of the New Testament, and that they had not the seal of the spirit, and this was spoken not as was pretended out of private conference, but out of conscience and warrant from scripture alleged the fear of man is a snare and seeing God had given her a calling to it she would freely speak. Some other speeches she used, as that the letter of the scripture held forth a covenant of works, and this is offered to be proved by probable grounds. If there be any thing else that the court hath to say they may speak.

[*At this point, a lengthy argument erupted when Hutchinson demanded that the ministers who testified against her be recalled as witnesses, put under oath, and repeat their accusations. One member of the court said that "the ministers are so well known unto us, that we need not take an oath of them."*]

GOV. I see no necessity of an oath in this thing seeing it is true and the substance of the matter confirmed by divers. Yet that all may be satisfied, if the elders will take an oath they shall have it given them. . . .

MRS. H. I will prove by what Mr. Wilson hath written[10] that they [the ministers] never heard me say such a thing.

MR. SIMS. We desire to have the paper and have it read.

MR. HARLAKENDEN. I am persuaded that is the truth that the elders do say and therefore I do not see it necessary how to call them to oath.

GOV. We cannot charge any thing of untruth upon them.

MR. HARLAKENDEN. Besides, Mrs. Hutchinson doth say that they are not able ministers of the New Testament.

MRS. H. They need not swear to that.

DEP. GOV. Will you confess it then?

MRS. H. I will not deny it or say it.

DEP. GOV. You must do one.

[*More on the oath followed.*]

DEP. GOV. Let her witnesses be called.

GOV. Who be they?

MRS. H. Mr. Leveret and our teacher and Mr. Coggeshall.

GOV. Mr. Coggeshall was not present.

MR. COGGESHALL. Yes, but I was. Only I desired to be silent till I should be called.

GOV. Will you, Mr. Coggeshall, say that she did not say so?

MR. COGGESHALL. Yes, I dare say that she did not say all that which they lay against her.

MR. PETERS. How dare you look into the court to say such a word?

10. Wilson had taken notes at the meeting between Hutchinson and the ministers. Hutchinson claimed that these notes would exonerate her. They were never produced and are now lost.

MR. COGGESHALL. Mr. Peters takes upon him to forbid me. I shall be silent.

MR. STOUGHTON. Ey, but she intended this that they say.

GOV. Well, Mr. Leveret, what were the words? I pray, speak.

MR. LEVERET. To my best remembrance when the elders did send for her, Mr. Peters did with much vehemency and intreaty urge her to tell what difference there was between Mr. Cotton and them, and upon his urging of her she said, "The fear of man is a snare, but they that trust upon the Lord shall be safe." And being asked wherein the difference was, she answered that they did not preach a covenant of grace so clearly as Mr. Cotton did, and she gave this reason of it: because that as the apostles were for a time without the spirit so until they had received the witness of the spirit they could not preach a covenant of grace so clearly.

[Here Hutchinson admitted that she might have said privately that the ministers were not able ministers of the New Testament.]

GOV. Mr. Cotton, the court desires that you declare what you do remember of the conference which was at the time and is now in question.

MR. COTTON. I did not think I should be called to bear witness in this cause and therefore did not labour to call to remembrance what was done; but the greatest passage that took impression upon me was to this purpose. The elders spake that they had heard that she had spoken some condemning words of their ministry, and among other things they did first pray her to answer wherein she thought their ministry did differ from mine. How the comparison sprang I am ignorant, but sorry I was that any comparison should be between me and my brethren and uncomfortable it was. She told them to this purpose that they did not hold forth a covenant of grace as I did. . . . I told her I was very sorry that she put comparisons between my ministry and theirs, for she had said more than I could myself, and rather I had that she had put us in fellowship with them and not have made the discrepancy. She said she found the difference. . . . And I must say that I did not find her saying they were under a covenant of works, not that she said they did preach a covenant of works.

[Here John Cotton tried to defend Hutchinson, mostly by saying he did not remember most of the events in question.]

MRS. H. If you please to give me leave I shall give you the ground of what I know to be true. Being much troubled to see the falseness of the constitution of the Church of England, I had like to have turned Separatist. Whereupon I kept a day of solemn humiliation and pondering of the thing, the scripture was brought unto me—he that denies Jesus Christ to be come in the flesh is antichrist. This I considered of and in considering found that the papists[11] did not deny him to come in the flesh, nor we did not deny him. Who then was antichrist? Was the Turk antichrist only? The Lord knows that I could not open scripture; he must by his prophetical office open it unto me. So after that being unsatisfied in the thing, the Lord was pleased to bring this scripture out of the Hebrews. He that denies the testament denies the testator, and in this did open unto me and give me to see that those which did not teach the new covenant had the spirit of antichrist, and upon this he did discover the ministry unto me, and ever since, I bless the Lord. He hath let me see which was the clear ministry and which the wrong. Since that time I confess I have been more choice and he hath left me to distinguish between the voice of my beloved and the voice of Moses, the voice of John Baptist and the voice of antichrist, for all those voices are spoken of in scripture. Now if you do condemn me for speaking what in my conscience I know to be truth I must commit myself unto the Lord.

MR. NOWEL. How do you know that that was the spirit?

MRS. H. How did Abraham know that it was God that bid him offer his son, being a breach of the sixth commandment?

DEP. GOV. By an immediate voice.

MRS. H. So to me by an immediate revelation.

DEP. GOV. How! an immediate revelation.

MRS. H. By the voice of his spirit to my soul. . . .

[*In spite of the general shock that greeted her claim that she had experienced an immediate revelation from God, Hutchinson went on to state that God had compelled her to take the course she had taken and that God had said to her, as He had to Daniel of the Old Testament, that "though I should meet with affliction, yet I am the same God that delivered Daniel out of the lion's den, I will also deliver thee."*]

MRS. H. You have power over my body but the Lord Jesus hath power over my body and soul, and assure yourselves thus much: you go on in this course you begin you will bring a curse upon you and your posterity, and the mouth of the Lord hath spoken it.

DEP. GOV. What is the scripture she brings?

11. *Papists* is a Protestant term for Roman Catholics, referring to the papacy.

MR. STOUGHTON. Behold I turn away from you.

MRS. H. But now having seen him which is invisible I fear not what man can do unto me.

GOV. Daniel was delivered by miracle. Do you think to be deliver'd so too?

MRS. H. I do here speak it before the court. I took that the Lord should deliver me by his providence.

MR. HARLAKENDEN. I may read scripture and the most glorious hypocrite may read them and yet go down to hell.

MRS. H. It may be so.

[*Hutchinson's "revelations" were discussed among the stunned court.*]

MR. BARTHOLOMEW. I speak as a member of the court. I fear that her revelations will deceive.

[*More on Hutchinson's revelations followed.*]

DEP. GOV. I desire Mr. Cotton to tell us whether you do approve of Mrs. Hutchinson's revelations as she hath laid them down.

MR. COTTON. I know not whether I do understand her, but this I say: If she doth expect a deliverance in a way of providence, then I cannot deny it.

DEP. GOV. No, sir. We did not speak of that.

MR. COTTON. If it be by way of miracle then I would suspect it.

DEP. GOV. Do you believe that her revelations are true?

MR. COTTON. That she may have some special providence of God to help her is a thing that I cannot bear witness against.

DEP. GOV. Good Sir, I do ask whether this revelation be of God or no?

MR. COTTON. I should desire to know whether the sentence of the court will bring her to any calamity, and then I would know of her whether she expects to be delivered from that calamity by a miracle or a providence of God.

MRS. H. By a providence of God I say I expect to be delivered from some calamity that shall come to me.

[*Hutchinson's revelations were further discussed.*]

DEP. GOV. These disturbances that have come among the Germans[12] have been all grounded upon revelations, and so they that have vented them have stirred up their hearers to take up arms against their prince and

12. This reference is to the bloody and violent fighting that took place between orthodox Protestants and the followers of the radical Anabaptist John of Leiden in 1534 and 1535.

to cut the throats of one another, and these have been the fruits of them, and whether the devil may inspire the same into their hearts here I know not, for I am fully persuaded that Mrs. Hutchinson is deluded by the devil, because the spirit of God speaks truth in all his servants.

GOV. I am persuaded that the revelation she brings forth is delusion.

[*All the court but some two or three ministers cried out, "We all believe—we all believe it." Hutchinson was found guilty. Coddington made a lame attempt to defend Hutchinson but was silenced by Governor Winthrop.*]

GOV. The court hath already declared themselves satisfied concerning the things you hear, and concerning the troublesomeness of her spirit and the danger of her course amongst us, which is not to be suffered. Therefore if it be the mind of the court that Mrs. Hutchinson for these things that appear before us is unfit for our society, and if it be the mind of the court that she shall be banished out of our liberties and imprisoned till she be sent away, let them hold up their hands.

[*All but three did so.*]

GOV. Those that are contrary minded hold up yours.

[*Only Mr. Coddington and Mr. Colborn did so.*]

MR. JENNISON. I cannot hold up my hand one way or the other, and I shall give my reason if the court require it.

GOV. Mrs. Hutchinson, the sentence of the court you hear is that you are banished from out of our jurisdiction as being a woman not fit for our society, and are to be imprisoned till the court shall send you away.

MRS. H. I desire to know wherefore I am banished?

GOV. Say no more. The court knows wherefore and is satisfied.

∽ QUESTIONS TO CONSIDER ∽

Now that you have examined the evidence, at least one point is very clear: the political and religious authorities of Massachusetts Bay were determined to get rid of Anne Hutchinson, whether or not she actually had broken any law. They tried to bait her, force admissions of guilt from her, confuse her, browbeat her. Essentially, they had already decided on the verdict before the trial began. So we know that Anne Hutchinson was a threat—and a serious one—to the colony.

And yet the colony had dealt quite differently with Roger Williams, a Puritan minister banished in 1635 because of his extreme religious beliefs. Williams was given every chance to mend his ways, Governor Winthrop remained his friend throughout Williams's appearances before the General Court, and it was only with great reluctance that the court finally decided to send him out into the "wilderness."

Why, then, was Anne Hutchinson such a threat, and why was her trial such an ordeal? Obviously, she did pose a religious threat. As you look back through the evidence, try to clarify the exact points of difficulty between Hutchinson and the ministers. What was the basis of the argument over covenants of grace and works? What was Hutchinson supposed to have said? Under what circumstances had she allegedly said this? To whom? What was the role of her own minister, John Cotton, in the trial?

Remember that Hutchinson's trial took place in the midst of the divisive Antinomian controversy. What threat did the Antinomians pose to Massachusetts Bay and Puritanism? Did Hutchinson say anything in her testi-mony that would indicate she was an Antinomian? How would you prove whether or not she was?

Hutchinson's place or role in the community also seems to have come into question during the trial. What do the questions about the meetings she held in her home reveal? Look beyond what the governor and members of the court are actually saying. Try to imagine what they might have been thinking. How might Hutchinson's meetings have eventually posed a threat to the larger community?

Finally, look through the transcript one more time. It provides some clues, often subtle ones, about the relationships between men and women in colonial Massachusetts. Puritan law and customs gave women approximately equal status with men, and of course women could join the church, just as men could. But in every society, there are unspoken assumptions about how men and women should behave. Can you find any evidence that Hutchinson violated these assumptions? If so, what did she do? Again, why would this be dangerous?

In conclusion, try to put together all you know from the evidence to answer the central question: Why was Anne Hutchinson such a threat to Massachusetts Bay colony?

EPILOGUE

Even after their banishment, misfortune continued to plague the Hutchinson family. After moving to Narragansett Bay, Hutchinson once again became pregnant. By then she was more than forty-five years old and had begun menopause. The fetus did not develop naturally and was aborted into a hydatidiform mole (resembling a cluster of grapes), which was expelled with considerable pain and difficulty. Many believed that the "birth" of this "monster baby" was proof of Hutchinson's religious heresy.

In 1642, Hutchinson's husband died, and she moved with her six youngest children to the Dutch colony of New Netherland in what is now the Bronx borough of New York City. The next year, she and all but one of her children were killed by Indians.

Ten years after Hutchinson was banished from Massachusetts Bay, John Winthrop died. Winthrop believed to the end of his life that he had had no choice other than to expel Hutchinson and her family. However, even Winthrop's most sympathetic biographer, historian Edmund S. Morgan, describes the Hutchinson trial and its aftermath as "the least attractive episode" in Winthrop's long public career.

Massachusetts Bay continued to try to maintain community cohesion for years after Anne Hutchinson and her family were expelled. But as the colony grew and prospered, change ultimately did come. New generations seemed unable to embrace the original zeal of the colony's founders. New towns increased the colony's size and made uniformity more difficult. Growth and prosperity also seemed to bring an increased interest in individual wealth and a corresponding decline in religious fervor. Reports of sleeping during sermons, fewer conversions of young people, blasphe-

mous language, and growing attention to physical pleasures were numerous, as were reports of election disputes, intrachurch squabbling, and community bickering.

To those who remembered the old ways of Massachusetts Bay, such straying from the true path was more than unfortunate. The Puritans believed that as the ancient Israelites had been punished by God when they broke their covenant, so they would have to pay for their indiscretions. As one Puritan minister said, "In the time of their prosperity, see how the Jews turn their backs and shake off the authority of the Lord." The comparison was lost on almost no one.

Jeremiads—stories that predicted disasters because of the decline in religious zeal and public morality—were especially popular in the 1660s. The minister and physician Michael Wigglesworth's poem "The Day of Doom" (specifically written for the general public) was "read to pieces," according to historian Perry Miller. Wigglesworth's more sophisticated but heartfelt poem "God's Controversy with New England" was equally popular among more educated readers. Hence it is not surprising that by the late 1680s (more than forty years after Anne Hutchinson's death), a wave of religious hysteria swept across Massachusetts Bay colony. Convinced that they had broken their covenant with God, many Puritans grimly awaited their punishment, spending long hours in churches listening to sermons. When in 1692 a few young girls in Salem Village began accusing some of their neighbors of being possessed by Satan, many were convinced that the day of punishment had arrived. Before that incident had run its course, twenty people had been killed, nineteen of them by hanging, and many more had been temporarily imprisoned. Although the Puritans' congregational church remained the official established church of Massachusetts until 1822, the original community cohesion had been altered long before that.

CHAPTER 3

RHYTHMS OF COLONIAL LIFE:
THE STATISTICS OF
COLONIAL MASSACHUSETTS BAY

 **THE PROBLEM**

An important benefit of studying history is the ability to measure both change over time and people's reactions or adjustments to those changes. Today's world is changing with incredible speed. Recently you probably drove a fuel-injected automobile along an interstate highway while listening to an FM stereo radio station or a cassette tape, exited from the highway for a fast-food snack, continued home and prepared a full meal in a microwave oven, and then watched a film or a previously taped television program on your videocassette recorder or worked with your personal computer. These are all activities that no American could have engaged in thirty years ago. Indeed, we live in a society that expects change, generally welcomes it, and tries to plan for it.

Centuries ago, change took place at a considerably slower pace. Yet change did occur in colonial America, sometimes with what for the colonists must have seemed like startling speed. Colonial Massachusetts Bay was such a society. A child born in that colony in 1650, whether male or female, experienced a profoundly different life from that of a child born in 1750. In some ways, the differences in those two children's lives were dramatic and unwelcome.

What were the differences in the lives of the people of Massachusetts Bay between 1650 and 1750? How can we account for those differences? How might those differences have affected those people's thoughts, attitudes, feelings, and behavior? In this chapter, you will be using statistics to measure change over time in colonial Massachusetts Bay and how men, women, and children reacted to and attempted to adapt to those changes. Then, using your historical imagination, you will explain how those changes and adaptations might have affected the emotions and actions of those colonists. More specifically, by the 1760s and early 1770s, an increasing number of Massachusetts Bay colonists were willing to protest and ultimately take up arms against Great Britain. Do the changes in the lives of the people of Massachusetts Bay help explain why these colonists made those momentous decisions?

BACKGROUND

The years between the settlement of the colonies and the American Revolution are critical ones in American history. In those years, which in some colonies stretched to more than a century,[1] stability was gradually achieved, economic bases were laid, political institutions were established, social structures and institutions evolved, and intellectual and cultural life eventually thrived. As the population increased and as older settlements matured, new towns and settlements were founded on the edge of the receding wilderness, thus repeating the process of settlement, stability, growth, and maturation. And although most colonists were still tied to England by bonds of language, economics, government, and affection, over the years those bonds gradually loosened until the colonists, many without fully realizing it, had become something distinctly different from simply English men and women who happened to reside in another land. In some ways, then, the American Revolution was the political realization of earlier economic, social, cultural, and political trends and events in colonial life.

These trends and events occurred, with some variations, in all the colonies, especially the Massachusetts Bay colony. Founded in 1630 by Puritans from England, Massachusetts Bay grew rapidly, aided in its first decade by 15,000 to 20,000 immigrants from England, and after that by natural increase.[2] By 1700, Massachusetts Bay's population had risen to almost 56,000 and by 1750, to approximately

1. The following colonies had been in existence for a century or more when the American Revolution broke out in 1775: Virginia, Massachusetts Bay, Rhode Island, Connecticut, Maryland, New York, and New Jersey. Settlements of Europeans also existed in New Hampshire and Delaware areas more than a century before the Revolution, although they did not formally become colonies until later.

2. The outbreak of the English Civil War in 1642 drastically reduced emigration from England to Massachusetts Bay, largely because Puritans in England believed it was important to stay and fight against Charles I. In 1649, when Charles I was deposed and beheaded, a Puritan commonwealth was established in England, which lasted until 1660.

CHAPTER 3

RHYTHMS OF
COLONIAL LIFE:
THE STATISTICS
OF COLONIAL
MASSACHUSETTS
BAY

188,000, making it one of Great Britain's most populous North American possessions.

This rapid population growth forced the government of Massachusetts Bay (called the General Court, which included the governor, the deputy governor, the executive council of assistants, and the representatives, all elected annually by the freemen)[3] to organize new towns. Within the first year of settlement, the six original towns of Massachusetts Bay were laid out: Dorchester, Roxbury, Watertown, Newtown (now Cambridge), Charlestown, and Boston, all on the Charles River. By the time Middlesex County (west of Boston) was organized in 1643, there were eight towns in that county alone, and by 1700, there were twenty-two.

The organization of towns was an important way for Puritan leaders to keep control of the rapidly growing population. Unlike settlers in the middle and southern colonies, colonists in Massachusetts Bay could not simply travel to an uninhabited area, select a parcel of land, and receive individual title to the land from the colonial governor. Instead, a group of men who wanted to establish a town had to apply to the General Court for a land grant for the entire town. Leaders of the prospective new town were then selected, and the single church was organized. Having received the grant from the General Court, the new town's leaders apportioned the avail-

able land among the male heads of households who were church members, holding in common some land for grazing and other uses (hence the "town common"). In this way, the Puritan leadership retained control of the fast-growing population, ensured Puritan economic and religious domination, and guaranteed that large numbers of dissenters—men and women who might divert the colony from its "holy mission" in the wilderness—would not be attracted to Massachusetts Bay.

Economically, Massachusetts Bay prospered from the very beginning, witnessing no "starving time" as did Virginia. Yet of all the major colonies, Massachusetts Bay fit the least well into England's mercantile system, whereby colonies supplied raw materials to the mother country and in turn purchased the mother country's manufactured products. Because comparatively rocky soil and a short growing season kept crop yields low and agricultural surpluses meager, many people in Massachusetts Bay had to seek other ways of making a living. Many men petitioned the General Court to organize new towns on the frontier; others turned to either the sea as fishermen, traders, shippers, and seamen or native manufacturing enterprises such as iron product manufacturing, rum distilling, shipbuilding, and rope-making. Except for fishing, none of these activities fit into England's mercantile plans for empire, and some undertakings were prohibited outright by the Navigation Acts (1660, 1663, and later, which set up the mercantile system), which most citizens of Massachusetts Bay ignored.

3. A freeman was an adult male who was accepted by his town (hence a landowner) and was a member of the Puritan congregational church.

The restoration of the English monarchy in 1660 in the person of Charles II greatly concerned the Massachusetts Bay colonists. It was no secret that Charles II loathed Puritanism. The new monarch also made it clear that the Navigation Acts would be enforced. After more than twenty years of wrangling among the colony, the king, and the Lords of Trade, in 1684 the Massachusetts Bay charter was revoked; in 1685, the colony was included in a grand scheme to reorganize the northern colonies into the Dominion of New England, with one royal governor and no elected assembly.[4] The dominion's governor, the undiplomatic Sir Edmund Andros, further alienated Massachusetts Bay colonists by levying taxes on them without consultation or consent, enforcing the Navigation Acts, favoring religious toleration in Massachusetts Bay, and calling their land titles into question. As a result, Massachusetts Bay colonists were only too glad to use the confusion and instability accompanying England's Glorious Revolution of 1688 to stage a bloodless coup that deposed Andros and returned the colony to its original form of government, an act that the mother country ultimately approved. Thus from almost the very beginning, the colonists of Massachusetts Bay were politically aware and jealously guarded their representative government.

Not only were the Massachusetts Bay colonists' political ideas sharp-

ened and refined decades before the American Revolution, but their other ways of thinking also were greatly affected. Two important intellectual movements in Europe, the Enlightenment and the Great Awakening, had an enormous impact in America. The Enlightenment was grounded in the belief that human reason could discover the natural laws that governed the universe, nature, and human affairs; human reason and scientific observation would reveal those natural laws to human beings. Although the Enlightenment's greatest impact was on the well-educated and therefore the wealthier citizens, even the "common" people were affected by it. The Great Awakening was a religious revival that swept through the colonies in the 1740s and 1750s. Touched off by English preacher George Whitefield, the Great Awakening emphasized humanity's utter sinfulness and need for salvation. In hundreds of emotional revival meetings, complete with shouting, moaning, and physical gyrations, thousands were converted. Because the Great Awakening undermined the traditional churches and their leaders, most clergymen (called "Old Lights") opposed the movement, but to little avail.

On the surface, the Enlightenment and the Great Awakening seemed to have nothing in common. The Enlightenment emphasized human reason, whereas the Great Awakening appealed more to emotion than to reason. Both movements, however, contained a strong streak of individualism: The Enlightenment emphasized the potential of the human mind, and the Great Awakening concentrated on

---

4. The Dominion of New England included the colonies of New Jersey, New York, Connecticut, Rhode Island, Plymouth, and Massachusetts Bay, which included lands that later became New Hampshire and Maine.

CHAPTER 3

RHYTHMS OF
COLONIAL LIFE:
THE STATISTICS
OF COLONIAL
MASSACHUSETTS
BAY

the individual soul. Each movement in its own way increased the colonists' sense of themselves as individuals who possessed both individual rights and individual futures. The colonists who once huddled together for protection and mutual assistance in tiny settlements had, by the mid-eighteenth century, grown, changed, and matured, as had the settlements they had built. They harbored new attitudes about themselves, their society, their individual futures, and, almost inevitably, their government. Hence the life and thought of a Massachusetts Bay colonist (or, indeed, any other colonist) born in 1750 was profoundly different from that of one born in 1650.

When most people think of the colonial period in America, they invariably think of the colonial leaders, men and women who held the economic, social, and political reins of the society. But these leaders—the John Winthrops and Anne Hutchinsons, the Jonathan Edwardses and Benjamin Franklins, the William Penns and Nathaniel Bacons—represent only a tiny fraction of the men and women who lived in the colonies between 1607 and 1775. And yet to understand the processes of growth, change, and maturation fully, it is necessary for us to study the lives of the "ordinary" men, women, and children, as well as those of their economic, social, and political "betters." How did the processes of growth, change, and maturation affect small farmers and artisans and their spouses, sons, and daughters? How did the situations of these people change over time? How did they react to those changes? Indeed, if we can learn more about the lives of all Americans, not just those of the prominent colonists, we will be able to understand better the extent to which growth, change, and maturation helped effect the American Revolution.

It is considerably easier to collect information about the leading colonial figures than the "average" men and women. Few of the farmers, artisans, or laborers left diaries or letters to provide clues to their thoughts and behavior; fewer made speeches or participated in decision making; fewer still talked with leaders like Washington and Jefferson, so their thoughts and actions were much less likely to be recorded for us by others. In some ways, then, a curtain has been drawn across a large part of American colonial history, obscuring the lives, thoughts, and feelings of the vast majority of the colonists. Sometimes even their names have been lost.

⟳ THE METHOD ⟳

How can we hope to reconstruct the lives, thoughts, and feelings of people who left no letters, diaries, sermons, speeches, or votes for us to analyze? Recently, historians have become more imaginative in using the relatively limited records at their disposal to examine the lives of ordinary men, women, and children who lived during the colonial period. Almost every per-

Table 1

Type of Record	Questions
Census	Is the population growing, shrinking, or stationary? Is the ratio of males to females roughly equal?[5] Does that ratio change over time?
Marriage	At what age are women marrying? Is that age changing over time?
Wills, probate	How are estates divided? Is that method changing over time? Based on real estate and personal property listed, is the collective standard of living rising, falling, or stationary? Based on dates of death, is the population living longer?
Land, tax	What percentage of the adult male population owns land? Is that percentage changing over time? Is the land evenly distributed among the adult male population?

son, even the poorest, left some record that she or he existed. That person's name may appear in any of a number of records, including church records stating when she or he was baptized, marriage records, property-holding records, civil- or criminal-court records, military records, tax records, and death or cemetery records. It is in these records that the lives of the ordinary men, women, and children of colonial America can be examined. An increasing number of historians have been carefully scrutinizing those records to re-create the lives and attitudes of those who left no other evidence.

How is this done? Most historians interested in the lives of the ordinary colonists rely heavily on statistics. Instead of trying to uncover all the records relating to one person or family (which might not be representative of the whole population), these historians use statistics to create *collective biographies*—that is, biographies of population groups (farmers in Andover, Massachusetts, for example) rather than biographies of certain individuals. The historians collect all (or a sample of all) the birth, death, and marriage records of a community and look at all (or a sample of all) the wills, probate records,[6] tax and landholding records, and census data. These historians are forming an aggregate or collective picture of a community and how that community has changed over time. Are women marrying later? What percentage of women remain unmarried? Are women having fewer children than they were in another time? Are inheritance patterns (the methods of dividing estates among heirs) changing over time? Are farms

5. Because males and females are born in roughly equal numbers, an unequal ratio of males to females (called a sex ratio) must be explained by events such as wars, out-migration, in-migration, or differing mortality rates for males and females.

6. Probate records are public records of processed wills.

CHAPTER 3

RHYTHMS OF
COLONIAL LIFE:
THE STATISTICS
OF COLONIAL
MASSACHUSETTS
BAY

increasing or decreasing in size? To the historian, each statistical summary of records (each set of statistics or *aggregate* picture) contains information that increases understanding of the community being studied.

After the statistics are compiled, what does the historian do next? Each set of statistics is examined separately to see what changes are occurring over time. Table 1 shows the types of questions historians ask of several different types of records.

Having examined each set of statistics, the historian places the sets in some logical order, which may vary depending on the available evidence, the central questions the historian is attempting to answer, and the historian's own preferences. Some historians prefer a "birth-to-death" ordering, beginning with age-at-marriage statistics for females and moving chronologically through the collective life of the community's population. Others prefer to isolate the demographic statistical sets (birth, marriage, migration, and death) from the economic sets (such as landholding and division of estates).

Up to this point, the historian has (1) collected the statistics and arranged them into sets, (2) examined each set and measured tendencies or changes over time, and (3) arranged the sets in some logical order. Now the historian must begin asking "why" for each set. For example:

1. Why does the method of dividing estates change over time?
2. Why are women marrying later?
3. Why are premarital pregnancies increasing?

In many cases, the answer to each question (and other "why" questions) is in one of the other statistical sets. That may cause the historian to alter his or her ordering of the sets to make the story clearer.

The historian is actually linking the sets to one another to form a chain. When two sets have been linked (because one set answers the "why" question of another set), the historian repeats the process until all the sets have been linked to form one chain of evidence. At that point, the historian can summarize the tendencies that have been discovered and, if desired, can connect those trends or tendencies with other events occurring in the period, such as the American Revolution.

One example of how historians link statistical sets together to answer the question "why" is sufficient. Source 1 in the Evidence section shows that the white population growth in Massachusetts Bay was extremely rapid between 1660 and 1770 (the growth rate actually approximates those of many non-Western developing nations today). How can we account for this rapid growth? Look at Source 4, which deals with the survival rate of children born in the town of Andover between 1640 and 1759. Note that between 1640 and 1699, the survival rate was very high (in Sweden between 1751 and 1799, 50 percent of the children born did not reach the age of fifteen). Also examine Source 16, the average number of births per marriage in Andover. Note that between 1655 and 1704, the average number of births per marriage was very high—between 5.3 and 7.6. Thus we can conclude that the population grew so rapidly in Massachusetts Bay between 1660 and 1700 because women gave birth to large numbers of children *and* a high percentage of those children survived. By following this process, you will be able to link together all the statistical sets.

Occasionally, however, you will need more information than statistics (some of which are unavailable) can provide. For example, notice in Sources 1 and 2 that the average annual growth rates were generally declining but there was a sharp *increase* in the population growth rates in the 1720s. This increase cannot be explained by the statistics in Sources 4 and 16, so another reason must be found. In fact, beginning in 1713, the number of religious dissenters who immigrated to Massachusetts Bay from Great Britain increased significantly, due to the end of intermittent warfare and to crop failures in northern Ireland. That swelling of immigration lasted for only about twenty years, after which it once again subsided. The town of Andover was host (albeit unwillingly) to some of those immigrants. Thus you can see that population increases in Massachusetts Bay and in Andover between 1713 and 1740 were the results of natural increase *plus* a temporary jump in immigration. If you have similar problems with other statistical sets, consult your instructor for assistance.

Remember that we are dealing with a society that was not as statistically oriented as ours. Several of the statistics you would like to have simply are not obtainable. The statistics we do have, however, provide a fascinating window for us to observe the lives of "ordinary" men, women, and children who lived centuries ago.

In this chapter, you will be using the statistics provided to identify important trends affecting the men, women, and children of Massachusetts Bay in the century preceding the American Revolution. Use the process described below:

1. Examine each statistical set, especially for a change over time.
2. Ask why that change took place.
3. Find the answer in another set, thereby establishing a linkage.
4. Repeat the process until all the sets have been linked together.
5. Then ask the central questions: What important trends affected the men, women, and children of colonial Massachusetts Bay in the century preceding the American Revolution? How were people likely to think and feel about those trends? Finally, how might those trends have contributed to the decision of Massachusetts Bay colonists to revolt against Great Britain?

As you will see, most of the statistical sets deal with Concord and Andover, two older towns in the Massachusetts Bay colony (see the following map). These two towns were chosen because historians Robert Gross and Philip Greven collected much statistical information about Concord and Andover, respectively; we have arranged the data in tabular form. Evidence suggests that these two towns are fairly representative of other towns in the eastern part of the colony. Concord, a farm town founded in 1635, was the first town in Massachu-

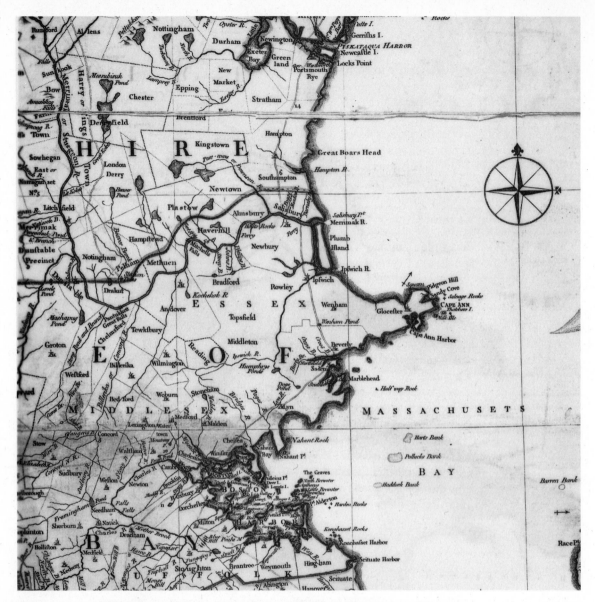

The eastern part of Massachusetts Bay colony, 1755. Reproduced from Thomas Jefferys's "A Map of the Most Inhabited Part of New England, Containing the Provinces of Massachusetts Bay, and New Hampshire, with the Colonies of Connecticut and Rhode Island. November 29, 1755"; in Jefferys's *A General Topography of North America and the West Indies* (London, 1768); courtesy of the Map Division, The New York Public Library, Astor, Lenox and Tilden Foundations.

setts Bay established away from the Charles River. The area was rich in furs, and settlers initially were able to trap the furs (especially beaver) for income. Andover was organized in 1646, the original settlers mainly from other towns in the colony. In Andover, the people lived in the village and walked out to farm their land, which was organized in the open-field system (landowners owned several strips of land in large open fields and worked the fields in common). In Concord, many settlers lived outside the village and near the fields, building clusters of houses along the Concord River (which was spanned by the soon-to-be-famous Old North Bridge).

As you examine the statistical sets from these two towns, note that the dates for the sets do not always match. Understand both *what* you are examining and *when* that particular factor is being measured. For example, the statistical set on premarital conceptions in Andover records that phenomenon from 1655 to 1739, whereas the same phenomenon in Concord is measured from 1740 to 1774 (see Source 17). Assuming that this trend is similar in both towns, how would you use those two sets of statistics?

At first the statistics appear cold and impersonal and seem to tell us little that is worth knowing. But we cannot just skip this problem and get on to the political events leading up to the American Revolution (such as the Boston Massacre) and the important battles of the Revolution. It is crucial

to remember that some of the men and boys who were on the streets of Boston on the evening of March 5, 1770, are counted in these statistics. And some of the men who participated in the Battles of Lexington and Concord also appear in these statistics. Are there any links between what the statistics represent and the subsequent behaviors of these people? Remember that in this chapter you are dealing not with numbers but with *people:* men, women, and children who had hopes, dreams, problems, and fears not unlike some of your own.

Working with historical statistics is not so difficult as it may first appear. Often it is helpful to establish a small study group with a few of your classmates, if your instructor permits it. As the study group talks through the problem, each individual can contribute something that possibly the other members of the group did not see, thereby broadening the group's understanding of the problem. Analyzing statistics is a challenging undertaking, but the results can be immensely satisfying, as you come to "see" the *people* the statistics represent.

You are bombarded almost daily with statistics—about teen pregnancies, inflation rates, illegal drug use, political polling results, and just about any other subject you can think of. In order to refer to yourself as a truly educated person, you must be able to analyze and understand these numbers, some of which are critical to your own life.

CHAPTER 3

RHYTHMS OF
COLONIAL LIFE:
THE STATISTICS
OF COLONIAL
MASSACHUSETTS
BAY

⚭ THE EVIDENCE ⚭

Source 1 reprinted from U.S. Bureau of the Census, *Historical Statistics of the United States, Colonial Times to 1957* (Washington, D.C.: U.S. Government Printing Office, 1960), p. 756.

1. Growth of White Population, Massachusetts Bay, 1660–1770.

Year	Population	Average Annual Growth Rate (%)
1660	20,082	—
1670	30,000	4.9
1680	39,752	3.3
1690	49,504	2.5
1700	55,941	1.3
1710	62,390	1.2
1720	91,008	4.6
1730	114,116	2.6
1740	151,613	3.3
1750	188,000	2.4
1760	222,600	1.8
1770	235,308	.57

Source 2 data from Philip J. Greven, Jr., *Four Generations: Population, Land, and Family in Colonial Andover, Massachusetts* (Ithaca, N.Y.: Cornell University Press, 1970), p. 179.

2. Growth of White Population, Town of Andover, 1680–1776.

Year	Population	Average Annual Growth Rate (%)
1680	435	—
1685	600	7.6
1695	710	1.8
1705	945	3.3
1715	1,050	1.1
1725	1,305	2.4
1735	1,630	2.5
1745	1,845	1.3
1755	2,135	1.6
1764	2,442	1.6
1776	2,953	1.8

Source 3 data from Robert A. Gross, *The Minutemen and Their World* (New York: Hill and Wang, 1976), p. 15.

3. Growth of Population, Town of Concord, 1679–1750.

Year	Population	Average Annual Growth Rate (%)
1679	480	—
1706	920	3.3
1710	c. 1,000	2.2
1725	c. 1,500	3.3
1750	c. 2,000	1.3

Sources 4 through 6 data from Greven, *Four Generations: Population, Land, and Family in Colonial Andover, Massachusetts,* pp. 191, 189, 177. Source 6 data also from Gross, *The Minutemen and Their World,* p. 209.

4. Children Born Between 1640 and 1759 Who Lived to at Least Age 10, Andover.

Years	Rate
1640–1669	917 per 1,000
1670–1699	855 per 1,000
1700–1729	805 per 1,000
1730–1759	695 per 1,000

5. Children Who Died Before Reaching Age 20, Andover, 1670–1759.

Years	Number	Mortality Rate[7]
1670–1699	87	225 per 1,000
1700–1729	206	381 per 1,000
1730–1759	142	534 per 1,000

7. The mortality rate is the ratio of the number of deaths per thousand people. It is used to compare the deaths in two or more populations of unequal size, such as those of Andover and Boston.

CHAPTER 3

RHYTHMS OF
COLONIAL LIFE:
THE STATISTICS
OF COLONIAL
MASSACHUSETTS
BAY

6. Population Density (persons per square mile), Concord and Andover, 1705–1776 (various years).

Year	Concord	Andover
1705		16.0
1706	14.7	
1754	44.2[8]	
1755		36.2
1764		41.0
1765	48.0	
1776	62.7	50.0

8. In 1729, the town of Bedford was formed from lands originally in Concord. Then, in 1735, the town of Acton was created from lands that had been part of Concord. Finally, in 1754, the town of Lincoln was set off from Concord. These losses of lands were taken into account when computing population density for 1754, 1765, and 1776.

Source 7 data from James A. Henretta, *The Evolution of American Society, 1700–1815: An Interdisciplinary Approach,* 1st ed. (Lexington, Mass.: D. C. Heath, 1973), p. 15.

7. Average New England Farm Size, 1650s and 1750s.

1650s: 200–300 acres (3–6 percent cultivated)
1750s: Under 100 acres (10–15 percent cultivated)

Sources 8 through 10 data from Gross, *The Minutemen and Their World,* pp. 210, 215, 214.

8. Average Landholding, Concord, 1663 and 1749.

Year	Amount of Land
1663	259 acres
1749	56 acres

9. Crop Yields per Acre, Concord, 1749 and 1771.

Year	Grain	Hay
1749	13.2 bushels	0.82 ton
1771	12.2 bushels	0.71 ton

10. Amount of Land Necessary to Pasture One Cow, Concord, 1749 and 1771.

Year	Average
1749	1.4
1771	2.2

CHAPTER 3

RHYTHMS OF
COLONIAL LIFE:
THE STATISTICS
OF COLONIAL
MASSACHUSETTS
BAY

Source 11 data from Henretta, *The Evolution of American Society,* p. 19.

11. Average Period of Fallow,[9] New England Farms, 1650 and 1770.

1650: Field left fallow between 7 and 15 years
1770: Field left fallow between 1 and 2 years

Source 12 data from Greven, *Four Generations: Population, Land, and Family in Colonial Andover, Massachusetts,* p. 216.

12. Abbot Family, Andover, Massachusetts, 1650 and 1750.

1650: George Abbot was only adult male Abbot
1750: 25 adult male Abbots in Andover

Source 13 data from Henretta, *The Evolution of American Society,* pp. 29–30.

13. Division of Estates, Andover, Massachusetts.[10]

First generation: 95 percent of all estates divided among all male heirs
Second generation: 75 percent of all estates divided among all male heirs
Third generation: 58 percent of all estates divided among all male heirs
Fourth generation (came to maturity after 1750): under 50 percent of all
  estates divided among all male heirs

Source 14 from Gross, *The Minutemen and Their World,* p. 216.

14. Insolvent Estates, Concord, 1740–1774.

Years	Total Estates	Number of Insolvent Estates
1740–1760	19	1
1760–1774	30	11

9. Fallow land is plowed and tilled but left unseeded during a growing season. Land is left fallow to replenish the soil's nutrients. Colonial farmers as a rule did not use fertilizer.
10. A widow inherited her late husband's estate only if the couple had no male heirs (sons). Otherwise, the land was passed down to the sons. Daughters received personal property (money, silverware, livestock, etc.).

Sources 15 through 17 data from Greven, *Four Generations: Population, Land, and Family in Colonial Andover, Massachusetts,* pp. 33, 23, 105, 183, 113. Source 17 data also from Gross, *The Minutemen and Their World,* p. 217.

15. Average Age at Marriage for Females, Andover, 1650–1724.

Year	Age
1650–1654	18.0
1660–1664	18.8
1670–1674	20.4
1680–1684	21.6
1690–1694	21.6
1700–1704	21.0
1710–1714	24.0
1720–1724	23.9

16. Average Births per Marriage, Andover, 1655–1764.

Year	Births
1655–1664	5.8
1665–1674	5.3
1675–1684	5.7
1685–1694	6.0
1695–1704	7.6
1705–1714	7.5
1715–1724	5.7
1725–1734	4.8
1735–1744	4.1
1745–1754	4.0
1755–1764	3.9

17. Percentage of Premarital Conceptions,[11] Andover, 1655–1739, and Concord, 1740–1774.

Years	Andover	Concord
1655–1674	0.0	
1675–1699	7.0	
1700–1739	11.3	
1740–1749		19
1750–1759		26
1760–1774		41

11. *Premarital conceptions* refers to first-born children who were born less than nine months from the date of marriage.

CHAPTER 3

RHYTHMS OF
COLONIAL LIFE:
THE STATISTICS
OF COLONIAL
MASSACHUSETTS
BAY

Source 18 data from Gary B. Nash, "Urban Wealth and Poverty in Pre-Revolutionary America," *Journal of Interdisciplinary History,* 6 (Spring 1976), pp. 545–584.

18. Percentage of Group Migration[12] into Boston, 1747, 1759, and 1771.

Group	1747	1759	1771
Single men	3.0%	8.5%	23.4%
Single women	4.0	16.8	20.0
Widows and widowers	7.9	8.9	4.4
Married couples	33.6	27.4	27.5
Children	51.5	38.4	24.7
	100.0%	100.0%	100.0%

Source 19 data from Gross, *The Minutemen and Their World,* p. 218.

19. Sex Ratio, Concord, 1765.

88 males to 100 females

Sources 20 through 22 data from Nash, "Urban Wealth and Poverty in Pre-Revolutionary America," pp. 545–584.

20. Distribution of Wealth by Percentage[13] in Boston, 1687 and 1771.

Wealth Distribution	1687	1771
Wealth possessed by the richest 5% of the people	30.2	48.7
Wealth possessed by the next wealthiest 5% of the people	16.1	14.7
Wealth possessed by the next wealthiest 30% of the people	39.8	27.4
Wealth possessed by the next wealthiest 30% of the people	11.3	9.1
Wealth possessed by the poorest 30% of the people	2.6	0.1

12. *Migration* refers to internal migration, not emigration from Europe.
13. See Questions to Consider for assistance in reading this source.

21. Taxables[14] in Boston, 1728–1771.

Year	Population	Taxables
1728	12,650	c. 3,000
1733	15,100	c. 3,500
1735	16,000	3,637
1738	16,700	3,395
1740	16,800	3,043
1741	16,750	2,972
1745	16,250	2,660
1750	15,800	c. 2,400
1752	15,700	2,789
1756	15,650	c. 2,500
1771	15,500	2,588

22. Poor Relief in Boston, 1700–1775.

Years	Population	Average Annual Expenditure in Pounds Sterling	Expenditure in Pounds Sterling per 1,000 Population
1700–1710	7,500	173	23
1711–1720	9,830	181	18
1721–1730	11,840	273	23
1731–1740	15,850	498	31
1741–1750	16,240	806	50
1751–1760	15,660	1,204	77
1761–1770	15,520	1,909	123
1771–1775	15,500	2,478	156

❦ QUESTIONS TO CONSIDER ❦

When using statistics, first look at each set individually. For each set, ask the following questions:

1. What does this set of statistics measure?
2. How does what is being measured change over time?

14. *Taxables* refers to the number of people who owned a sufficient amount of property (real estate and buildings) to be taxed.

3. Why does that change take place? As noted, the answer to this question can be found in another set or sets. When you connect one set to another, statisticians say that you have made a *linkage*.

A helpful way of examining the statistical sets is to think of three children born in Massachusetts Bay: one in 1650, a second in 1700, and the

CHAPTER 3

RHYTHMS OF
COLONIAL LIFE:
THE STATISTICS
OF COLONIAL
MASSACHUSETTS
BAY

third in 1750. As you look at the statistical evidence, ask yourself how the lives of these three children (male or female) were different. What factors accounted for those differences?

Begin by examining Sources 1 through 3, which deal with population increase in Massachusetts Bay as a whole, in Andover, and in Concord. How did population growth change over time? How can Sources 4, 5, 15, and 16 help you answer the "why" question for population growth?

Because immigration to Massachusetts Bay from Europe declined drastically in the 1640s and did not resume significantly until the early 1700s, population increases in the period in between can be explained only by migration from other colonies (which was negligible) or by natural increase. How did natural increase change over time (Sources 4, 5, and 16)? How would you explain this change? To answer that question, you will have to use your historical imagination as well as *all* the rest of the sources. For example, how might you explain the dramatic increase in child mortality, as seen in Sources 4 and 5? Look again at Sources 6 through 12 and Source 14, this time with that specific question in mind. As you now see, the same statistics can be used to answer different questions.

We can see that one result of population growth in Andover and Concord was a rise in population density. What were the *results* of that increase in population density? Begin by examining Sources 6 through 11. How did farming change over time? Why was this so (see earlier sources plus Source 12, on the Abbot family)? How did

those changes affect the division of estates (Source 13) and the number of insolvent estates (Source 14), and why? Did economic changes have any effect on the female life cycle? Consider the following demographic changes: the average age at marriage for Andover females (Source 15), the number of births per marriage (Source 16), and the significant increase in premarital conceptions (Source 17).

At this point, it helps to pause and take stock of what you have learned. What was the relationship between population growth and farming? Between changes in farming and social conditions? Would you say that the lifestyle of Massachusetts Bay colonists was improving, declining, or stationary during the first century of the colony's history? How would you prove your answer?

As noted at the beginning of this chapter, one important factor that historians study is the ability of people to adapt to changes in their environment or circumstances. In your view, how were Massachusetts Bay colonists attempting to adapt to these changes? Would you say they were or were not successful?

Many of the people we have been examining chose to adapt by leaving their towns and migrating to the frontier to set up new communities where they could make fresh starts. Many others, however, adapted by migrating to Boston (Source 18). How could you prove this? How did migration to Boston change in character between 1747 and 1771? How did migration affect the towns from which these people migrated (see Source 19)? What were the likely results of that migration?

Our attention now should follow those migrants to Boston. Were these migrants able to improve their collective situation in that large seaport? How could you prove your answer to that question?

At this point, we are at Source 20, wealth distribution in Boston. Note that Boston was not a farming village like Andover and Concord. Read the set this way: the richest 5 percent of those living in Boston in 1687 owned 30.2 percent of the town's taxable wealth (essentially real estate and buildings), but by 1771 the richest 5 percent owned 48.7 percent of the town's taxable wealth; the poorest 30 percent of those living in Boston in 1687 owned 2.6 percent of the town's taxable wealth, but by 1771 the poorest 30 percent owned 0.1 percent of the town's taxable wealth. Read the chart the same way for the groups in between. As you examine the chart, note which groups were gaining in wealth and which groups were losing in wealth.

Sources 21 and 22 are different ways of looking at the same problem. How are those sources related to one another? How can you link them back to the chain you have made?

At this point, you should be able to answer these central questions:

1. What important trends regarding growth, change, and maturation affected the people of colonial Massachusetts Bay?
2. How were people likely to think and feel about those trends?
3. How might those trends have contributed to the decision of Massachusetts Bay colonists to revolt against Great Britain?

 EPILOGUE

Many of the men who fought on the Patriot side in either Continental Line (the troops under the central government) or the Massachusetts Bay militia came from the towns, farms, and seaports of Massachusetts Bay. If asked why they would endure hardships to fight against the mother country, most probably would have said that they were fighting for liberty and independence—and undoubtedly they were. But we now realize that a number of other factors were present that may very well have provided strong reasons for these men to contest the British. Whether they fully understood these forces can never be known with certainty because very few left any written record that might help us comprehend their thoughts or behavior.

The American Revolution was a momentous event not just for Americans but ultimately for many other people as well. As Ralph Waldo Emerson wrote years later, it was a "shot heard 'round the world." The American Revolution was the first anticolonial rebellion that was successful on the first try, and as such it provided a model for others in Latin America and elsewhere. As a revolt against author-

CHAPTER 3

RHYTHMS OF
COLONIAL LIFE:
THE STATISTICS
OF COLONIAL
MASSACHUSETTS
BAY

ity, the American Revolution made many European rulers tremble because if the ideas contained in the Declaration of Independence (especially that of the right of revolution against unjust rulers) ever became widespread, their own tenures might well be doomed. And, beginning with the French Revolution, this is precisely what happened; gradually, crowns began to topple all across the Continent. Indeed, many would have agreed with the Frenchman Turgot, who, writing of America in the 1780s, noted the following:

> This people is the hope of the human race. It may become the model. It ought to show the world, by facts, that men can be free and yet peaceful, and may dispense with the chains in which tyrants and knaves . . . have presumed to bind them. . . . The Americans should be an example of political, religious, commercial and industrial liberty. The asylum they offer to the oppressed of every nation, the

avenue of escape they open, will compel governments to be just and enlightened.[15]

The Revolution obviously brought independence and in the long run became one of the significant events in world history. But did it alter or reverse the economic and social trends that, as we have seen, were affecting the men, women, and children of colonial New England? In 1818, the U.S. Congress passed an act providing pensions for impoverished veterans of the War of Independence and their widows. Congressmen believed that there were approximately 1,400 poor veterans and widows who were still alive. Yet an astounding 30,000 applied for pensions, 20,000 of whom were ultimately approved to receive these benefits. Clearly, the American Revolution, although an event that had worldwide significance, did not necessarily change the lives of all the men and women who participated in it. Or did it?

15. Richard Price, *Observations on the Importance of the American Revolution, and the Means of Making It a Benefit to the World* (London: printed for T. Cadell, 1785), pp. 102, 123.

CHAPTER 4

WHAT REALLY HAPPENED IN THE BOSTON MASSACRE? THE TRIAL OF CAPTAIN THOMAS PRESTON

⤻ THE PROBLEM ⤸

On the chilly evening of March 5, 1770, a small group of boys began taunting a British sentry (called a "Centinel" or "Sentinel") in front of the Boston Custom House. Pushed to the breaking point by this goading, the soldier struck one of his tormentors with his musket. Soon a crowd of fifty or sixty gathered around the frightened soldier, prompting him to call for help. The officer of the day, Captain Thomas Preston, and seven British soldiers hurried to the Custom House to protect the sentry.

Upon arriving at the Custom House, Captain Preston must have sensed how precarious his position was. The crowd had swelled to more than one hundred, some anxious for a fight, oth-

ers simply curiosity seekers, and still others called from their homes by the town's church bells, a traditional signal that a fire had broken out. Efforts by Preston and others to calm the crowd proved useless. And because the crowd had enveloped Preston and his men as it had the lone sentry, escape was nearly impossible.

What happened next is a subject of considerable controversy. One of the soldiers fired his musket into the crowd, and the others followed suit, one by one. The colonists scattered, leaving five dead[1] and six wounded,

1. Those killed were Crispus Attucks (a black seaman in his forties, who also went by the name of Michael Johnson), James Caldwell

[71]

CHAPTER 4

WHAT REALLY
HAPPENED IN
THE BOSTON
MASSACRE?
THE TRIAL OF
CAPTAIN
THOMAS
PRESTON

some of whom were probably innocent bystanders. Preston and his men quickly returned to their barracks, where they were placed under house arrest. They were later taken to jail and charged with murder.

Preston's trial began on October 24, 1770, delayed by the authorities in an attempt to cool the emotions of the townspeople. Soon after the March 5 event, however, a grand jury had taken sworn depositions from Preston, the soldiers, and more than ninety Bostonians. The depositions leaked out (in a pamphlet, probably published by anti-British extremists), helping to keep emotions at a fever pitch.

John Adams, Josiah Quincy, and Robert Auchmuty had agreed to defend Preston,[2] even though the first two were staunch Patriots. They believed that the captain was entitled to a fair trial and did their best to defend

him. After a difficult jury selection, the trial began, witnesses for the prosecution and the defense being called mostly from those who had given depositions to the grand jury. The trial lasted for four days, an unusually long trial for the times. The case went to the jury at 5:00 P.M. on October 29. Although it took the jury only three hours to reach a verdict, the decision was not announced until the following day.

In this chapter, you will be using portions of the evidence given at the murder trial of Captain Thomas Preston to reconstruct what actually happened on that March 5, 1770, evening in Boston, Massachusetts. Was Preston guilty as charged? Or was he innocent? Only by reconstructing the event that we call the Boston Massacre will you be able to answer these questions.

BACKGROUND

The town of Boston[3] had been uneasy throughout the first weeks of 1770. Tension had been building since the early 1760s because the town was increasingly affected by the forces of migration, change, and maturation. The protests against the Stamp Act had been particularly bitter there, and men such as Samuel Adams were encouraging their fellow Bostonians to be even bolder in their remonstrances. In response, in 1768 the British government ordered two regiments of soldiers to Boston to restore order and enforce the laws of Parliament. "They

---

(a sailor), Patrick Carr (an immigrant from Ireland who worked as a leather-breeches maker), Samuel Gray (a rope-maker), and Samuel Maverick (a seventeen-year-old apprentice).

2. Adams, Quincy, and Auchmuty (pronounced Aŭk′mŭty) also were engaged to defend the soldiers, a practice that would not be allowed today because of the conflict of interest (defending more than one person charged with the same crime).

3. Although Boston was one of the largest urban centers in the colonies, the town was

---

not incorporated as a city. Several attempts were made, but residents opposed them, fearing they would lose the institution of the town meeting.

will not *find* a rebellion," quipped Benjamin Franklin of the soldiers, "they may indeed *make* one" (italics added).

Instead of bringing calm to Boston, the presence of soldiers only increased tensions. Incidents between Bostonians and redcoats were common on the streets, in taverns, and at the places of employment of British soldiers who sought part-time jobs to supplement their meager salaries. Known British sympathizers and informers were harassed, and Crown officials were openly insulted. Indeed, the town of Boston seemed to be a powder keg just waiting for a spark to set off an explosion.

On February 22, 1770, British sympathizer and informer Ebenezer Richardson tried to tear down an anti-British sign. He was followed to his house by an angry crowd that proceeded to taunt him and break his windows with stones. One of the stones struck Richardson's wife. Enraged, he grabbed a musket and fired almost blindly into the crowd. Eleven-year-old Christopher Seider[4] fell to the ground with eleven pellets of shot in his chest. The boy died eight hours later. The crowd, by now numbering about one thousand, dragged Richardson from his house and through the streets, finally delivering him to the Boston jail. Four days later, the town conducted a huge funeral for Christopher Seider, probably arranged and organized by Samuel Adams. Seider's casket was carried through the streets by children, and approximately two thousand mourners (one-seventh of Boston's total population) took part.

All through the next week Boston was an angry town. Gangs of men and boys roamed the streets at night looking for British soldiers foolish enough to venture out alone. Similarly, off-duty soldiers prowled the same streets looking for someone to challenge them. A fight broke out at a ropewalk between some soldiers who worked there part time and some unemployed colonists.

With large portions of both the Boston citizenry and the British soldiers inflamed, an incident on March 5 touched off an ugly confrontation that took place in front of the Custom House, a symbol of British authority over the colonies. Both sides sought to use the event to support their respective causes. But Samuel Adams, a struggling attorney with a flair for politics and propaganda, clearly had the upper hand. The burial of the five "martyrs" was attended by almost every resident of Boston, and Adams used the event to push his demands for British troop withdrawal and to heap abuse on the mother country. Therefore, when the murder trial of Captain Thomas Preston finally opened in late October, emotions had hardly diminished.

Crowd disturbances had been an almost regular feature of life, in both England and America. Historian John Bohstedt has estimated that England was the scene of at least one thousand crowd disturbances and riots between 1790 and 1810.[5] Colonial American towns were no more placid; demon-

---

4. Christopher Seider is sometimes referred to as Christopher Snider.

5. John Bohstedt, *Riots and Community Politics in England and Wales, 1790–1810* (Cambridge, Mass.: Harvard University Press, 1983), p. 5.

CHAPTER 4

WHAT REALLY
HAPPENED IN
THE BOSTON
MASSACRE?
THE TRIAL OF
CAPTAIN
THOMAS
PRESTON

strations and riots were almost regular features of the colonists' lives. Destruction of property and burning of effigies were common in these disturbances. In August 1765 in Boston, for example, crowds protesting against the Stamp Act burned effigies and destroyed the homes of stamp distributor Andrew Oliver and Massachusetts Lieutenant Governor Thomas Hutchinson. Indeed, it was almost as if the entire community was willing to countenance demonstrations and riots as long as they were confined to parades, loud gatherings, and limited destruction of property. In almost no cases were there any deaths, and the authorities seldom fired on the crowds. Yet on March 5, 1770, both the crowd and the soldiers acted uncharacteristically. The result was the tragedy that colonists dubbed the "Boston Massacre." Why did the crowd and the soldiers behave as they did?

To repeat, your task is to reconstruct the so-called Boston Massacre so as to understand what really happened on that fateful evening. Spelling and punctuation in the evidence have been modernized only to clarify the meaning.

❧ THE METHOD ❧

Many students (and some historians) like to think that facts speak for themselves. This is especially tempting when analyzing a single incident like the Boston Massacre, many eyewitnesses of which testified at the trial. However, discovering what really happened, even when there are eyewitnesses, is never quite that easy. Witnesses may be confused at the time, they may see only part of the incident, or they may unconsciously "see" only what they expect to see. Obviously, witnesses also may have some reasons to lie. Thus the testimony of witnesses must be carefully scrutinized, for both what the witnesses *mean* to tell us and other relevant information as well. Therefore, historians approach such testimony with considerable skepticism and are concerned not only with the testimony itself but also with the possible motives of the witnesses.

Neither Preston nor the soldiers testified at the captain's trial because English legal custom prohibited defendants in criminal cases from testifying in their own behalf (the expectation was that they would perjure themselves). One week after the massacre, however, in a sworn deposition, or statement, Captain Preston gave his side of the story. Although the deposition was not introduced at the trial and therefore the jury was not aware of what Preston himself had said, we have reproduced a portion of Preston's deposition for you to examine. How does Preston's deposition agree or disagree with other eyewitnesses' accounts?

No transcript of Preston's trial survives, if indeed one was ever made.

Trial testimony comes from an anonymous person's summary of what each person said, the notes of Robert Treat Paine (one of the lawyers for the prosecution), and one witness's (Richard Palmes's) reconstruction of what his testimony and the cross-examination had been. Although historians would prefer to use the original trial transcript and would do so if one were available, the anonymous summary, Paine's notes, and one witness's recollections are acceptable substitutes because probably all three people were present in the courtroom (Paine and Palmes certainly were) and the accounts tend to corroborate one another.

Almost all the witnesses were at the scene, yet not all their testimony is of equal merit. First try to reconstruct the scene itself: the actual order in which the events occurred and where the various participants were standing. Whenever possible, look for corroborating testimony: two or more reliable witnesses who heard or saw the same things.

Be careful to use all the evidence. You should be able to develop some reasonable explanation for the conflicting testimony and those things that do not fit into your reconstruction very well.

Almost immediately you will discover that some important pieces of evidence are missing. For example, it would be useful to know the individual backgrounds and political views of the witnesses. Unfortunately, we know very little about the witnesses themselves, and we can reconstruct the political ideas of only about one-third of them. Therefore, you will have to rely on the testimonies given, deducing which witnesses were telling the truth, which were lying, and which were simply mistaken.

The fact that significant portions of the evidence are missing is not disastrous. Historians seldom have all the evidence they need when they attempt to tackle a historical problem. Instead, they must be able to do as much as they can with the evidence that is available, using it as completely and imaginatively as they can. They do so by asking questions of the available evidence. Where were the witnesses standing? Which one seems more likely to be telling the truth? Which witnesses were probably lying? When dealing with the testimony of the witnesses, be sure to determine what is factual and what is a witness's opinion. A rough sketch of the scene has been provided. How can it help you?

Also included in the evidence is Paul Revere's famous engraving of the incident, probably plagiarized from a drawing by artist Henry Pelham. It is unlikely that either Pelham or Revere was an eyewitness to the Boston Massacre, yet Revere's engraving gained widespread distribution, and most people—in 1770 and today—tend to recall that engraving when they think of the Boston Massacre. Do not examine the engraving until you have read the trial account closely. Can Revere's engraving help you find out what really happened that night? How does the engraving fit the eyewitnesses' accounts? How do the engraving and the accounts differ? Why?

Keep the central question in mind: What really happened in the Boston Massacre? Throughout this exercise,

CHAPTER 4

WHAT REALLY
HAPPENED IN
THE BOSTON
MASSACRE?
THE TRIAL OF
CAPTAIN
THOMAS
PRESTON

you will be trying to determine whether an order to fire was actually given. If so, by whom? If not, how can you explain why shots were fired? As commanding officer, Thomas Preston was held responsible and charged with murder. You might want to consider the evidence available to you as either a prosecution or defense attorney. Which side had the stronger case?

∞ THE EVIDENCE ∞

1. Site of the Boston Massacre, Town House Area, 1770.

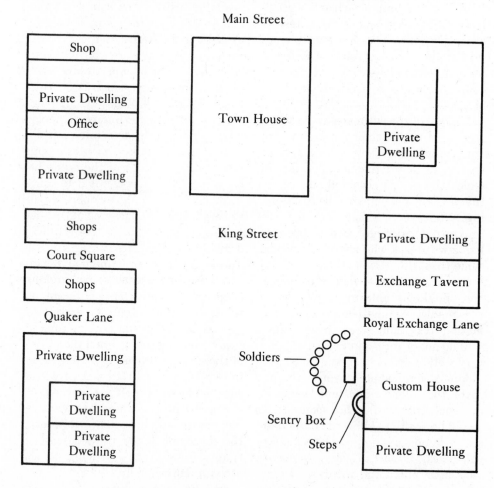

Source 2 from *Publications of The Colonial Society of Massachusetts,* Vol. VII (Boston: The Colonial Society of Massachusetts, 1905), pp. 8–9.

2. Deposition of Captain Thomas Preston, March 12, 1770 (Excerpt).

The mob still increased and were outrageous, striking their clubs or bludgeons one against another, and calling out, come on you rascals, you bloody backs, you lobster scoundrels, fire if you dare, G-d damn you, fire and be damned, we know you dare not, and much more such language was used. At this time I was between the soldiers and the mob, parleying with, and endeavoring all in my power to persuade them to retire peaceably, but to no purpose. They advanced to the points of the bayonets, struck some of them and even the muzzles of the pieces, and seemed to be endeavoring to close with the soldiers. On which some well behaved persons asked me if the guns were charged. I replied yes. They then asked me if I intended to order the men to fire. I answered no, by no means, observing to them that I was advanced before the muzzles of the men's pieces, and must fall a sacrifice if they fired; that the soldiers were upon the half cock[6] and charged bayonets, and my giving the word fire under those circumstances would prove me to be no officer. While I was thus speaking, one of the soldiers having received a severe blow with a stick, stepped a little to one side and instantly fired. . . . On this a general attack was made on the men by a great number of heavy clubs and snowballs being thrown at them, by which all our lives were in imminent danger, some persons at the same time from behind calling out, damn your bloods—why don't you fire. Instantly three or four of the soldiers fired. . . . On my asking the soldiers why they fired without orders, they said they heard the word fire and supposed it came from me. This might be the case as many of the mob called out fire, fire, but I assured the men that I gave no such order; that my words were, don't fire, stop your firing. . . .[7]

6. The cock of a musket had to be fully drawn back (cocked) for the musket to fire. In half cock, the cock was drawn only halfway back so that priming powder could be placed in the pan. The musket, however, would not fire at half cock. This is the origin of "Don't go off half cocked." See Source 5.

7. Depositions also were taken from the soldiers, three of whom claimed, "We did our Captain's orders and if we don't obey his commands should have been confined and shot." As with Preston's deposition, the jury was not aware of that statement. In addition, ninety-six depositions were taken from townspeople.

CHAPTER 4

WHAT REALLY
HAPPENED IN
THE BOSTON
MASSACRE?
THE TRIAL OF
CAPTAIN
THOMAS
PRESTON

Source 3 from Hiller B. Zobel, ed., *The Legal Papers of John Adams* (Cambridge, Mass.: Belknap Press of Harvard University Press, 1965), Vol. III, pp. 46–98.

3. The Trial of Captain Thomas Preston (*Rex v. Preston*), October 24–29 (Excerpt).

Witnesses for the King (Prosecution)

Edward Gerrish (or Garrick)

I heard a noise about 8 o'clock and went down to Royal Exchange Lane. Saw some Persons with Sticks coming up Quaker Lane. I said [to the sentry] Capt. Goldsmith owed my fellow Apprentice. He said he was a Gentleman and would pay every body. I said there was none in the Regiment.[8] He asked for me. I went to him, was not ashamed of my face. . . . The Sentinel left his Post and Struck me. I cried. My fellow Apprentice and a young man came up to the Sentinel and called him Bloody back.[9] He called to the Main Guard. . . . There was not a dozen people when the Sentinel called the Guard.

Ebenezer Hinkley

Just after 9 o'clock heard the Cry of Fire. I saw the party come out of the Guard House. A Capt. cried out of the Window "fire upon 'em damn 'em." I followed 'em down before the Custom House door. Capt. Preston was out and commanded 'em. They drew up and charged their Bayonets. Montgomery[10] pushed at the people advancing. In 2 or 3 minutes a Boy threw a small stick over hand and hit Montgomery on Breast. Then I heard the word fire in ¼ minute he fired. I saw some pieces of Snow as big as Egg thrown. 3 or 4 thrown at the same time of pushing on the other End of the file, before 1st gun fired. The body of People about a Rod[11] off. People said Damn 'em they durst not fire don't be afraid. No threats . . . I was a Rod from Capt. Preston. Did not hear him give Order to fire. ½ minute from 1st Gun to 2d. same to 3d. The others quicker. I saw no people striking the Guns or Bayonets nor pelting 'em. I saw Preston between people and Soldiers. I did not see him when 1st firing.

---

8. To say that there was no gentleman in the regiment was an insult to the sentry's superior officer, Captain Goldsmith.
9. British soldiers' coats were red.
10. Montgomery, one of the soldiers, undoubtedly fired the first shot.
11. A rod equals 16.5 feet.

Peter Cunningham

Upon the cry of fire and Bells ringing went into King Street, heard the Capt. say Turn out the Guard.[12] Saw the Centinel standing on the steps of the Custom house, pushing his Bayonet at the People who were about 30 or 40. Captain came and ordered the Men to prime and load.[13] He came before 'em about 4 or 5 minutes after and put up their Guns with his Arm. They then fired and were priming and loading again. I am pretty positive the Capt. bid 'em Prime and load. I stood about 4 feet off him. Heard no Order given to fire. The Person who gave Orders to Prime and load stood with his back to me, I did not see his face only when he put up their Guns. I stood about 10 or 11 feet from the Soldiers, the Captain about the midway between.

William Wyatt

I heard the bell, . . . saw People running several ways. The largest part went down to the North of the Townhouse. I went the South side, saw an officer leading out 8 or 10 Men. Somebody met the officer and said, Capt. Preston for Gods sake mind what you are about and take care of your Men. He went down to the Centinel, drew up his Men, bid them face about, Prime and load. I saw about 100 People in the Street huzzaing, crying fire, damn you fire. In about 10 minutes I heard the Officer say fire. The Soldiers took no notice. His back was to me. I heard the same voice say fire. The Soldiers did not fire. The Officer then stamped and said Damn your bloods fire be the consequences what it will. Immediately the first Gun was fired. I have no doubt the Officer was the same person the Man spoke to when coming down with the Guard. His back was to me when the last order was given. I was then about 5 or 6 yards off and within 2 yards at the first. He stood in the rear when the Guns were fired. Just before I heard a Stick, which I took to be upon a Gun. I did not see it. The Officer had to the best of my knowledge a cloth coloured Surtout[14] on. After the firing the Captain stepd forward before the Men and struck up their Guns. One was loading again and he damn'd 'em for firing and severely reprimanded 'em. I did not mean the Capt. had the Surtout but the Man who spoke to him when coming with the Guard.

12. To dress and equip so as to be ready for duty.
13. Muskets were loaded from the muzzle with powder, wadding, a ball, and more wadding. The hammer was drawn back halfway, and powder was poured into the small pan under the hammer. There was a small piece of flint attached to the cock (see Source 5) so that when the trigger was pulled, the cock would come down and the flint would spark and ignite the gunpowder in the pan. The fire would then ignite the gunpowder in the breech and fire the gun. If the powder in the pan exploded but did not ignite the powder in the breech, the result was a "flash in the pan" and a musket that did not fire.
14. A type of overcoat.

CHAPTER 4

WHAT REALLY
HAPPENED IN
THE BOSTON
MASSACRE?
THE TRIAL OF
CAPTAIN
THOMAS
PRESTON

Theodore Bliss

At home. I heard the Bells for fire.[15] Went out. Came to the Town House. The People told me there was going to be a Rumpus[16] with the Soldiers. Went to the Custom house. Saw Capt. Preston there with the Soldiers. Asked him if they were loaded. He said yes. If with Ball. He said nothing. I saw the People throw Snow Balls at the Soldiers and saw a Stick about 3 feet long strike a Soldier upon the right. He sallied[17] and then fired. A little time a second. Then the other[s] fast after one another. One or two Snow balls hit the Soldier, the stick struck, before firing. I know not whether he sallied on account of the Stick or step'd back to make ready. I did not hear any Order given by the Capt. to fire. I stood so near him I think I must have heard him if he had given an order to fire before the first firing. I never knew Capt. Preston before. I can't say whether he had a Surtout on, he was dressed in red. I know him to be the Man I took to be the Officer. The Man that fired first stood next to the Exchange lane. I saw none of the People press upon the Soldiers before the first Gun fired. I did after. I aimed a blow at him myself but did not strike him. I am sure the Captain stood before the Men when the first Gun was fired. I had no apprehension[18] the Capt. did give order to fire when the first Gun was fired. I thought, after the first Gun, the Capt. did order the Men to fire but do not certainly know.

Benjamin Burdick

When I came into King Street about 9 o'Clock I saw the Soldiers round the Centinel. I asked one if he was loaded and he said yes. I asked him if he would fire, he said yes by the Eternal God and pushd his Bayonet at me. After the firing the Captain came before the soldiers and put up their Guns with his arm and said stop firing, dont fire no more or dont fire again. I heard the word fire and took it and am certain that it came from behind the Soldiers. I saw a man passing busily behind who I took to be an Officer. The firing was a little time after. I saw some persons fall. Before the firing I saw a stick thrown at the Soldiers. The word fire I took to be a word of Command. I had in my hand a highland broad Sword which I brought from home. Upon my coming out I was told it was a wrangle[19] between the Soldiers and people, upon that I went back and got my Sword. I never used

15. Colonial American towns did not have fire departments. When fires broke out, church bells would be rung, and citizens were expected to come out with buckets to help extinguish the fire.
16. A disturbance.
17. Leaped forward suddenly.
18. Had no doubt.
19. A quarrel.

to go out with a weapon. I had not my Sword drawn till after the Soldier pushed his Bayonet at me. I should have cut his head off if he had stepd out of his Rank to attack me again. At the first firing the People were chiefly in Royal Exchange lane, there being about 50 in the Street. After the firing I went up to the Soldiers and told them I wanted to see some faces that I might swear to them another day. The Centinel in a melancholy tone said perhaps Sir you may.

Diman Morton

Between 9 and 10 I heard in my house the cry of fire but soon understood there was no fire but the Soldiers were fighting with the Inhabitants. I went to King Street. Saw the Centinel over the Gutter, his Bayonet breast high. He retired to the steps—loaded. The Boys dared him to fire. Soon after a Party came down, drew up. The Captain ordered them to load. I went across the Street. Heard one Gun and soon after the other Guns. The Captain when he ordered them to load stood in the front before the Soldiers so that the Guns reached beyond him. The Captain had a Surtout on. I knew him well. The Surtout was not red. I think cloth colour. I stood on the opposite corner of Exchange lane when I heard the Captain order the Men to load. I came by my knowledge of the Captain partly by seeing him lead the Fortification Guard.

Nathaniel Fosdick

Hearing the Bells ring, for fire I supposed I went out and came down by the Main Guard. Saw some Soldiers fixing their Bayonets on. Passed on. Went down to the Centinel. Perceived something pass me behind. Turned round and saw the Soldiers coming down. They bid me stand out of the way and damnd my blood. I told them I should not for any man. The party drew up round the Centinel, faced about and charged their Bayonets. I saw an Officer and said if there was any disturbance between the Soldiers and the People there was the Officer present who could settle it soon. I heard no Orders given to load, but in about two minutes after the Captain step'd across the Gutter. Spoke to two Men—I don't know who—then went back behind his men. Between the 4th and 5th men on the right. I then heard the word fire and the first Gun went off. In about 2 minutes the second and then several others. The Captain had a Sword in his hand. Was dressd in his Regimentals. Had no Surtout on. I saw nothing thrown nor any blows given at all. The first man on the right who fired after attempting to push the People slipped down and drop'd his Gun out of his hand. The Person who stepd in between the 4th and 5th Men I look upon it gave the orders

CHAPTER 4

WHAT REALLY
HAPPENED IN
THE BOSTON
MASSACRE?
THE TRIAL OF
CAPTAIN
THOMAS
PRESTON

to fire. His back was to me. I shall always think it was him. The Officer had a Wig on. I was in such a situation that I am as well satisfied there were no blows given as that the word fire was spoken.

Witnesses for the Prisoner (Preston)

Edward Hill

After all the firing Captain Preston put up the Gun of a Soldier who was going to fire and said fire no more you have done mischief enough.

Richard Palmes

Somebody there said there was a Rumpus in King Street. I went down. When I had got there I saw Capt. Preston at the head of 7 or 8 Soldiers at the Custom house drawn up, their Guns breast high and Bayonets fixed. Found Theodore Bliss talking with the Captain. I heard him say why don't you fire or words to that effect. The Captain answered I know not what and Bliss said God damn you why don't you fire. I was close behind Bliss. They were both in front. Then I step'd immediately between them and put my left hand in a familiar manner on the Captains right shoulder to speak to him. Mr. John Hickling then looking over my shoulder I said to Preston are your Soldiers Guns loaded. He answered with powder and ball. Sir I hope you dont intend the Soldiers shall fire on the Inhabitants. He said by no means. The instant he spoke I saw something resembling Snow or Ice strike the Grenadier[20] on the Captains right hand being the only one then at his right. He instantly stepd one foot back and fired the first Gun. I had then my hand on the Captains shoulder. After the Gun went off I heard the word fire. The Captain and I stood in front about half between the breech and muzzle of the Guns. I dont know who gave the word fire. I was then looking on the Soldier who fired. The word was given loud. The Captain might have given the word and I not distinguish it. After the word fire in about 6 or 7 seconds the Grenadier on the Captains left fired and then the others one after another. . . .

Q. Did you situate yourself before Capt. Preston, in order that you might be out of danger, in case they fired?
A. I did not apprehend myself in any danger.
Q. Did you hear Captain Preston give the word *Fire?*
A. I have told your Honors, that after the first gun was fired, I heard the word, *fire!* but who gave it, I know not.

20. A soldier in the British Grenadier Guards.

Matthew Murray

I heard no order given. I stood within two yards of the Captain. He was in front talking with a Person, I don't know who. I was looking at the Captain when the Gun was fired.

Andrew, a Negro servant to Oliver Wendell[21]

I jump'd back and heard a voice cry fire and immediately the first Gun fired. It seemed to come from the left wing from the second or third man on the left. The Officer was standing before me with his face towards the People. I am certain the voice came from beyond him. The Officer stood before the Soldiers at a sort of a corner. I turned round and saw a Grenadier who stood on the Captain's right swing his Gun and fire. . . .

Jane Whitehouse

A Man came behind the Soldiers walked backwards and forward, encouraging them to fire. The Captain stood on the left about three yards. The man touched one of the Soldiers upon the back and said fire, by God I'll stand by you. He was dressed in dark colored clothes. . . . He did not look like an Officer. The man fired directly on the word and clap on the Shoulder. I am positive the man was not the Captain. . . . I am sure he gave no orders. . . . I saw one man take a chunk of wood from under his Coat throw it at a Soldier and knocked him. He fell on his face. His firelock[22] was out of his hand. . . . This was before any firing.

Newton Prince, a Negro, a member of the South Church

Heard the Bell ring. Ran out. Came to the Chapel. Was told there was no fire but something better, there was going to be a fight. Some had buckets and bags and some Clubs. I went to the west end of the Town House where [there] were a number of people. I saw some Soldiers coming out of the Guard house with their Guns and running down one after another to the Custom house. Some of the people said let's attack the Main Guard, or the Centinel who is gone to King street. Some said for Gods sake don't lets touch the main Guard. I went down. Saw the Soldiers planted by the Custom house two deep. The People were calling them Lobsters, daring 'em to fire saying damn you why don't you fire. I saw Capt. Preston out from behind the Soldiers. In the front at the right. He spoke to some people.

21. Andrew was actually Wendell's slave, and Wendell appeared in court to testify that Andrew was honest and truthful.
22. Musket.

CHAPTER 4

WHAT REALLY
HAPPENED IN
THE BOSTON
MASSACRE?
THE TRIAL OF
CAPTAIN
THOMAS
PRESTON

The Capt. stood between the Soldiers and the Gutter about two yards from the Gutter. I saw two or three strike with sticks on the Guns. I was going off to the west of the Soldiers and heard the Guns fire and saw the dead carried off. Soon after the Guard Drums beat to arms.[23] The People whilst striking on the Guns cried fire, damn you fire. I have heard no Orders given to fire, only the people in general cried fire.

James Woodall

I saw one Soldier knocked down. His Gun fell from him. I saw a great many sticks and pieces of sticks and Ice thrown at the Soldiers. The Soldier who was knocked down took up his Gun and fired directly. Soon after the first Gun I saw a Gentleman behind the Soldiers in velvet of blue or black plush trimmed with gold. He put his hand toward their backs. Whether he touched them I know not and said by God I'll stand by you whilst I have a drop of blood and then said fire and two went off and the rest to 7 or 8. . . . The Captain, after, seemed shocked and looked upon the Soldiers. I am very certain he did not give the word fire.

Cross-Examination of Captain James Gifford

Q. Did you ever know an officer order men to fire with their bayonets charged?

A. No, Officers never give order to fire from charged bayonet. They would all have fired together, or most of them.

---

23. A special drumbeat that signaled soldiers to arm themselves.

Source 4 from Anthony D. Darling, *Red Coat and Brown Bess,* Historical Arms Series, No. 12 (Bloomfield, Ontario). Courtesy of Museum Restoration Service, © 1970, 1981.

4. The Position of "Bayonets Charged."

Source 5 from Robert Helm, *Age of Firearms* (1957), p. 93. Drawing by Nancy Jenkins. Reprinted by permission of the author.

5. Detail of a Musket.

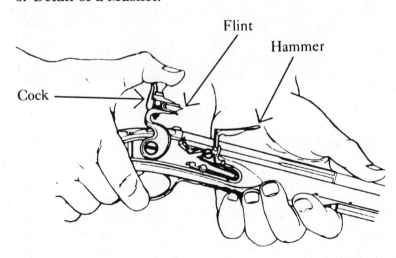

CHAPTER 4

WHAT REALLY
HAPPENED IN
THE BOSTON
MASSACRE?
THE TRIAL OF
CAPTAIN
THOMAS
PRESTON

Source 6: Library of Congress.

6. Paul Revere's Engraving of the Boston Massacre.
[Notice how he dubbed the Custom House "Butcher's Hall."]

∽ QUESTIONS TO CONSIDER ∽

In reconstructing the event, begin by imagining the positions of the various soldiers and witnesses. Where were the soldiers standing? Where was Captain Preston standing? Which witnesses were closest to Preston (that is, in the best positions to see and hear what happened)? Where were the other witnesses? Remember that the event took place around 9:00 P.M., when Boston was totally dark.

Next, read closely Preston's deposition and the trial testimony. What major points did Preston make in his own defense? Do you find those points plausible? More important, do the witnesses who were closest to Preston agree or disagree with his recounting, or with each other's? On what points? Be as specific as possible.

Now consider the other witnesses, those who were not so near. What did they hear? What did they see? To what degree do their testimonies agree or disagree, both with each other and with Preston and those closest to him?

Lawyers for both sides spent considerable time trying to ascertain what Captain Preston was wearing on that evening. Why did they consider this important? Based on the evidence, what do you think Preston was wearing on the evening of March 5, 1770? What conclusions could you draw from that?

The attorneys also were particularly interested in the crowd's behavior *prior to* the firing of the first musket. Why did they consider that important? How would you characterize the crowd's behavior? Are you suspicious of testimony that is at direct odds with your conclusion about this point?

Several witnesses (especially Jane Whitehouse) tell a quite different story. To what extent is her recounting of the event plausible? Is it corroborated by other witnesses?

We included Paul Revere's engraving, even though he probably was not an eyewitness, because by the time of Preston's trial, surely all the witnesses would have seen it and, more important, because later Americans have obtained their most lasting visual image of the event from that work. How does the engraving conform to what actually happened? How does it conflict with your determination of what actually took place? If there are major discrepancies, why do you think this is so? (Revere certainly knew a number of the eyewitnesses and could have ascertained the truth from them.)

After you have answered these questions and carefully weighed the eyewitnesses' evidence, answer the central question: What really happened in the Boston Massacre?

⟶ EPILOGUE ⟵

In his closing arguments in defense of Captain Preston, John Adams noted that the crowd not only had been harassing the soldiers but also had actually threatened to attack them. Yet there was no reliable evidence to prove that Preston had ordered his men to fire into the crowd, Adams insisted. In such doubtful cases, he concluded, the jury must vote for an acquittal. The prosecution's closing summary portrayed Preston as a murderer. The

crowd's actions, the prosecution maintained, were "a few Snow-balls, thrown by a parcel of *Boys*." According to the prosecution, the rest of the people who gathered in the square were peaceful and simply curious about what was happening.

In the trial of Thomas Preston, the jury took only three hours to reach its verdict: not guilty. Some of the jurors were sympathetic to the British, and thus were determined to find

CHAPTER 4

WHAT REALLY
HAPPENED IN
THE BOSTON
MASSACRE?
THE TRIAL OF
CAPTAIN
THOMAS
PRESTON

Preston innocent no matter what evidence was presented. Also, the leaking of the grand jury depositions ultimately helped Preston's defense, since defense attorneys knew in advance what the potentially most damaging witnesses would say in court. Finally, defense attorney John Adams's tactics (to create so much confusion in the minds of the jurors that they could not be certain what actually had taken place) were extremely effective. As it turned out, Preston had the advantage from the very beginning.

As for Thomas Preston himself, the British officer was quickly packed off to England, where he received a pension of £200 per year from the king "to compensate him for his suffering." He did not participate in the American Revolution and died in 1781. Of the eight soldiers (the sentry plus the seven men Preston brought to the Custom House), six were acquitted, and two were convicted of manslaughter and punished by being branded on the thumb. From there they disappeared into the mists of history.

On the road to the American Revolution, many events stand out as important or significant. The Boston Massacre is one such event. However, we must be careful in assessing its importance. After all, the colonists and the mother country did not finally resort to arms until five years after this dramatic event. By that time, most of those killed on King Street on March 5 had been forgotten.

Yet the Boston Massacre and other events have helped shape Americans' attitudes as to what their own Revolution was all about. To most Americans, the British were greedy, heartless tyrants who terrorized a peaceful citizenry. More than one hundred years after the event, the Massachusetts legislature authorized a memorial honoring the "martyrs" to be placed on the site of the "massacre." The Bostonians' convictions were bolstered by Irish immigrants whose ancestors had known British "tyranny" firsthand, and the Bostonians remained convinced that the American Revolution had been caused by Britain's selfishness and oppression. As we can see in the Boston Massacre, the road to the Revolution was considerably more complicated than that.

Today the site of the Boston Massacre is on a traffic island beside the Old State House (formerly called the Town House and seen in the background of Paul Revere's famous engraving) in the midst of Boston's financial district. With the exception of the State House (now a tasteful museum), the site is ringed by skyscrapers that house, among other institutions, BankBoston and Fleet Bank of Massachusetts. Thousands of Bostonians and tourists stand on the Boston Massacre site every day, waiting for the traffic to abate.

Many years ago, John Adams said that "the foundation of American independence was laid" on the evening of March 5, 1770. Although he may have overstated the case, clearly many Americans have come to see the event as a crucial one in the coming of their Revolution against Great Britain.

Now that you have examined the evidence, do you think the Boston Massacre of March 5, 1770, was a justifiable reason for rebellion against the mother country? Could the crowd action on that evening secretly have been directed by the Patriot elite, or was it a spontaneous demonstration of anti-British fury? Why was Paul Revere's engraving at such variance with what actually took place?

Few Americans have stopped to ponder what actually happened on that fateful evening. Like the American Revolution itself, the answer to that question may well be more complex than we think.

CHAPTER 5

THE FIRST AMERICAN PARTY SYSTEM: THE PHILADELPHIA CONGRESSIONAL ELECTION OF 1794

∽ THE PROBLEM ∽

For weeks prior to the federal congressional elections of 1794, the city of Philadelphia, the nation's temporary capital, was in a state of extreme political excitement. Not since the battle in Pennsylvania over the ratification of the United States Constitution had the city been the scene of such political tension and argument. The political factions that had appeared like small clouds over the first administration of President George Washington had grown immensely, and by 1794 in Philadelphia, they were on the verge of becoming distinct political parties.

Federalist Thomas Fitzsimons, a congressman since the beginning of the new government, was challenged by wealthy merchant and Democratic-Republican John Swanwick. Friends of the two contestants filled the air with vicious charges and countercharges in hopes of attracting voters to their respective candidates. Fitzsimons's supporters called Swanwick an "unstable, avaricious upstart who was unknown as a public figure until he 'herded with [the people's] enemies [the Democratic-Republicans], and became their tools.'" Swanwick's friends nicknamed Fitzsimons "Billy the Fidler" and portrayed him as a mindless sycophant of Secretary of the Treasury Alexander Hamilton. Meetings were held in various parts of the city to endorse one candidate or the other, and Philadelphia's newspapers were filled with charges and countercharges. Although many people were disturbed by these eruptions in what they considered a still fragile nation, unquestionably the growing factions had broken the political calm. Would political parties shatter the new republic or strengthen it? In Philadelphia in 1794, opinion was divided.

Challenger John Swanwick won a stunning victory over incumbent Thomas Fitzsimons, carrying seven of the city's twelve wards and collecting 56 percent of the votes cast. Federalism in Philadelphia had been dealt a severe blow.

In this chapter, you will be analyzing the evidence to determine why the lesser-known Swanwick won the election. What factors do you think were responsible for his victory? You will not be relying on just one or two types of evidence, as in previous chapters. Instead, you will be examining myriad pieces of evidence to answer that question.

BACKGROUND

The years between 1789 and 1801 were crucial ones for the young nation. To paraphrase a comment by Benjamin Franklin, Americans by 1789 (the first year of the Washington administration) had proved themselves remarkably adept at *destroying* governments: In the American Revolution, they had ended British rule of the thirteen colonies, and in the Constitutional Convention of 1787, they had ultimately destroyed the United States' first attempt at self-government, the Articles of Confederation. But they had yet to prove that they could *build* a central government that could protect their rights and preserve order and independence. For that reason, the period from 1789 to 1801 was important in terms of the survival of the new republic.

Many important questions confronted the nation's citizens during those difficult years. Could the new government create a financial system that would pay off the public debt; encourage commerce, manufacturing, and investments; and establish a workable federal tax program? Was the central government strong enough to maintain order and protect citizens on the expanding frontier? Could the nation's leaders conceive a foreign policy that would maintain peace, protect international trade, and honor previous treaty commitments? To what extent should national interests overrule the interests and views of the several states?

A much larger question concerned republicanism itself. No republican experiment of this magnitude had ever been tried before, and a number of Americans expressed considerable fears that the experiment might not survive. Some people, such as Rufus King of New York,[1] wondered whether the people possessed sufficient intelligence and virtue to be trusted to make

1. Rufus King (1755–1827) was a native of Massachusetts who moved to New York in 1786. He was a U.S. senator from 1789 to 1796 and minister to Great Britain from 1796 to 1803. He supported Alexander Hamilton's financial plans. In 1816, he was the Federalist candidate for president, losing in a landslide to James Monroe.

CHAPTER 5

THE FIRST
AMERICAN
PARTY SYSTEM:
THE
PHILADELPHIA
CONGRESSIONAL
ELECTION OF
1794

wise decisions and choose proper leaders. Others, such as John Adams of Massachusetts, doubted that a government without titles, pomp, and ceremony would command the respect and allegiance of common men and women. Still others, such as William L. Smith of South Carolina,[2] feared that the new government was not strong enough to maintain order and enforce its will throughout the huge expanse of its domain. And finally, men such as Patrick Henry of Virginia and Samuel Adams of Massachusetts were afraid that the national government would abandon republican principles in favor of an aristocratic despotism. Hence, although most Americans were republican in sentiment, they strongly disagreed about the best ways to preserve republicanism and the dangers it faced. Some Americans openly distrusted "the people"—Alexander Hamilton of New York once called them a "headless beast." Others were wary of the government itself, even though George Washington had been chosen as its first president.

Much of the driving force of the new government came from Alexander Hamilton, the first secretary of the treasury. Hamilton used his closeness to Washington and his boldness and imagination to fashion policies that set the new nation on its initial course.

Hamilton's first task was to deal with the massive public debt. The defunct Confederation government had an unpaid debt going back to the War of Independence of more than $54 mil-

lion. In addition, the various states had amassed an additional $21.5 million of their own debts. In a bold move in 1790, the secretary of the treasury proposed that the new federal government assume the debts of both its predecessor and the states, thus binding creditors to the central government. After considerable debate and some compromising, Congress passed Hamilton's plan virtually intact. At one stroke, the "credit rating" of the new government became among the best in the world.

To pay for this ambitious proposal, as well as to give the federal government operating capital, Hamilton recommended a system of taxation that rested primarily on taxes on foreign imports (tariffs) and an excise tax on selected products manufactured in the United States (tobacco products such as snuff and pipe tobacco, sugar products, and whiskey). The excise tax, however, raised considerable protest, especially in western Pennsylvania, where whiskey was an important commodity. In that area, farmers tried to prevent the collection of the tax, a protest that eventually grew into the Whiskey Rebellion of 1794. Prompted by Hamilton (see Source 4 in the Evidence section), President Washington called out fifteen thousand troops and dispatched them to western Pennsylvania, but the rebellion had fizzled out by the time the troops arrived.

Thus by 1794 (when he announced that he was leaving office), Hamilton had put his "system" in place. Revenue was coming into the government coffers; the debt was being serviced; and the semipublic Bank of the United States had been created in 1791 to handle government funds, make avail-

2. William L. Smith (1758–1812) was a Federalist congressman from South Carolina and later U.S. minister to Portugal. He was a staunch supporter of Alexander Hamilton.

able investment capital, and expand the nation's currency in the form of bank notes. The collapse of the Whiskey Rebellion had proved that the new federal government could enforce its laws throughout the nation. Finally, by meddling in the business of Secretary of State Thomas Jefferson, Hamilton had been able to redirect American foreign policy to a more pro-British orientation. This was because Hamilton believed the new, weak republic needed British protection of its commerce, British revenue (in the form of tariffs), and a friendly neighbor to the north (Canada, a British possession). Using the popular Washington as a shield (as he later admitted), Hamilton became the most powerful figure in the new government and the one most responsible for making that new government work.

It is not surprising, however, that these issues and policies provoked sharp disagreements that eventually created two rival political factions: the Federalists (led by Hamilton) and the Democratic-Republicans (led by James Madison and Thomas Jefferson). Federalists generally advocated a strong central government, a broad interpretation of the Constitution, full payment of national and state debts, the establishment of the Bank of the United States, encouragement of commerce, and a pro-British foreign policy. Democratic-Republicans generally favored a central government with limited powers, a strict interpretation of the Constitution, and a pro-French foreign policy; they opposed the bank.[3]

3. These are general tendencies. Some Federalists and Democratic-Republicans did not stand with their respective factions on all these issues.

First appearing in Congress in the early 1790s, these two relatively stable factions gradually began taking their ideas to the voters, creating the seeds of what would become by the 1830s America's first political party system. Although unanticipated by the men who drafted the Constitution, this party system became a central feature of American political life, so much so that today it would probably be impossible to conduct the affairs of government or hold elections without it.

Yet Americans of the 1790s did not foresee this evolution. Many feared the rise of these political factions, believing that the new government was not strong enough to withstand their increasingly vicious battles. Most people did not consider themselves members of either political faction, and there were no highly organized campaigns or platforms to bind voters to one faction or another. It was considered bad form for candidates openly to seek office (one *stood* for office but never *ran* for office), and appeals to voters were usually made by friends or political allies of the candidates. Different property qualifications for voting in each state limited the size of the electorate, and in the 1790s, most states did not let the voters select presidential electors. All these factors impeded the rapid growth of the modern political party system.

Still, political battles during the 1790s grew more intense and ferocious. As Hamilton's economic plans and Federalism's pro-British foreign policy (the climax of which was the Jay Treaty of 1795) became clearer, Democratic-Republican opposition grew more bitter. Initially, the Federalists

[93]

CHAPTER 5

THE FIRST
AMERICAN
PARTY SYSTEM:
THE
PHILADELPHIA
CONGRESSIONAL
ELECTION OF
1794

had the upper hand, perhaps because of that group's identification with President Washington. But gradually, the Democratic-Republicans gained strength, so much so that by 1800 their titular leader, Thomas Jefferson, was able to win the presidential election and put an end to Federalist control of the national government.

How can we explain the success of the Democratic-Republicans over their Federalist opponents? To answer this question, it is necessary to study in depth several key elections of the 1790s. Although many such contests are important for understanding the eventual Democratic-Republican victory in 1800, we have selected for fur-

ther examination the 1794 race for the federal congressional seat from the city of Philadelphia. Because that seat had been held by a Federalist since the formation of the new government, this election was both an important test of strength of the rival Democratic-Republicans and representative of similar important contests being held in that same year in New York, Massachusetts, Maryland, and elsewhere. Because Philadelphia was the nation's capital in 1794, political party development was more advanced there than in other towns and cities of the young republic, thus offering us a harbinger of things to come nationwide.

 THE METHOD

Observers of modern elections use a variety of methods to analyze political contests and determine why particular candidates won or lost. Some of the more important methods are:

1. *Study the candidates.* How a candidate projects himself or herself may be crucial to the election's outcome. Candidates have backgrounds, voting records, personalities, and idiosyncrasies voters can assess. Candidates travel extensively, are seen by voters either in person or on television, and have several opportunities to appeal to the electorate. Postelection polls have shown that many voters respond as much to the candidates as people (a strong leader, a warm person, a confident leader, and so forth) as they do to the candidates' ideas. For exam-

ple, in 1952, voters responded positively to Dwight Eisenhower, even though many were not sure of his positions on a number of important issues. Similarly, in 1980, Ronald Reagan proved to be an extremely attractive presidential candidate, as much for his personal style as for his ideas and policies.

2. *Study the issues.* Elections often give citizens a chance to clarify their thinking on leading questions of the day. To make matters more complicated, certain groups (economic, ethnic, and interest groups, for example) respond to issues in different ways. The extent to which candidates can identify the issues that concern voters and can speak to these issues in an acceptable way can well mean the difference between victory and defeat.

For example, in 1976, candidate Jimmy Carter was able to tap voters' post-Watergate disgust with corruption in the federal government and defeat incumbent Gerald Ford by speaking to that issue.

3. *Study the campaigns.* Success in devising and implementing a campaign strategy in modern times has been a crucial factor in the outcomes of elections. How does the candidate propose to deal with the issues? How are various interest groups to be lured under the party banner? How will money be raised, and how will it be spent? Will the candidate debate her or his opponent? Will the candidate make many personal appearances, or will she or he conduct a "front-porch" campaign? How will the candidate's family, friends, and political allies be used? Which areas (neighborhoods, regions, states, sections) will be targeted for special attention? To many political analysts, it is obvious that a number of superior candidates have been unsuccessful because of poorly run campaigns. By the same token, many less-than-superior candidates have won elections because of effectively conducted campaigns.

4. *Study the voters.* Recently, the study of elections has become more sophisticated. Polling techniques have revealed that people similar in demographic variables such as age, sex, race, income, marital status, ethnic group, and religion tend to vote in similar fashions. For example, urban blacks voted overwhelmingly for Jimmy Carter in 1976.

These sophisticated polling techniques, also used for Gallup polls, Nielsen television ratings, and predicting responses to new consumer products, rest on important assumptions about human behavior. One assumption is that human responses tend to be strongly influenced (some say *determined*) by demographic variables; similar people tend to respond similarly to certain stimuli (such as candidates and campaigns). Another assumption is that these demographic patterns are constant and do not change rapidly. Finally, it is assumed that if we know how some of the people responded to certain stimuli, we can calculate how others possessing the same demographic variables will respond to those same stimuli.

Although there are many such patterns of voting behavior, they are easily observable. After the demographic variables that influence these patterns have been identified, a demographic sample of the population is created. Thus fifty white, male, middle-aged, married, Protestant, middle-income voters included in a sample might represent perhaps 100,000 people who possess these same variables. The fifty in the sample would then be polled to determine how they voted, and from this information we could infer how the 100,000 voted. Each population group in the sample would be polled in a similar fashion. By doing this, we can know with a fair amount of precision who voted for whom, thereby understanding which groups within the voting population were attracted to which candidate. Of course, the answer to why they were attracted still must be sought with one of the other methods: studying the candidates, studying the issues, and studying the campaigns.

CHAPTER 5

THE FIRST
AMERICAN
PARTY SYSTEM:
THE
PHILADELPHIA
CONGRESSIONAL
ELECTION OF
1794

These four approaches are methods for analyzing modern electoral contests. In fact, most political analysts use a combination of these approaches. But can these methods be used to analyze the 1794 congressional election in Philadelphia? Neither candidate openly sought the office, and neither made appearances in his own behalf. Although there certainly were important issues, neither political faction drew up a platform to explain to voters where its candidate stood on those issues. Neither political faction conducted an organized campaign. No polls were taken to determine voter concerns. At first glance, then, it appears that most if not all of these approaches to analyzing modern elections are useless in any attempt to analyze the 1794 Fitzsimons-Swanwick congressional contest.

These approaches, however, are not as useless as they initially appear. Philadelphia in 1794 was not a large city—it contained only about 45,000 people—and many voters knew the candidates personally because both were prominent figures in the community. Their respective backgrounds were generally well known. Moreover, Fitzsimons, as the incumbent, had a voting record in Congress, and most voters would have known how Swanwick stood on the issues, either through Swanwick's friends or through the positions he took as a member of the Democratic Society. Furthermore, the Federalists and Democratic-Republicans had taken general positions on some of the important issues. In addition, we are able to establish with a fair amount of certainty which voters cast ballots for Fitzsimons and which supported Swanwick. Finally, it is possible to identify important trends and events occurring in Philadelphia. In sum, although we might not have all the evidence we would like to have (historians almost never do), intelligent use of the evidence at our disposal enables us to analyze the 1794 election with all or most of the approaches used in analyzing modern political contests.

As you examine the various types of evidence, divide it into four groups, one group for each general approach used in analyzing elections (candidates, issues, campaign, voters). For example, there are two excerpts from Philadelphia newspapers (one Federalist and one Democratic-Republican) dealing with the excise tax and the Whiskey Rebellion in western Pennsylvania. In what group would you put this evidence? Follow this procedure for all the evidence, noting that occasionally a piece of evidence could fit into more than one group. Such an arrangement of the evidence will give you four ways to analyze why the 1794 congressional election in Philadelphia turned out the way it did. Then, having examined and analyzed the evidence by groups, you will have to assess what principal factors explain Swanwick's upset victory.

THE EVIDENCE

1. The Candidates.

Thomas Fitzsimons (1741–1811) was born in Ireland and migrated to the colonies sometime before the Revolution, probably in 1765. He entered commerce as a clerk, worked his way up in his firm, and secured his position by marrying into the principal merchant's family. Fitzsimons served as a captain of the Pennsylvania militia during the Revolution, was a member of the Continental Congress in 1782 and 1783, and was elected to the Pennsylvania House of Representatives in 1786 and 1787. He was a delegate to the Constitutional Convention in 1787, was a signer of the Constitution, and was elected to the federal House of Representatives in 1788. He was a member of the Federalist inner circle in Philadelphia and a firm supporter of Alexander Hamilton's policies. He was a strong supporter of the excise tax (see approach 2 in the Questions to Consider section), was an instrumental figure in the compromise that brought the national capital to Philadelphia for ten years (1790–1800), and helped draft the legislation chartering the Bank of the United States in 1791. He was one of the original founders and directors of the Bank of North America, the director and president of the Insurance Company of North America, and a key figure in dispensing federal patronage in Philadelphia. He was a Roman Catholic.

John Swanwick (1740–1798) was born in England. He and his family arrived in the colonies in the early 1770s. His father was a wagon master and minor British government official. During the Revolution, his father became a Tory and was exiled, but John Swanwick embraced the Patriot cause. In 1777, he was hired as a clerk in the merchant firm of Robert Morris. His fluency in both French and German made him invaluable to the firm, and he quickly rose to full partnership in 1783, the firm then being known as Willing, Morris & Swanwick. In 1794, he bought out Morris's share in the company. He was one of Philadelphia's leading export merchants, was a stockholder in the Bank of North America, and held a number of minor offices (under Morris) in the Confederation government. He supported the federal Constitution and Hamilton's early financial policies. Swanwick was elected to the state legislature in 1792. By 1793, he had drifted away from Federalism and had become a Democratic-Republican. In 1794, he joined the Pennsylvania Democratic Society[4] and was soon

---

4. Democratic Societies were organizations composed principally of artisans and laborers and founded by Democratic-Republican leaders as political pressure groups against the Washington

CHAPTER 5

THE FIRST
AMERICAN
PARTY SYSTEM:
THE
PHILADELPHIA
CONGRESSIONAL
ELECTION OF
1794

made an officer. Swanwick also was an officer in a society that aided immigrants. He opposed the excise tax but thought the Whiskey Rebellion (see approach 2 in the Questions to Consider section) in western Pennsylvania was the wrong method of protest. He wrote poetry and was never admitted to Philadelphia's social elite. He owned a two-hundred-acre country estate. He was a member of the Protestant Episcopal church.

Source 2 from *Gazette of the United States* (a pro-Federalist Philadelphia newspaper), August 10, 1794.

2. A Pro–Federalist View of the Excise Tax and the Whiskey Rebellion.

. . . These Societies [the Democratic Societies], strange as it may seem, have been formed in a free elective government for the sake of *preserving liberty*. And what is the liberty they are striving to introduce? It is the liberty of reviling the rulers who are chosen by the people and the government under which they live. It is the liberty of bringing the laws into contempt and persuading people to resist them [a reference to the Whiskey Rebellion]. It is the liberty of condemning every system of Taxation because they have resolved that they will not be subject to laws—that they will not pay any taxes. To suppose that societies were formed with the purpose of opposing and with the hope of destroying government, might appear illiberal provided they had not already excited resistance to the laws and provided some of them had not publicly avowed their opinions that they *ought not to pay any taxes.* . . .

Source 3 from *General Advertiser* (a pro–Democratic-Republican Philadelphia newspaper), August 20, 1794.

3. A Pro–Democratic-Republican View of the Excise Tax and the Whiskey Rebellion.

As violent means appear the desire of high toned government men, it is to be hoped that those who derive the most benefit from our revenue laws

---

administration. Many Federalists believed that some Democratic Society members had been behind the Whiskey Rebellion. President Washington condemned the societies in 1794.

will be the foremost to march against the Western insurgents. Let stock-holders, bank directors, speculators and revenue officers arrange themselves immediately under the banner of the treasury, and try their prowess in arms as they have done in calculation. The prompt recourse to hostilities which two certain great characters [Hamilton and Washington?] are so anxious for, will, no doubt, operate upon the knights of our country to appear in military array, and then the poor but industrious citizen will not be obliged to spill the blood of his fellow citizen before conciliatory means are tried. . . .

Source 4 from Harold C. Syrett, ed., *The Papers of Alexander Hamilton* (New York: Columbia University Press, 1972), Vol. XVII, pp. 15–19.

4. Alexander Hamilton to President Washington, August 2, 1794.

If the Judge shall pronounce that the case described in the second section of that Act exists, it will follow that a competent force of Militia should be called forth and employed to suppress the insurrection and support the Civil Authority in effectuating Obedience to the laws and punishment of Offenders.

It appears to me that the very existence of Government demands this course and that a duty of the highest nature urges the Chief Magistrate to pursue it.[5]

Source 5 from Paul L. Ford, ed., *Writings of Thomas Jefferson* (New York: G. P. Putnam's Sons, 1895), Vol. VI, pp. 516–519.

5. Thomas Jefferson to James Madison, December 28, 1794.

And with respect to the transactions against the excise law [the Whiskey Rebellion], it appears to me that you are all swept away in the torrent of governmental opinion, or that we do not know what these transactions

5. The Militia Act ("that Act") of 1792 required that a Supreme Court justice ("the Judge," in this case Justice James Wilson) certify that the disturbance could not be controlled by civil authorities (as defined in the "second section" of the Act) before the president could order out the state militia. The "Chief Magistrate" referred to is President Washington. The majority of the U.S. Army was in the Northwest Territory, about to engage the Native Americans in the Battle of Fallen Timbers (August 20, 1794). Justice Wilson released his opinion that Washington could call out the troops on August 4, two days after Hamilton wrote to Washington.

CHAPTER 5

THE FIRST
AMERICAN
PARTY SYSTEM:
THE
PHILADELPHIA
CONGRESSIONAL
ELECTION OF
1794

have been. We know of none which, according to the definitions of the law, have been anything more than riotous. . . . The excise law is an infernal one. . . . The information of our militia, returned from the Westward, is uniform, that the people there let them pass quietly; they were objects of their laughter, not of their fear.

Sources 6 through 8 from Ronald M. Baumann, "Philadelphia's Manufacturers and the Excise Tax of 1794: The Forging of the Jeffersonian Coalition," *Pennsylvania Magazine of History and Biography,* Vol. 106 (January 1982), pp. 26, 28–30.

6. Excise Tax Statistics.

There were 23 tobacconists and snuffmakers in Philadelphia in 1794 who owned real property from £26 to over £2501 and who employed over 400 workers. In addition, there were sugar refiners in the city, and Philadelphia also had 21 brewers and distillers.

7. Swanwick and the Democratic Society.

Swanwick was a member of the Democratic Society of Pennsylvania. The society passed a resolution opposing the excise tax. President Washington condemned the society in 1794, saying that he believed that it and other similar societies were responsible for the Whiskey Rebellion. The society endorsed Swanwick in 1794 and worked actively in his behalf.

8. Philadelphia Wards, 1794.

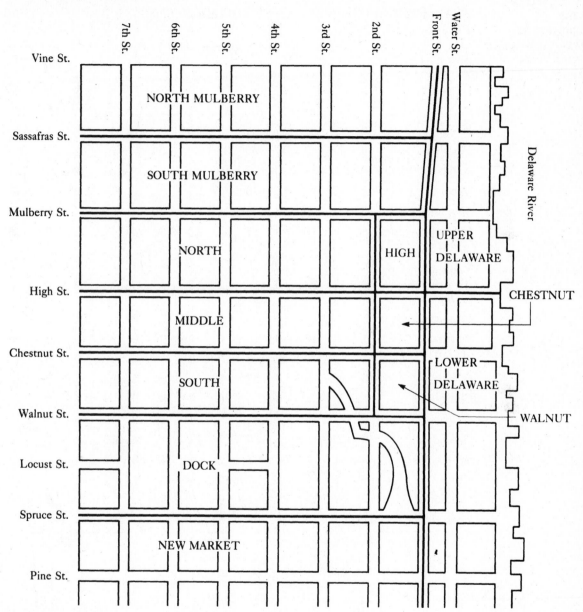

CHAPTER 5

THE FIRST
AMERICAN
PARTY SYSTEM:
THE
PHILADELPHIA
CONGRESSIONAL
ELECTION OF
1794

Source 9 from James Hardie, *Philadelphia City Directory* (Philadelphia, 1794).

9. A Sample of Occupations by Ward (Males Only), Philadelphia, 1794.[6]

	Upper Delaware	North Mulberry	South Mulberry	High	North	Chestnut	Middle	Walnut	South	Dock	New Market	Lower Delaware	Occupation Totals
Gentleman	3	22	31	7	21	1	15	2	8	17	25	5	157
Merchant	76	47	65	47	90	38	63	20	26	101	83	43	699
Artisan	95	353	338	333	183	46	164	48	73	131	222	71	1,757
Laborer	18	93	103	10	70	7	27	8	12	38	56	1	443
Shopkeeper	13	24	39	24	44	9	23	4	6	7	35	8	236
Inn and tavern keeper	8	17	12	3	13	5	22	3	4	12	11	6	116
Captain	6	17	14	0	3	0	1	4	1	7	37	0	90
Government employee	2	12	13	0	16	2	13	1	7	14	18	0	98
Seaman	7	15	5	1	3	1	2	2	2	9	21	2	70
Teacher	1	5	12	0	6	0	2	0	3	5	6	0	40
Doctor	1	3	10	3	5	3	2	3	6	10	9	0	55
Grocer	10	22	20	3	37	2	20	0	5	25	34	6	184
Clergy	0	5	8	0	0	0	3	0	3	4	4	0	27
Lawyer	0	3	11	2	1	0	4	1	13	12	5	1	53
Clerk	5	16	18	3	7	1	12	1	4	10	12	1	90
Broker	0	1	2	0	3	2	4	4	3	2	1	0	22
Other	1	5	0	1	3	1	0	0	1	1	2	0	15
Unknown	1	7	14	1	1	0	2	0	1	2	8	0	37
Ward totals	247	667	715	138	506	118	379	101	178	407	589	144	

6. Sample taken from the Philadelphia city directory for 1794. Poor people were notoriously undercounted in city directories, as were nonpermanent residents, such as seamen.

Sources 10 and 11 from Billy G. Smith, *The "Lower Sort": Philadelphia's Laboring People, 1750–1800* (Ithaca, N.Y.: Cornell University Press, 1990), pp. 101, 110, 114, 116, 121, 232. For household budgets, Smith calculated the costs of food, rent, fuel, and clothing and then established how much of these items were consumed.

10. Cost of Living Index,[7] Philadelphia (Base Year 1762 = 100).

Year	Food	Rent	Firewood	Clothing	Household Budget
1788	99		74	139	123
1789	107	165[8]	76	82	115
1790	134		79	92	131
1791	130		97	92	131
1792	131		106	110	136
1793	143		111	119	144
1794	161		130	137	158

11. Index of Real Wages,[9] Philadelphia (Base Year 1762 = 100).

Year	Laborers	Sailors	Tailors	Shoemakers
1788	95	—	68	63
1789	77	—	69	63
1790	66	59	76	44
1791	74	59	63	48
1792	88	70	80	55
1793	81	84	57	143
1794	90	161	78	77

7. An index number is a statistical measure designed to show changes in a variable (such as wages or prices) over time. A base year is selected and given the value of 100. The index for subsequent years is then expressed as a percentage of the base year.

8. No other rent index is available for 1788 through 1794. The rent index in 1798, however, was 184.

9. Real wages are wages that are actually paid, adjusted for the cost of living. To find a person's real wage, one would take the index of that person's actual wage divided by the index of household budget and multiply that figure by 100. Real wages allow us to see whether a person's wages are exceeding or falling behind the cost of living.

CHAPTER 5

THE FIRST
AMERICAN
PARTY SYSTEM:
THE
PHILADELPHIA
CONGRESSIONAL
ELECTION OF
1794

Source 12 from James Hardie, *The Philadelphia Directory and Register* (Philadelphia, 1794).

12. First-Person Account of the Yellow Fever.

Having mentioned this disorder to have occasioned great devastation in the year 1793, a short account of it may be acceptable to several of our readers. . . .

This disorder made its first appearance toward the latter end of July, in a lodging house in North Water Street,[10] and for a few weeks seemed entirely confined to that vicinity. Hence it was generally supposed to have been imported and not generated in the city. This was the opinion of Doctors Currie, Cathrall and many others. It was however combated by Dr. Benjamin Rush, who asserts that the contagion was generated from the stench of a cargo of damaged coffee. . . .

But from whatever fountain we trace this poisoned stream, it has destroyed the lives of many thousands—and many of those of the most distinguished worth. . . . During the month of August the funerals amounted to upwards of three hundred. The disease had then reached the central streets of the city and began to spread on all sides with the greatest rapidity. In September its malignance increased amazingly. Fear pervaded the stoutest heart, flight became general, and terror was depicted on every countenance. In this month 1,400 more were added to the list of mortality. The contagion was still progressive and towards the end of the month 90 & 100 died daily. Until the middle of October the mighty destroyer went on with increasing havoc. From the 1st to the 17th upwards of 1,400 fell victims to the tremendous malady. From the 17th to the 30th the mortality gradually decreased. In the whole month, however, the dead amounted to upwards of 2,000—a dreadful number, if we consider that at this time near one half of the inhabitants had fled. Before the disorder became so terrible, the appearance of Philadelphia must to a stranger have seemed very extraordinary. The garlic, which chewed as a preventative[,] could be smelled at several yards distance, whilst other[s] hoped to avoid infection by a recourse to smelling bottles, handkerchiefs dipped in vinegar, camphor bags, &c. . . .

During this melancholy period the city lost ten of her most valuable physicians, and most of the others were sick at different times. The number of deaths in all amounted to 4041.[11]

---

10. See Source 8. Working-class areas were particularly hard hit. On Fetter Lane (near North Water Street), 50 percent of the residents died. See Smith, *The "Lower Sort,"* pp. 25–26.
11. The population of Philadelphia (including its suburbs) was 42,444 in 1790.

Sources 13 and 14 from L. H. Butterfield, ed., *Letters of Benjamin Rush*[12] (Princeton, N.J.: Published for the American Philosophical Society, 1951), Vol. II, pp. 644–645, 657–658.

13. Benjamin Rush to Mrs. Rush, August 29, 1793, on the Yellow Fever.

Be assured that I will send for you if I should be seized with the disorder, for I conceive that it would be as much your duty not to desert me in that situation as it is now mine not to desert my patients. . . .

Its symptoms are very different in different people. Sometimes it comes on with a chilly fit and a high fever, but more frequently it steals on with headache, languor, and sick stomach. These symptoms are followed by stupor, delirium, vomiting, a dry skin, cool or cold hands and feet, a feeble slow pulse, sometimes below in frequency the pulse of health. The eyes are at first suffused with blood, they afterwards become yellow, and in most cases a yellowness covers the whole skin on the 3rd or 4th day. Few survive the 5th day, but more die on the 2 and 3rd days. In some cases the patients possess their reason to the last and discover much less weakness than in the last stage of common fevers. One of my patients stood up and shaved himself on the morning of the day he died. Livid spots on the body, a bleeding at the nose, from the gums, and from the bowels, and a vomiting of black matter in some instances close the scenes of life. The common remedies for malignant fevers have all failed. Bark, wine, and blisters make no impression upon it. Baths of hot vinegar applied by means of blankets, and the cold bath have relieved and saved some. . . .

This day I have given mercury, and I think with some advantage. . . .

12. Dr. Benjamin Rush (1745–1813) was a Pennsylvanian who was graduated from the College of New Jersey (Princeton, 1760) and studied medicine at the College of Philadelphia and the University of Edinburgh. Practicing medicine in Philadelphia, he was elected to the Continental Congress in 1776 and was a signer of the Declaration of Independence. He supported the ratification of the Constitution. By 1794, he had changed allegiances and was considered a Democratic-Republican. He participated in many reform movements, including the abolition of slavery, the end to capital punishment, temperance, an improved educational system, and prison reform. His protégé, Dr. Michael Leib, was extremely active in Democratic-Republican politics. Most physicians in Philadelphia in 1794 were Federalists. The majority fled the city when the fever broke out. Of the doctors who stayed, Rush was one of the most prominent.

CHAPTER 5

THE FIRST
AMERICAN
PARTY SYSTEM:
THE
PHILADELPHIA
CONGRESSIONAL
ELECTION OF
1794

**14. Benjamin Rush to Mrs. Rush, September 10, 1793, on the
Yellow Fever.**

My dear Julia,

Hereafter my name should be Shadrach, Meshach, or Abednego, for I am
sure the preservation of those men from death by fire was not a greater
miracle than my preservation from the infection of the prevailing disorder.
I have lived to see the close of another day, more awful than any I have yet
seen. Forty persons it is said have been buried this day, and I have visited
and prescribed for more than 100 patients. Mr. Willing is better, and Jno.
Barclay is out of danger. Amidst my numerous calls to the wealthy and
powerful, *I do not forget the poor, . . .*[13]

15. Yellow Fever Committee.

Of the 18 people cited for contributions to the Citizens' Committee on the
Fever, 9 were definitely Democratic-Republicans. Of the remaining 9, only
one was an avowed Federalist.

Source 16 from J. H. Powell, *Bring Out Your Dead: The Great Plague of Yellow
Fever in Philadelphia in 1793* (Philadelphia: University of Pennsylvania Press,
1949), p. 123.

16. Federalist Comment on Rush.

Rush "is become the darling of the common people and his humane forti-
tude and exertions will render him deservedly dear."

13. Italics added.

17. Sampling of Deaths from Yellow Fever, Philadelphia, 1793 Epidemic.[14]

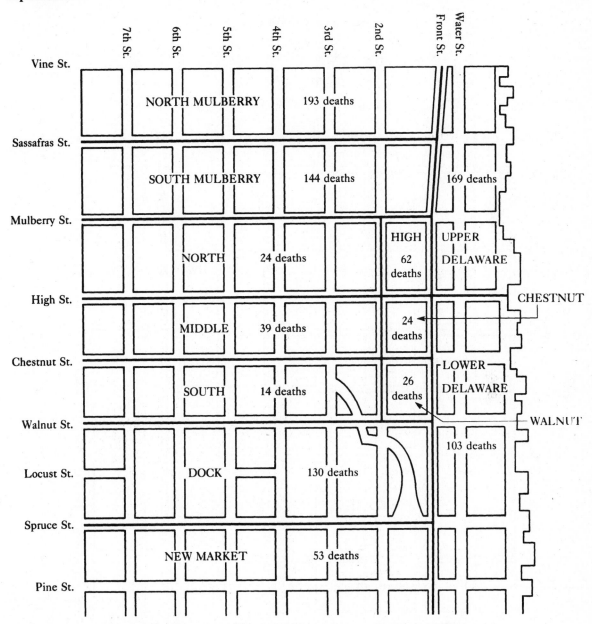

14. Sample taken from Philadelphia newspapers. After a time, officials simply stopped recording the names of those who died, except for prominent citizens. Therefore, although James Hardie reported that 4,041 people had died, one scholar has estimated the death toll at as high as 6,000, roughly one out of every seven Philadelphians.

Source 18 from Baumann, "Philadelphia's Manufacturers and the Excise Tax," p. 27.

18. Congressional Election, Philadelphia, 1794.[15]

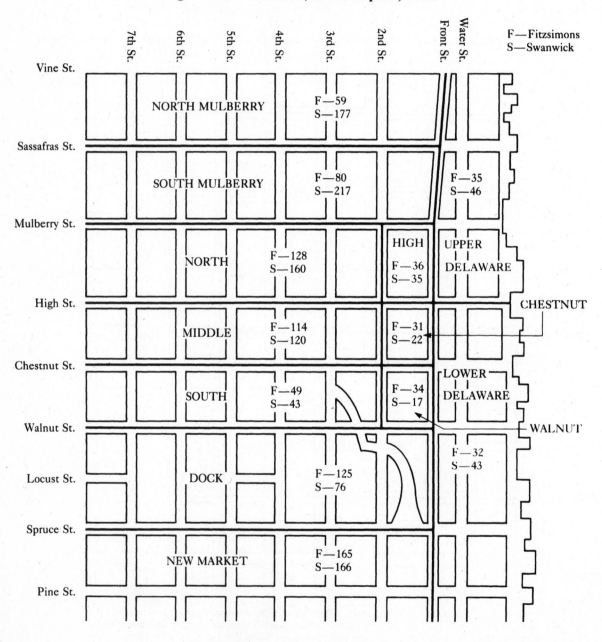

❧ QUESTIONS TO CONSIDER ❧

No single method of analyzing elections will give you the answer to the central question of why John Swanwick was able to defeat Thomas Fitzsimons. Instead, you must use all four approaches, grouping the evidence by approach and determining what each approach tells you about why the election turned out as it did.

Before examining each group of evidence, however, try to discover who tended to vote for each candidate. Source 9 shows occupations by ward. Although there are exceptions, occupations can often be used to establish a person's wealth and status. Today many people introduce themselves by telling their name, occupation, and address. What are these people really saying? Examine carefully the occupational makeup of each ward. This can be done by matching the figures in Source 9 to the map in Source 8. For example, look at the artisan (skilled labor) population. Only a very few lived in High, Chestnut, and Walnut wards, areas that tended to be more upper-class neighborhoods. Instead, most artisans lived on the city's fringes, in North Mulberry, South Mulberry, North, Middle, Dock, and New Market wards. Follow the same procedure for merchants, laborers, shopkeepers, and so on. Although early American cities were not as residentially segregated by socioeconomic class as today's cities, you will be able to see general tendencies that will allow you to characterize each of Philadelphia's wards in 1794.

Keeping those characterizations in mind (or by using notes), turn to Source 18, the election results. How could you use these three sources (8, 9, 18) to determine who tended to support Fitzsimons and Swanwick? Historians call this process *overlaying evidence* because they are overlaying one source on another.

Pennsylvania had one of the most liberal suffrage laws in the nation. All adult white males who had lived in the state for two years preceding an election *and* had paid any state or county taxes could vote. Of the occupational groups listed in Source 9, only laborers and seamen contained large percentages of men who could not vote. Keep this in mind as you overlay the evidence.

Having established who tended to vote for Fitzsimons and who tended to vote for Swanwick, you are ready to answer the question of why one of the candidates was more appealing to the majority of Philadelphia voters. Here is where the four major approaches explained earlier can be brought into play.

1. *Candidates*. Source 1 supplies biographical information about the two candidates. Do not neglect to study the additional material on Swanwick (Source 7); this is material that voters not personally acquainted with the candidates still would have known. What are the significant points of comparison and contrast between the candidates?

CHAPTER 5

THE FIRST
AMERICAN
PARTY SYSTEM:
THE
PHILADELPHIA
CONGRESSIONAL
ELECTION OF
1794

One significant point of difference is religion. Fitzsimons was a Roman Catholic, and Swanwick belonged to the Protestant Episcopal church. Most of Philadelphia's voters were Protestant, the two largest denominations being Lutheran and Quaker. Very few voters belonged to either the Roman Catholic or the Episcopal church. Was religion a factor in this election? How can you prove that it was or was not?

One interesting point in Swanwick's biographical sketch is that, although wealthy, he was never admitted to Philadelphia's social elite circles, a fact that some of the voters probably knew. Do you think this was an important consideration in the voters' minds? How would you prove your point?

2. *Issues.* There were a number of issues in this election, and it was fairly clear how each faction stood on those issues. Two of the most important issues were the excise tax (Sources 2, 3, 6, 7) and the Whiskey Rebellion (Sources 4, 5).

As noted above, to raise money, Hamilton proposed, Congress passed, and President Washington signed a bill placing an excise tax on selected domestic manufactured products, an act that eventually touched off the Whiskey Rebellion of 1794. Indeed, there is some evidence that Hamilton actually anticipated such a reaction to the excise tax when he proposed it, convinced that the crushing of such an uprising would prove that the new government had the power to enforce its laws. When examining the impact of the excise tax and the Whiskey Re-

bellion on the election, use the sources to answer the following questions:

a. Which groups in Philadelphia did the excise tax affect most? How? Remember to think of people as both workers and consumers.
b. How did each candidate stand on the excise tax?
c. Which groups of Philadelphians would have been likely to favor their respective positions?
d. How did each faction stand on the Whiskey Rebellion? (See Sources 2 through 5.)
e. How did the candidates stand on this issue?
f. Which groups of Philadelphians would have been likely to favor their respective positions?

3. *Campaign.* Although there were a few mass meetings and some distribution of literature, there was no real campaign in the modern sense. In the absence of an organized campaign, how did voters make up their minds?

4. *Voters.* At the time of the election, other important trends in Philadelphia might have influenced voters. For example, review the evidence on the cost of living and on real wages compiled by Billy G. Smith (Sources 10 and 11). On cost of living, if the cost of living index in 1762 was 100, were the indexes for food, firewood, and clothing rising or falling? Using household budget indexes, how much more expensive was it to live in Philadelphia in 1794 than it was in 1788 (158 minus 123 equals 35, divided by 123 equals 28.5 percent)?

Remember that real wages are actual wages adjusted for the cost of living. As you can see in Source 11, tailors and shoemakers (called "cordwainers" at this time) experienced modest gains in real wages from 1788 to 1794. Note, however, that real wages were extremely volatile and could fluctuate wildly. For example, real wages for shoemakers fell 30.2 percent between 1788 and 1790, then began a gradual recovery, due in part to a protective tariff on shoes passed by Congress in 1790. In 1793, the retail prices for shoes jumped 64.8 percent, largely because war in Europe created a great international demand for American shoes. As a result, real wages for shoemakers spiraled from 55 to 143, a gain of 160 percent. But in 1794, real wages dropped 46.2 percent. As for sailors, their wages skyrocketed from 1793 to 1794 (almost 80 percent). Keep in mind, however, that the war between Great Britain and France that broke out in 1793 made that occupation an extremely dangerous one. In sum, can the cost of living and real wage indexes give you any clues to how these occupational groups might have voted?

The pieces of evidence that appear at first glance to have nothing to do with the Fitzsimons-Swanwick contest are Sources 12 through 17, on the 1793 yellow fever epidemic that virtually paralyzed the city. After all, the fever broke out more than a year prior to the election and was over by the end of October 1793. Most of those who had fled the city had returned and were in Philadelphia during the "campaign" and voting.

Yet a closer analysis of Sources 12 through 17 offers some fascinating insights, although you will have to use some historical imagination to relate them to the election. To begin with, James Hardie (Source 12) reported that the fever initially appeared "in a lodging house in North Water Street; and for a few weeks seemed entirely confined to that vicinity." Where was North Water Street (Source 8)? Who would have lived there (Sources 8 and 9)? So long as the fever was confined to that area, Hardie does not appear to have been overly concerned. What does that tell you? Hardie further reported that almost half the total population had fled the city. Which groups would have been most likely to flee (approximately 20,000 of Philadelphia's 45,000 fled)? Who could not leave? If businessmen closed their businesses when they fled, what was the situation of workers who could not afford to leave? What impact might this have had on the election a year later?

Although perhaps a bit too graphic, Dr. Benjamin Rush's August 29, 1793, letter to his wife (Source 13) is valuable because it establishes the fact that Rush, although he could have abandoned the sick, refused to do so and stayed in Philadelphia. This was an act of remarkable courage, for no one knew what caused yellow fever and people believed that it struck its victims almost completely at random. Consider, however, not what Rush *says* in Source 13 but rather *who he was* (a prominent Democratic-Repub-

CHAPTER 5

THE FIRST
AMERICAN
PARTY SYSTEM:
THE
PHILADELPHIA
CONGRESSIONAL
ELECTION OF
1794

lican). Refer again to footnote 12. Also examine Rush's letter of September 10, 1793 (Source 14), especially the last sentence. Do you think Rush might have been a factor in the Fitzsimons Swanwick election? In what way?

Sources 15 and 16 attempt to tie the fever epidemic to party politics in Philadelphia. How might Philadelphia voters have reacted to the two parties (the Federalists and the Democratic-Republicans) after the fever? How might the voters have reacted to Dr. Rush (an avowed Democratic-Republican)?

Finally, examine Source 17 with some care. Where did the fever victims tend to reside? What types of people lived in those wards?

Now you are ready to answer the question of why the 1794 congressional election in Philadelphia turned out the way it did (Source 18). Make sure, however, that your opinion is solidly supported by evidence.

⟨⟩ EPILOGUE ⟨⟩

As the temporary national capital in 1794, Philadelphia was probably somewhat more advanced than the rest of the nation in the growth of political factions. However, by the presidential election of 1800, most of the country had become involved in the gradual process of party building. By that time, the Democratic-Republicans were the dominant political force, aided by more aggressive campaign techniques, their espousal of a limited national government (which most Americans preferred), their less elitist attitudes, and their ability to brand their Federalist opponents as aristocrats and pro-British monocrats.[16] Although Federalism retained considerable strength in New England and the Middle States, by 1800 it no longer was a serious challenge to the Democratic-Republicans on the national level.

16. A monocrat is a person who favors a monarchy. It was considered a disparaging term in the United States during the period.

For his part, John Swanwick never saw the ultimate triumph of Democratic-Republicanism because he died in the 1798 yellow fever epidemic in Philadelphia. Fitzsimons never again sought political office, preferring to concentrate his energies on his already successful mercantile and banking career. Hamilton died in a duel with Aaron Burr in 1804. After he left the presidency in 1809, Jefferson retired to his estate, Monticello, to bask in the glories of being an aging founding father. He died in 1826 at the age of eighty-three.

By 1826, many of the concerns of the Federalist era had been resolved. The War of 1812 had further secured American independence, and the death of the Federalist faction had put an end to the notion of government by an entrenched (established) and favored elite. At the same time, however, new issues had arisen to test the durability of the republic and the collective wisdom of its people. After a brief political calm, party battles once again were growing fiercer, as the rise of Andrew Jackson threatened to split the brittle Jeffersonian coalition. Westward expansion was carrying Americans into territories owned by other nations, and few doubted that an almost inevitable conflict lay ahead. American cities, such as Philadelphia, were growing in both population and socioeconomic problems. The twin specters of slavery and sectional conflict were claiming increasing national attention. Whether the political system fashioned in the 1790s could address these crucial issues and trends and at the same time maintain its republican principles was a question that would soon have to be addressed.

CHAPTER 6

ASSESSING HISTORICAL ALTERNATIVES: THE REMOVAL OF THE CHEROKEES, 1838–1839

∽ THE PROBLEM ∽

In the spring of 1838, General Winfield Scott and several units of the U.S. Army (including artillery regiments) were deployed to the Southeast to collect Native Americans known as Cherokees[1] and remove them to lands west of the Mississippi River. Employing bilingual Cherokees to serve as interpreters at $2.50 per day, Scott constructed eleven makeshift stockades and on May 23 began rounding up Native Americans and herding them into these temporary prisons. According to John G. Burnett, a soldier who participated in the removal,

> Men working in the fields were arrested and driven to the stockades. Women were dragged from their homes by soldiers whose language they could not understand. Children were often separated from their parents and driven into the stockades with the sky for a blanket and the earth for a pillow. And often the old and infirm were prodded with bayonets to hasten them to the stockades.[2]

Just behind the soldiers came whites, eager to claim homesteads, search for gold, or pick over the belongings that

---

1. The Cherokees referred to themselves as Ani'Yun'wiya ("principal people"). The origin of the term *Cherokee* is unknown, but the name almost certainly was given to them by Native American neighbors. See Russell Thornton, *The Cherokees: A Population History* (Lincoln: University of Nebraska Press, 1990), pp. 7–8.

2. See John G. Burnett, "The Cherokee Removal Through the Eyes of a Private Soldier," *Journal of Cherokee Studies* 3 (1978): 180–185.

the Cherokees did not have time to carry away.

On August 23, 1838, the first of thirteen parties of Cherokees began their forced march to the West, arriving in what had been designated as Indian Territory (later Oklahoma) on January 17, 1839. With some traveling by boat while others journeyed overland, a total of approximately thirteen thousand Cherokees participated in what became known as the Trail of Tears. (See Map 1.) It has been estimated that over four thousand died in the squalid stockades or along the way.[3] But recent research has determined that the figure may have been higher than that, in part because of shoddy record keeping and in part because numerous Cherokees died in an epidemic almost immediately on reaching their destination. In addition, conflict broke out between new arrivals and those Cherokees (around six thousand) who had earlier moved. And, once in the West, those who opposed removal took out their vengeance on the leaders of the Cherokee removal faction. Cherokee advocates of removal (including leaders Major Ridge, John Ridge, Elias Boudinot, and Thomas Watie) were murdered.[4]

One of the most determined advocates of removal of Native Americans was Andrew Jackson. Ignoring strong opposition in Congress and one Supreme Court decision (*Worcester v. Georgia,* 1832), Jackson was determined to remove all Native Americans to the West.

Your task in this chapter is to identify and assess the alternatives available to Andrew Jackson regarding Cherokee removal. Jackson never wavered in his advocacy of Native American removal to the West. And yet he consistently claimed that his policy was best for the Native Americans themselves. (Having no children, Jackson and his wife adopted a Creek orphan in 1814; he died of tuberculosis in 1828 at the age of sixteen.) What alternatives were available to President Andrew Jackson regarding Cherokee removal? What were the strengths and weaknesses of each alternative? Could removal have been avoided?

⟨∽ BACKGROUND ∽⟩

The origins of the Cherokees are clouded in mystery. Linguistically related to the Iroquois of New England and northern New York, it is thought that the Cherokees migrated south into present-day Georgia, Tennessee (itself a derivation of the name of a Cherokee town, Tanasi), South Carolina, and North Carolina and settled the area somewhere between the years 600 and 1000, centuries before the

3. The official U.S. Army count of those removed to Indian Territory totaled 13,149, of whom 11,504 actually arrived in the West. Based on the tribal census of 1835, at least 2,000 died in the stockades.

4. See Russell Thornton, "The Demography of the Trail of Tears Period: A New Estimate of Cherokee Population Losses," in William L. Anderson, ed., *Cherokee Removal: Before and After* (Athens, Ga.: University of Georgia Press, 1991), pp. 75–95.

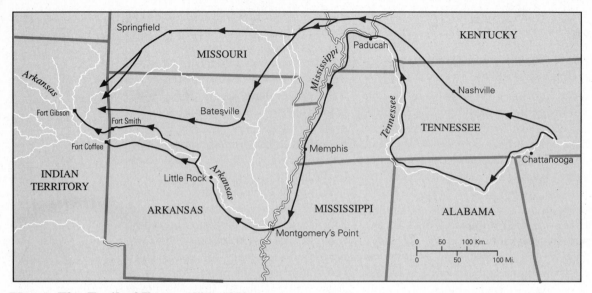

Map 1. The Trail of Tears, 1838–1839.
Adapted from Grace Steele Woodward, *The Cherokees* (Norman: University of Oklahoma Press, 1963), pp. 206–207.

first regular contact with white people, in the late 1600s. Spread across much of the Southeast, the Cherokees were divided into three main groups: the Lower Towns, along the upper Savannah River in South Carolina; the Middle Towns, along the Little Tennessee River and its tributaries in western North Carolina; and the Overhill Towns, in eastern Tennessee and extreme western North Carolina. (See Map 2.)

Sometime before their regular contact with Europeans, the Cherokees became sedentary. Women performed most of the farm duties, raising corn and beans, while men hunted deer and turkey and caught fish to complete their diet. The Cherokees built towns organized around extended families. Society was *matrilineal,* meaning that property and position passed from

generation to generation through the mother's side of the family. Each town theoretically was autonomous, and there were no leaders (or chiefs, in European parlance) who ruled over all the towns. Local leaders led by persuasion and example, and all adults, including women, could speak in town councils. Indeed, Cherokee governing practices were considerably more democratic and consensual than the Europeans' hierarchical ways.

Initial contacts with Europeans were devastating. Europeans brought with them measles and smallpox, against which Native Americans were not immune. Also, Cherokees were attracted to European goods such as fabrics, metal hoes and hatchets, firearms, and (tragically) alcohol. In order to acquire these goods, Cherokees traded deerskins for them. By the

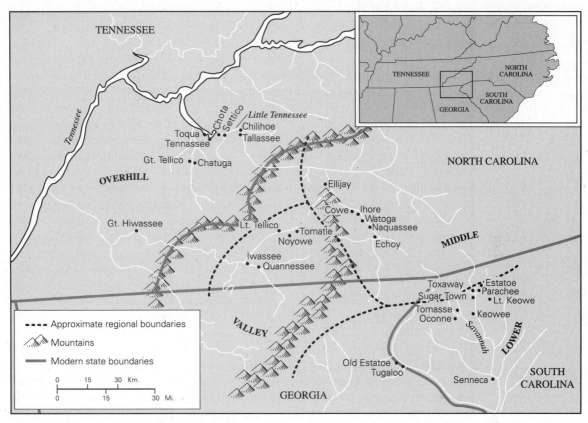

Map 2. Cherokee Settlements, 1775.
From Duane H. King, ed., *The Cherokee Nation: A Troubled History* (Knoxville:
University of Tennessee Press, 1979), p. 50.

early 1700s, Cherokees were killing an average of fifty thousand deer each year to secure their hides for barter, and estimates are that by 1735 over 1 million deer had been killed, almost certainly depleting the herds. Gradually, the Cherokees were losing their self-sufficiency and becoming increasingly dependent on European goods.

With European colonization and expansion in North America, the Cherokees inevitably became swept up into European peoples' wars. Initially siding with the British against the French, the Cherokees turned against the British when the colonial governor of South Carolina called thirty-two chieftains to a conference and then killed twenty-nine of them. The British retaliated against a Cherokee outburst by destroying the Lower Towns, killing over one hundred Cherokee warriors, and driving the survivors into the mountains. In the American Revolution, the Cherokees, hoping to stem white western expansion, again

CHAPTER 6

ASSESSING
HISTORICAL
ALTERNATIVES:
THE REMOVAL
OF THE
CHEROKEES,
1838–1839

sided with the British. American patriots destroyed over fifty Cherokee towns, scalping men and women indiscriminately.

After the American Revolution, the new U.S. government pursued a policy of attempting to "civilize" the Cherokees. Aided by government Indian agent Return J. Meigs (who lived with the Cherokees from 1801 to 1823) and a number of missionaries, the Cherokee Nation was able to adapt to many of the "white man's ways." Anglo-European gender roles were adopted, as men gave up hunting and took over agriculture from women. Plows, spinning wheels, and looms were introduced, and Cherokee women took up the making of cloth and clothing. As it did with white settlers, landownership and agriculture produced a class system. By 1824, the most affluent Cherokees owned 1,277 African American slaves, and most Cherokees were living in log homes similar to those of their white neighbors.

Cherokees were becoming "civilized" culturally as well. Mission boarding schools, supported by white contributions, dotted the landscape, and Cherokee children learned to read, write, and compute and also learned Anglo-European gender roles. Around 1809 the Native American Sequoyah began devising a Cherokee alphabet (he called it a syllabary) of eighty-five phonetic symbols that allowed Cherokees to become literate in their own language. In 1828, the first edition of the newspaper the *Cherokee Phoenix* appeared, edited by Cherokee Elias Boudinot.

Governmental and political forms also were modeled after Anglo-European institutions. A Native American police force was instituted in 1808, and in the following year a detailed census was taken. In 1827 a formal constitution was adopted, modeled on the United States Constitution, setting up a representative government and courts for the Cherokee Nation. Women, who were more nearly equal to men in traditional Cherokee society, saw their position deteriorate, as they were prohibited from voting or serving as representatives by the new constitution. In many ways, then, Cherokees had remade their economy, society, culture, and government. And although some people clung stubbornly to the old ways, Cherokee adaptation was generally widespread.

As it turned out, adaptation to the white persons' ways would not save the Cherokees. In 1802, the U.S. government and the state of Georgia reached an agreement whereby the federal government promised to "extinguish, for the use of Georgia, as early as the same can be peaceably obtained upon reasonable terms . . . the Indian titles to all lands lying within the limits of the state."[5] The Louisiana Purchase (1804) acquired territory in the West that theoretically could be used for the relocation of the eastern Native Americans. Slowly the federal government began purchasing Cherokee lands in Tennessee, southern Kentucky, northern Alabama, South Carolina, and northeastern Georgia. In 1818, a trickle of Chero-

5. Quoted in Samuel Carter III, *Cherokee Sunset, A Nation Betrayed: A Narrative of Travail and Triumph, Persecution and Exile* (Garden City, N.Y.: Doubleday, 1976), p. 28.

kees began to migrate to lands west of the Mississippi River.

The vast majority of Cherokees, however, refused to move. They had built farms, sawmills, tanneries, ferries, stores, and towns. The Treaty of Hopewell (1785) had promised that they would be able to hold onto their land "forever." In addition, Christian missionaries who lived among the Cherokees strengthened their resolve to resist removal, believing that the Cherokees were making great strides at becoming "civilized" where they were.

Yet one Cherokee chieftain's 1775 statement turned out to be prophetic: "Indian Nations before the Whites are like balls of snow before the sun."[6] In 1828, three events took place that would change the Cherokee Nation forever. First, gold was discovered in Cherokee lands in Georgia, setting off a rush of around four thousand whites into Cherokee territory.[7] Cherokees fought back by attacking and burning the houses of the white prospectors, and federal troops had to be dispatched to restore order. Then, in November 1828, Tennessean Andrew Jackson was elected president. Although Cherokees had been his allies in the earlier war against the Creeks, Jackson had made no secret of the fact that he strongly favored the removal

of all Native Americans to lands west of the Mississippi River. As a person who had made a great deal of money in land speculation, it is possible that Jackson recognized the potential profits that could be made by acquiring Cherokee lands and was interested in helping other land speculators.

With Jackson as president, the state of Georgia realized that it could now move with impunity. In December 1828, over three months before Jackson's inauguration, the Georgia legislature passed a bill declaring that as of June 1, 1830, all Cherokee territory would be subject to Georgia laws, and Cherokee laws (including their constitution) would be null and void. The Georgia legislature also made provisions for a lottery to distribute Cherokee lands to whites. In 1829, the Georgia legislature passed an act requiring all whites living in Cherokee territory to secure licenses, an obvious attempt to expel white missionaries who, many Georgians believed, were urging the Native Americans to resist white encroachment.

In his annual message to Congress of December 8, 1829 (see Source 2), President Jackson made his case for the "voluntary" removal of all Native Americans east of the Mississippi River.[8] Responding to the president's wishes, in February 1830 the House of Representatives took up the Indian Removal Bill. The bill touched off a furious debate both in Congress and among the general public. Hundreds

6. J. G. M. Ramsey, *Annals of Tennessee* (Charleston, S.C.: Walker and James, 1853), pp. 117–118.
7. Some of those who made a great deal of money from the Georgia gold rush included the South Carolina political leader John C. Calhoun, his son-in-law Thomas G. Clemson (who used some of the profits to found Clemson College in South Carolina), and future governor of New York and Democratic presidential candidate Samuel J. Tilden.

8. Approximately sixty Native American nations still resided east of the Mississippi, the largest among them being the Choctaws, Creeks, Chickasaws, and Seminoles, all in the southeastern United States.

CHAPTER 6

ASSESSING
HISTORICAL
ALTERNATIVES:
THE REMOVAL
OF THE
CHEROKEES,
1838–1839

of petitions were sent to Congress, the majority from religious groups and benevolent societies opposed to removal. Many congressional opponents of the bill were genuinely concerned with the welfare of Native Americans (see Source 3, from the speech by New Jersey congressman Theodore Frelinghuysen), but at least an equal number were Jackson's political opponents who sought to embarrass the president. On April 23, 1830, the Senate approved the Indian Removal Bill by a vote of 28–19, the House following suit on May 24 by the close margin of 102–97. Jackson signed the bill on May 28, 1830.[9] The act empowered the president to trade land in the West for lands on which Native Americans east of the Mississippi then resided, to pay Native Americans for improvements they had made to lands they were giving up, to assist and protect Native Americans during their migration, and to superintend and care for them once they had reached their destinations.

Cherokees were divided over how to respond to the imminent loss of their lands. Believing the fight was over, about two thousand voluntarily moved west to join some Cherokees who had moved even earlier. But the majority resisted removal, appealing twice to the U.S. Supreme Court. In *Cherokee Nation v. Georgia* (1831), Chief Justice John Marshall dismissed the Cherokees' suit on technical grounds.[10] In his written opinion,

however, he hinted that he might be sympathetic to the Cherokee cause if they could bring a case to the Supreme Court in another way, and the next year, in *Worcester v. Georgia* (1832), Marshall declared that Georgia's laws did not extend to the Cherokees.[11] But President Jackson refused to enforce the Court's decision, and many Cherokees came to realize that their cause was lost.

In 1835 a minority of Cherokees signed the Treaty of New Echota whereby the Cherokees promised that, in return for $5 million and land in the West, they would give up all claims to lands they occupied in Georgia, North Carolina, Tennessee, and Alabama.[12] Outraged over actions of this minority (who were derisively labeled the "Treaty Party"), 15,665 Cherokees purportedly signed a petition to the U.S. Congress protesting their removal. The Senate, which earlier had ratified the Treaty of New Echota by a single vote, tabled the petition on April 9, 1838, and General Winfield Scott was given his orders.

About 1,100 Cherokees were permitted to remain in North Carolina, principally because a white merchant named William Holland Thomas had used money from the Treaty of New

---

9. For the text of the Removal Act, see Wilcomb E. Washburn, ed., *The American Indian and the United States: A Documentary History* (New York: Random House, 1973), Vol. III, pp. 2169–2171.
10. Marshall ruled that the Supreme Court could not be the court of original jurisdiction,

since the Cherokee Nation was not a sovereign nation such as France or Great Britain, within the meaning of Article III, Section 2, of the Constitution, and therefore the case had to originate in a lower court.
11. Samuel Worcester was a white missionary who refused to secure a Georgia license to live among the Cherokees. He and a fellow missionary were thrown into jail and appealed their case to the Supreme Court.
12. The Cherokee census of 1835 reported 8,946 living in Georgia, 3,644 in North Carolina, 2,528 in Tennessee, and 1,424 in Alabama, for a total of 16,542.

Echota to purchase thousands of acres in western North Carolina on which he encouraged Cherokees to settle (he kept the land title in his own name). In 1837 the North Carolina General Assembly acknowledged the Cherokees' right to remain in North Carolina. The fact that the land Thomas purchased for the Cherokees was land that virtually no one else wanted probably was a factor in the legislature's decision. In addition to the 1,100 Cherokees who were allowed to stay in North Carolina, an additional 300 remained scattered throughout Georgia, Alabama, and Tennessee. Some had hidden themselves from Scott's soldiers, while others were related by blood and marriage to their white neighbors.

Eyewitness accounts of the Trail of Tears, by both Native Americans and U.S. Army escorts, make for grim reading. As many as 2,500 or more died in the makeshift stockades prior to the journey. And of the 13,149 (cited by army records) who began the trip, only 11,504 arrived in Indian Territory. In addition, several hundred died soon after their arrival, by either disease or violence between the new arrivals and earlier migrants or between the "accommodationists" and the last-ditch resisters.

What other alternatives were available to President Jackson and Congress? Could removal have been avoided? Your task in this chapter is to examine the evidence to determine Jackson's alternatives.

THE METHOD

Normally historians concern themselves with what actually *did* happen rather than what *might have* happened. In certain circumstances, however, it is helpful in assessing a person's or a group's decisions by considering what other choices or options were available to the person or group—in this case, what alternatives to Cherokee removal were available to President Andrew Jackson.

The first thing you will have to do is to identify the alternatives to removal. In his annual message to Congress (Source 2), Jackson himself stated what he thought his alternatives were, so it would be wise to begin there. Remember, however, that the president was arguing in favor of Cherokee removal. Therefore, he might not have

explained what he saw as his alternatives completely or fairly.

Each additional piece of evidence then identifies or implies an alternative to Cherokee removal. Examine each piece of evidence carefully in order to identify the particular alternative it contains. Occasionally you may have to read between the lines (especially in Sources 5 and 6, but in others as well). Make a list of alternatives as you go along, together with the principal arguments in their favor or against them.

Once you have identified the alternatives available to President Jackson, the difficult work begins. In order to answer the question of whether removal could have been avoided, you will have to ask certain questions of

CHAPTER 6

ASSESSING
HISTORICAL
ALTERNATIVES:
THE REMOVAL
OF THE
CHEROKEES,
1838–1839

each alternative. How realistic was that alternative? What might have been the results of choosing that alternative? What benefits might that alternative have offered? If there were any liabilities, what were they? Try to put yourself in the position of a person living in the 1830s, not the late 1990s. Also try to be as objective and dispassionate as possible. Take notes as you go along.

∽ THE EVIDENCE ∽

Source 1 from Andrew A. Lipscomb and Albert Ellergy Bergh, eds., *The Writings of Thomas Jefferson* (Washington, D.C.: Thomas Jefferson Memorial Association, 1903), Vol. XVI, pp. 450–454.

1. President Thomas Jefferson to Captain Hendrick, the Delawares, Mohicans, and Munries, December 21, 1808.

. . . The picture which you have drawn, my son, of the increase of our numbers and the decrease of yours is just, the causes are very plain, and the remedy depends on yourselves alone. You have lived by hunting the deer and buffalo—all these have been driven westward; you have sold out on the sea-board and moved westwardly in pursuit of them. As they became scarce there, your food has failed you; you have been a part of every year without food, except the roots and other unwholesome things you could find in the forest. Scanty and unwholesome food produce diseases and death among your children, and hence you have raised few and your numbers have decreased. Frequent wars, too, and the abuse of spirituous liquors, have assisted in lessening your numbers. The whites, on the other hand, are in the habit of cultivating the earth, of raising stocks of cattle, hogs, and other domestic animals, in much greater numbers than they could kill of deer and buffalo. Having always a plenty of food and clothing they raise abundance of children, they double their numbers every twenty years, the new swarms are continually advancing upon the country like flocks of pigeons, and so they will continue to do. Now, my children, if we wanted to diminish our numbers, we would give up the culture of the earth, pursue the deer and buffalo, and be always at war; this would soon reduce us to be as few as you are, and if you wish to increase your numbers you must give up the deer and buffalo, live in peace and cultivate the earth. You see then, my children, that it depends on yourselves alone to become a numerous and great people. Let me entreat you, therefore, on the lands now given you to begin to give every man a farm; let him enclose it, cultivate it, build a warm house on it, and when he dies, let it belong to his wife and children after him. Nothing is so easy as to learn to cultivate the earth; all your women understand it, and to make it easier, we are always ready to teach you how to make ploughs, hoes, and necessary utensils. If the men will take the labor of the earth from the women they will learn to spin and weave and to clothe their families. In this way you will also raise many children, you will double your numbers every twenty years, and soon fill the land your friends have given you, and your children will never be tempted to sell the spot on which they have been born, raised, have labored and called their own. When once you have property, you will want laws and magistrates to protect your property and persons, and to punish those among you who commit crimes. You will find that our laws are good for this purpose; you will wish to live under them, you will unite yourselves with us, join in our Great Councils and form one people with us, and we shall all be Americans; you will mix with us by marriage, your blood will run in our veins, and will spread with us over this great island. Instead, then, my children, of the gloomy prospect you have drawn of your total disappearance from the face of the earth, which is true, if you continue to hunt the deer and buffalo and go to war, you see what a brilliant aspect is offered to your future history, if you give up war and hunting. Adopt the culture of the earth and raise domestic animals; you see how from a small family you may become a great nation by adopting the course which from the small beginning you describe has made us a great nation. . . .

Source 2 from Anthony F. C. Wallace, *The Long, Bitter Trail: Andrew Jackson and the Indian* (New York: Hill and Wang, 1993), pp. 121–124.

2. Excerpt from Jackson's Message to Congress, December 8, 1829.

The condition and ulterior destiny of the Indian Tribes within the limits of some of our States, have become objects of much interest and importance. It has long been the policy of Government to introduce among them the arts of civilization, in the hope of gradually reclaiming them from a wandering life. This policy has, however, been coupled with another, wholly incompatible with its success. Professing a desire to civilize and settle them, we have, at the same time, lost no opportunity to purchase their lands, and thrust them further into the wilderness. By this means they have not only been kept in a wandering state, but been led to look upon us as unjust and indifferent to their fate. Thus, though lavish in its expen-

CHAPTER 6

ASSESSING
HISTORICAL
ALTERNATIVES:
THE REMOVAL
OF THE
CHEROKEES,
1838–1839

ditures upon the subject, Government has constantly defeated its own policy; and the Indians, in general, receding further and further to the West, have retained their savage habits. A portion, however, of the Southern tribes, having mingled much with the whites, and made some progress in the arts of civilized life, have lately attempted to erect an independent government, within the limits of Georgia and Alabama. These States, claiming to be the only Sovereigns within their territories, extended their laws over the Indians; which induced the latter to call upon the United States for protection.

Under these circumstances, the question presented was, whether the General Government had a right to sustain those people in their pretensions? The Constitution declares, that "no new State shall be formed or erected within the jurisdiction of any other State," without the consent of its legislature. If the General Government is not permitted to tolerate the erection of a confederate State within the territory of one of the members of this Union, against her consent; much less could it allow a foreign and independent government to establish itself there. Georgia became a member of the Confederacy which eventuated in our Federal Union, as a sovereign State, always asserting her claim to certain limits; which having been originally defined in her colonial charter, and subsequently recognised in the treaty of peace, she has ever since continued to enjoy, except as they have been circumscribed by her own voluntary transfer of a portion of her territory to the United States, in the articles of cession of 1802. Alabama was admitted into the Union on the same footing with the original States, with boundaries which were prescribed by Congress. There is no constitutional, conventional, or legal provision, which allows them less power over the Indians within their borders, than is possessed by Maine or New York. Would the People of Maine permit the Penobscot tribe to erect an Independent Government within their State? and unless they did, would it not be the duty of the General Government to support them in resisting such a measure? Would the People of New York permit each remnant of the Six Nations within her borders, to declare itself an independent people under the protection of the United States? Could the Indians establish a separate republic on each of their reservations in Ohio? and if they were so disposed, would it be the duty of this Government to protect them in the attempt? If the principle involved in the obvious answer to these questions be abandoned, it will follow that the objects of this Government are reversed; and that it has become a part of its duty to aid in destroying the States which it was established to protect.

Actuated by this view of the subject, I informed the Indians inhabiting parts of Georgia and Alabama, that their attempt to establish an independent government would not be countenanced by the Executive of the United States; and advised them to emigrate beyond the Mississippi, or submit to the laws of those States.

Our conduct towards these people is deeply interesting to our national character. Their present condition, contrasted with what they once were, makes a most powerful appeal to our sympathies. Our ancestors found them the uncontrolled possessors of these vast regions. By persuasion and force, they have been made to retire from river to river, and from mountain to mountain; until some of the tribes have become extinct, and others have left but remnants, to preserve, for a while, their once terrible names. Surrounded by the whites, with their arts of civilization, which, by destroying the resources of the savage, doom him to weakness and decay; the fate of the Mohegan, the Narragansett, and the Delaware, is fast overtaking the Choctaw, the Cherokee, and the Creek. That this fate surely awaits them, if they remain within the limits of the States, does not admit of a doubt. Humanity and national honor demand that every effort should be made to avert so great a calamity. It is too late to inquire whether it was just in the United States to include them and their territory within the bounds of new States whose limits they could control. That step cannot be retraced. A State cannot be dismembered by Congress, or restricted in the exercise of her constitutional power. But the people of those States, and of every State, actuated by feelings of justice and a regard for our national honor, submit to you the interesting question, whether something cannot be done, consistently with the rights of the States, to preserve this much injured race?

As a means of effecting this end, I suggest, for your consideration, the propriety of setting apart an ample district West of the Mississippi, and without the limits of any State or Territory, now formed, to be guarantied to the Indian tribes, as long as they shall occupy it: each tribe having a distinct control over the portion designated for its use. There they may be secured in the enjoyment of governments of their own choice, subject to no other control from the United States than such as may be necessary to preserve peace on the frontier, and between the several tribes. There the benevolent may endeavor to teach them the arts of civilization; and, by promoting union and harmony among them, to raise up an interesting commonwealth, destined to perpetuate the race, and to attest the humanity and justice of this Government.

This emigration should be voluntary: for it would be as cruel as unjust to compel the aborigines to abandon the graves of their fathers, and seek a home in a distant land. But they should be distinctly informed that, if they remain within the limits of the States, they must be subject to their laws. In return for their obedience, as individuals, they will, without doubt, be

CHAPTER 6

ASSESSING
HISTORICAL
ALTERNATIVES:
THE REMOVAL
OF THE
CHEROKEES,
1838–1839

protected in the enjoyment of those possessions which they have improved by their industry. But it seems to me visionary to suppose, that, in this state of things, claims can be allowed on tracts of country on which they have neither dwelt nor made improvements, merely because they have seen them from the mountain, or passed them in the chace [sic]. Submitting to the laws of the States, and receiving, like other citizens, protection in their persons and property, they will, ere long, become merged in the mass of our population.

Source 3 from *Speeches on the Passage of the Bill for the Removal of the Indians, Delivered in the Congress of the United States, April and May, 1830* (Boston: Perkins and Marvin, 1830), pp. 25–28.

3. Excerpt from Speech of Senator Theodore Frelinghuysen of New Jersey.

. . . It is alleged, that the Indians cannot flourish in the neighborhood of a white population—that whole tribes have disappeared under the influence of this propinquity. As an abstract proposition, it implies reproach some-where. Our virtues certainly have not such deadly and depopulating power. It must, then, be our vices that possess these destructive energies—and shall we commit injustice, and put in, as our plea for it, that our intercourse with the Indians has been so demoralizing that we must drive them from it, to save them? True, Sir, many tribes have melted away—they have sunk lower and lower—and what people could rise from a condition to which policy, selfishness, and cupidity, conspired to depress them?

Sir, had we devoted the same care to elevate their moral condition, that we have to degrade them, the removal of the Indians would not now seek for an apology in the suggestions of humanity. But I ask, as to the matter of fact, how stands the account? Wherever a fair experiment has been made, the Indians have readily yielded to the influences of moral cultivation. Yes, Sir, they flourish under this culture, and rise in the scale of being. They have shown themselves to be highly susceptible of improvement, and the ferocious feelings and habits of the savage are soothed and reformed by the mild charities of religion. They can very soon be taught to understand and appreciate the blessings of civilization and regular government. And I have the opinions of some of our most enlightened statesmen to sustain me. . . .

[*Here Frelinghuysen quoted from the messages to Congress of Presidents Jefferson (1801, 1803, 1806, 1808), Madison (1809), and Monroe (1824), all of whom reported on the rapid adaptation by Native Americans of Anglo-European "civilization."*]

Now, Sir, when we consider the large space which these illustrious men have filled in our councils, and the perfect confidence that is due to their official statements, is it not astonishing to hear it gravely maintained that the Indians are retrograding in their condition and character; that all our public anxieties and cares bestowed upon them have been utterly fruitless; and that, for very pity's sake, we must get rid of them, or they will perish on our hands? Sir, I believe that the confidence of the Senate has been abused by some of the letter-writers, who give us such sad accounts of Indian wretchedness. I rejoice that we may safely repose upon the statements contained in the letters of Messrs. J. L. Allen, R. M. Livingston, Rev. Cyrus Kingsbury, and the Rev. Samuel A. Worcester.[13] The character of these witnesses is without reproach; and their satisfactory certificates of the improvement of the tribes continue and confirm the history furnished to us in the several messages from which I have just read extracts.

It is further maintained, "that one of the greatest evils to which the Indians are exposed, is that incessant pressure of population, that forces them from seat to seat, without allowing time for moral and intellectual improvement." Sir, this is the very reason—the deep, cogent reason—which I present to the Senate, now to raise the barrier against the pressure of population, and, with all the authority of this nation, say to the urging tide, "Thus far, and no farther." Let us save them now, or we never shall. For is it not clear as the sunbeam, Sir, that a removal will aggravate their woes? If the tide is nearly irresistible at this time; when a few more years shall fill the regions beyond the Arkansas with many more millions of enterprising white men, will not an increased impulse be given, that shall sweep the red men away into the barren prairies, or the Pacific of the west?

If these constant removals are so afflictive, and allow no time for moral improvement; if this be the cause why the attempts at Indian reformation are alleged to have been so unavailing; do not the dictates of experience, then, plead most powerfully with us, to drive them no farther?—to grant them an abiding place, where these moral causes may have a fair and uninterrupted operation in moulding and refining the Indian character? And, Sir, weigh a moment the considerations that address us on behalf of the Cherokees especially. Prompted and encouraged by our counsels, they have in good earnest resolved to become men, rational, educated, Christian men; and they have succeeded beyond our most sanguine hopes. They have established a regular constitution of civil government, republican in its principles. Wise and beneficent laws are enacted. The people acknowledge their authority, and feel their obligation. A printing press, conducted by one

13. Friends of the Cherokees and missionaries who worked with them. Samuel A. Worcester was the principal figure in *Worcester v. Georgia* (1832).

CHAPTER 6

ASSESSING
HISTORICAL
ALTERNATIVES:
THE REMOVAL
OF THE
CHEROKEES,
1838–1839

of the nation, circulates a weekly newspaper, printed partly in English, and partly in the Cherokee language. Schools flourish in many of their settlements. Christian temples, to the God of the Bible, are frequented by respectful, devout, and many sincere worshippers. God, as we believe, has many people among them, whom he regards as the "apple of his eye." They have become better neighbors to Georgia. She made no complaints during the lapse of fifty years, when the tribes were a horde of ruthless, licentious and drunken savages; when no law controlled them; when the only judge was their will, and their avenger the tomahawk.

Then Georgia could make treaties with them, and acknowledge them as nations; and in conventions trace boundary lines, and respect the landmarks of her neighbor: and now, when they begin to reap the fruits of all the paternal instructions, so repeatedly and earnestly delivered to them by the Presidents; when the Cherokee has learned to respect the rights of the white man, and sacredly to regard the obligations of truth and conscience; is this the time, Sir, to break up a peaceful community, to put out its council fires, to annul its laws and customs, to crush the rising hopes of its youth, and to drive the desponding and discouraged Indian to despair? Although it be called a sickly humanity to sympathize with Indians—every freeman in the land, that has one spark of the spirit of his fathers, will denounce the proposed measure as an unparalleled stretch of cruel injustice—unparalleled certainly in our history. And if the deed be done, Sir, how it is regarded in heaven will, sooner or later, be known on earth; for this is the judgment place of public sins. And all these ties are to be broken asunder, for a State that was silent, and acquiesced in the relations of the Indians to our present government; that pretended to no right of direct interference, whilst these tribes were really dangerous; when their ferocious incursions justly disturbed the tranquillity of the fireside, and waked the "sleep of the cradle;"—for a State that seeks it now against an unoffending neighbor, which implores, by all that is dear in the graves of her fathers, in the traditions of by-gone ages; that beseeches by the ties of nature, of home, and of country, to let her live unmolested, and die near the dust of her kindred!

Our fears have been addressed in behalf of those States, whose legislation we resist: and it is inquired with solicitude, Would you urge us to arms with Georgia? No, Sir. This tremendous alternative will not be necessary. Let the general government come out, as it should, with decided and temperate firmness, and officially announce to Georgia, and the other States, that if the Indian tribes choose to remain, they will be protected against all interference and encroachment; and such is my confidence in the sense of justice, in the respect for law, prevailing in the great body of this portion of our fellow-citizens, that I believe they would submit to the authority of the nation. I can expect no other issue. . . .

Sources 4, 5, and 6 from Theda Perdue and Michael D. Green, eds., *The Cherokee Removal: A Brief History with Documents* (Boston: Bedford Books, 1995), pp. 98–102, 38–41, 124.

4. Excerpt from William Penn (pseudonym for Jeremiah Evarts of the American Board of Commissioners for Foreign Missions), "A Brief View of the Present Relations Between the Government and People of the United States and the Indians Within Our National Limits," November 1829.

. . . The positions here recited are deemed to be incontrovertible. It follows, therefore,

That the removal of any nation of Indians from their country by force would be an instance of gross and cruel oppression:

That all attempts to accomplish this removal of the Indians by bribery or fraud, by intimidation and threats, by withholding from them a knowledge of the strength of their cause, by practising upon their ignorance, and their fears, or by vexatious opportunities, interpreted by them to mean nearly the same thing as a command;—all such attempts are acts of oppression, and therefore entirely unjustifiable:

That the United States are firmly bound by treaty to protect the Indians from force and encroachments on the part of a State; and a refusal thus to protect them would be equally an act of bad faith as a refusal to protect them against individuals: and

That the Cherokees have therefore the guaranty of the United States, solemnly and repeatedly given, as a security against encroachments from Georgia and the neighboring States. By virtue of this guaranty the Cherokees may rightfully demand, that the United States shall keep all intruders at a distance, from whatever quarter, or in whatever character, they may come. Thus secured and defended in the possession of their country, the Cherokees have a perfect right to retain that possession as long as they please. Such a retention of their country is no just cause of complaint or offence to any State, or to any individual. It is merely an exercise of natural rights, which rights have been not only acknowledged but repeatedly and solemnly confirmed by the United States.

Although these principles are clear and incontrovertible, yet many persons feel an embarrassment from considering the Cherokees *as living in*

CHAPTER 6

ASSESSING
HISTORICAL
ALTERNATIVES:
THE REMOVAL
OF THE
CHEROKEES,
1838–1839

the State of Georgia. All this embarrassment may be removed at once by bearing in mind, that the Cherokee country is not in Georgia. . . .

[*Here Penn argued that the Cherokees owned their land by treaty with the U.S. government, that in 1825 the state of Georgia made a treaty with the Creek Nation to acquire their land, and hence would have to do so with the Cherokees as well.*]

If the separate existence of the Indian tribes *were* an inconvenience to their neighbours, this would be but a slender reason for breaking down all the barriers of justice and good faith. Many a rich man has thought it very inconvenient, that he could not add the farm of a poor neighbour to his possessions. Many a powerful nation has felt it to be inconvenient to have a weak and dependent state in its neighbourhood, and has therefore forcibly joined the territory of such state to its own extensive domains. But this is done at the expense of honour and character, and is visited by the historian with his severest reprobation.

In the case before us the inconvenience is altogether imaginary. If the United States were examined, with a view to find a place where Indians could have a residence assigned them, so that they might be as little as possible in the way of the whites, not a single tract, capable of sustaining inhabitants, could be found more secluded than the present country of the Cherokees. It is in the mountains, among the head waters of rivers diverging in all directions; and some parts of it are almost inaccessible. The Cherokees have ceded to the United States all their best land. Not a twentieth part of what remains is of a very good quality. More than half is utterly worthless. Perhaps three tenths may produce moderate crops. The people of the United States have a free passage through the country, secured by treaty. What do they want more? If the Cherokee country were added to Georgia, the accession would be but a fraction joined to the remotest corner of that great State;—a State now scarcely inferior in size to any State in the Union except Virginia; a State having but six or seven souls to a square mile, counting whites and blacks, and with a soil and climate capable of sustaining a hundred to the square mile with the greatest of ease. There is no mighty inconvenience, therefore, in the arrangement of Providence, by which the Cherokee claim a resting place on the land which God gave to their fathers. . . .

There is one remaining topic, on which the minds of many benevolent men are hesitating; and that is, *whether the welfare of the Indians would not be promoted by a removal.* Though they have a right to remain where they are; though the whole power of the United States is pledged to defend them in their possessions; yet it is supposed by some, that they would act wisely, if they would yield to the pressure, quietly surrender their territory to the United States, and accept a new country beyond the Mississippi, with a new guaranty.

In support of this supposition, it is argued, that they can never remain quiet where they are; that they will always be infested by troublesome whites; and that the states, which lay claim to their territory, will persevere in measures to vex and annoy them.

Let us look a moment at this statement. Is it indeed true, that, in the very prime and vigour of our republican government, and with all our boasted reliance upon constitutions and laws, we cannot enforce as plain an act of Congress as is to be found in our national statute-book? Is it true, that while treaties are declared in the constitution to be the supreme law of the land, a whole volume of these supreme laws is to be at once avowedly and utterly disregarded? Is the Senate of the United States, that august body, as our newspapers have called it a thousand times, to march in solemn procession, and burn a volume of treaties? Are the archives of state to be searched, and a hundred and fifty rolls, containing treaties with the Indians, to be brought forth and consigned to the flames on Capitol Hill, in the presence of the representatives of the people, and all the dignitaries of our national government? When ambassadors from foreign nations inquire, *What is the cause of all this burning?* are we to say, "Forty years ago President Washington and the Senate made treaties with the Indians, which have been repeated and confirmed by successive administrations. The treaties are plain, and the terms reasonable. But the Indians are weak, and their white neighbors will be lawless. The way to please these white neighbours is, therefore, to burn the treaties, and then call the Indians our dear children, and deal with them precisely as if no treaties had ever been made." Is this answer to be given to the honest inquires of intelligent foreigners? Are we to declare to mankind, that in our country law is totally inadequate to answer the great end for which human laws are made, that is, the protection of the weak against the strong? And is this confession to be made without feeling and without shame? It cannot be. The people of the United States will never subject themselves to so foul a reproach. They will not knowingly affix to the character of a republican government so indelible a stigma. Let it not be said, then, that the laws of the country cannot be executed. Let it never be admitted, that the faith of the nation must be violated, lest the government should come into collision with white intruders upon Indian lands:—with intruders, whose character is admitted to be lawless; and who can be invested with power, in no other way than by tamely yielding to their acts of encroachment and aggression.

The laws can be executed with perfect ease. The Indians can be defended. The faith of the nation can be preserved. Let the President of the United States, whenever the Indians shall be threatened, issue his proclamation,

CHAPTER 6

ASSESSING
HISTORICAL
ALTERNATIVES:
THE REMOVAL
OF THE
CHEROKEES,
1838–1839

describing the danger and asserting the majesty of the laws. Let him refer to the treaties and the acts of Congress, which his oath of office obliges him to enforce; let him recite the principal provisions of these treaties and acts, and declare, in the face of the world, that he shall execute the laws, and that he shall confidently rely upon the aid and co-operation of all good citizens:—let him do this, and neither he, nor the country, will be disappointed. Law will triumph, and oppression will hide its head.

5. John Ridge (a Cherokee leader) to Albert Gallatin,[14] February 27, 1826.

Superstition is the portion of all uncivilized Nations and Idolatry is only engendered in the Brain of rudeness. The Cherokees in their most savage state, never worshipped the work of their own hands—neither fire or water nor any one or portion of splendid fires that adorn heaven's Canopy above. They believed in a great first cause or Spirit of all Good & in a great being the author of all evil. These [were] at variance and at war with each other, but the good Spirit was supposed to be superior to the bad one. These immortal beings had on both sides numerous intelligent beings of analogous dispositions to their chieftains. They had a heaven, which consisted of a visible world to those who had undergone a change by death. This heaven was adorned with all the beauties which a savage imagination could conceive: An open forest, yet various, giving shade & fruit of every kind; Flowers of various hues & pleasant to the Smell; Game of all kinds in great abundance, enough of feasts & plenty of dances, & to crown the whole, the most beautiful women, prepared & adorned by the great Spirit, for every individual Indian that by wisdom, hospitality & Bravery was introduced to this happy & immortal region. The Bad place was the reverse of this & in the vicinity of the good place, where the wretched, compelled to live in hunger, hostility & darkness, could hear the rejoicings of the happy, without the possibility of reaching its shores.

Witches or wizards were in existence and pretended to possess Supernatural powers & intercourse with the Devil or bad Spirit. They were supposed capable of transforming themselves into the beasts of the forest & fowls of the air & take their nocturnal excursions in pursuit of human

14. Albert Gallatin (1761–1849) was a congressman, secretary of the treasury, and diplomat. When Ridge wrote to Gallatin, Gallatin had just been nominated as U.S. minister to Great Britain.

victims, particularly those suffering from disease, & it was often necessary for their friends to employ witch shooters to protect the sick from such visitors. Such characters were the dread of the Country, & many a time have I trembled at the croaking of a frog, hooting of an owl or guttural hoarseness of a Raven by night in my younger days. After the people began to be a little more courageous, these witches had a bad time of it. They were often on suspicion butchered or tomahawked by the enraged parents, relatives or friends of the deceased, particularly if the sickness was of short duration. The severity of revenge fell most principally on the grey hairs of aged persons of both sexes. To stop this evil, it was necessary to pass a law considering all slaughters of this kind in the light of murder, which has effected the desired remedy. There [are] yet among us who pretend to possess powers of milder character, Such as making rain, allaying a storm or whirlwinds, playing with thunder & foretelling future events with many other trifling conjurations not worth mentioning, but they are generally living monuments of fun to the young and grave Ridicule for those in maturer years. There [are] about 8 churches, where the gospel is preached on sabbath days with in the Nation. They are missionary stations supported by moravians, Presbyterians, Baptists and methodists and each of these churches have a goodly number of pious & exemplary members and others, not professors, attend to preaching with respectable deportment. I am not able to say the precise number of actual christians, but they are respectable in point of number & character. And many a drunken, idle & good for nothing Indian has been converted from error & have become useful Citizens: Portions of Scripture & sacred hymns are translated and I have frequently heard with astonishment a Cherokee, unacquainted with the English take his text & preach, read his hymn & sing it, Joined by his audience, and pray to his heavenly father with great propriety & devotion. The influence of Religion on the life of the Indians is powerful & lasting. I have an uncle, who was given to all the vices of savagism in drunkenness, fornication and roguery & he is now tho' poorer in this world's goods but rich in goodness & makes his living by hard labor & is in every respect an honest praying christian.

In respect to marriage, we have no law regulating it & polygamy is still allowed to Native Cherokees. Increase of morality among the men, the same among the women & a respect for their characters & matrimonial happiness is fast consuming this last vestige of our ignorance. We attempted to pass a law regulating marriage, but as nearly all the members of our Legislature, tho' convinced of the propriety, had been married under the old existing ceremony, [and] were afraid it would reflect dishonor on them, it failed. Time will effect the desired change in this system & it is worthy of mention,

CHAPTER 6

ASSESSING
HISTORICAL
ALTERNATIVES:
THE REMOVAL
OF THE
CHEROKEES,
1838–1839

even now, that the most respectable portion of our females prefer, tho' not required by law to be united in marriage attended by the solemnities of the Christian mode. Indians, tho' naturally highminded, are not addicted to as much revenge as they have been represented, and I can say this, much it is paid for them to endure an intended Insult but they are ready to forgive if they discover marks of repentance in the countenance of an enemy. In regard to Intemperance, we are still as a nation grossly degraded. We are however on the improve. Five years ago our best chiefs during their official labors would get drunk & continue so for two or three days. It is now not the case & any member who should thus depart from duty would now be expelled from the Council. Among the younger class, a large number are of fine habits, temperate & genteel in their deportment. The females aspire to gain the affection of such men & to the females we may always ascribe the honor of effecting the civilization of man. There are about 13 Schools established by missionaries in the Nation and may contain 250 students. They are entirely supported by the humane Societies in different parts of the U. States. The Nation has not as yet contributed to the support of these Schools. Besides this, some of our most respectable people have their children educated at the academies in the adjoining states. Two cherokee females have recently completed their Education, at the expense of their father, at a celebrated female Academy in Salem, North Carolina. They are highly accomplished & in point of appearance & deportment; they would pass for the genteel & wellbred ladies in any Country.

I know of some others who are preparing for an admission in the same institution. I suppose that there are one third of our Citizens, that can read & write in the English Language. George Guess[15] a Cherokee who is unacquainted with the English has invented 86 characters, in which the cherokees read & write in their own Language and regularly correspond with their Arkansas friends. This mode of writing is most extensively adopted by our people particularly by those who are ignorant of the English Language. A National Academy of a high order is to be soon established by law at our seat of Government. The edifice will be of Brick & will be supported by the Nation. It is also in contemplation to establish an English & Cherokee printing press & a paper edited in both languages at our seat of Government. In our last Session, $1500 was appropriated to purchase the press and regulations adopted to carry the object into effect. We have also a Society organized called the "Moral & Literary Society of the Cherokee Nation." A library is attached to this Institution. . . .

15. George Guess: Sequoyah.

6. Petition of Cherokee Women, May 2, 1817.

The Cherokee ladys now being present at the meeting of the chiefs and warriors in council have thought it their duty as mothers to address their beloved chiefs and warriors now assembled.

Our beloved children and head men of the Cherokee Nation, we address you warriors in council. We have raised all of you on the land which we now have, which God gave us to inhabit and raise provisions. We know that our country has once been extensive, but by repeated sales has become circumscribed to a small track [sic], and [we] never have thought it our duty to interfere in the disposition of it till now. If a father or mother was to sell all their lands which they had to depend on, which their children had to raise their living on, which would be indeed bad & to be removed to another country. We do not wish to go to an unknown country [to] which we have understood some of our children wish to go over the Mississippi, but this act of our children would be like destroying your mothers.

Your mothers, your sisters ask and beg of you not to part with any more of our land. We say ours. You are our descendants; take pity on our request. But keep it for our growing children, for it was the good will of our creator to place us here, and you know our father, the great president,[16] will not allow his white children to take our country away. Only keep your hands off of paper talks for its our own country. For [if] it was not, they would not ask you to put your hands to paper, for it would be impossible to remove us all. For as soon as one child is raised, we have others in our arms, for such is our situation & will consider our circumstance.

Therefore, children, don't part with any more of our lands but continue on it & enlarge your farms. Cultivate and raise corn & cotton and your mothers and sisters will make clothing for you which our father the president has recommended to us all. We don't charge any body for selling any lands, but we have heard such intentions of our children. But your talks become true at last; it was our desire to forwarn you all not to part with our lands. . . .

QUESTIONS TO CONSIDER

Remember that your task in this chapter is to identify and assess the alternatives to Cherokee removal that were available to President Andrew Jackson. To assess each alternative, you will have to judge the strengths and

16. President James Monroe.

[135]

CHAPTER 6

ASSESSING
HISTORICAL
ALTERNATIVES:
THE REMOVAL
OF THE
CHEROKEES,
1838–1839

weaknesses (the pros and cons) of each option. Finally, you should be able to reach a conclusion as to whether removal could have been avoided.

President Thomas Jefferson's letter of December 21, 1808 (Source 1), while not specifically relating to the Cherokees, is a good summary of his general policy with regard to Native Americans living within the boundaries of the United States. What did Jefferson believe were the causes of population decline among the Delawares, Mohicans, and Munries? How, in his view, could that situation be reversed? In return for staying on their lands, what would Native Americans have to give up? What do you make of the phrase, "you will unite yourselves with us, join in our Great Councils and form one people with us"? What alternative was Jefferson proposing? What were the strengths and weaknesses of that option?

President Andrew Jackson began his annual message to Congress (Source 2) by dismissing the alternative of allowing the Cherokees to remain where they were as a political entity separate from the state of Georgia. Why was that option unacceptable to Jackson? In his opinion, what would be the results of permitting the Cherokees to remain in the East? Do you think his argument was a strong one? What were the strengths and weaknesses of the alternative that Jackson offered? Finally, President Jackson strongly maintained that any such emigration "should be voluntary." According to Jackson, what would happen to the Cherokees who refused to leave?

Senator Theodore Frelinghuysen was deeply and genuinely concerned about the fate of Native Americans. The speech excerpted here (Source 3) took six hours to deliver. Frelinghuysen begins by admitting that many Native Americans living in close proximity to whites had experienced great difficulties. Yet why does he say this has happened? Why does Frelinghuysen believe that removal will *not* work and is not necessary? What alternative (by inference) does he support? What were its strengths and weaknesses?

Jeremiah Evarts (Source 4) was an ally of Senator Frelinghuysen. Yet notice that in this excerpt Evarts does not speak about "civilizing" the Cherokees. Can one infer that another possible alternative was to allow the Native Americans to remain on their lands but *not* try to "civilize" them? Since many Cherokees had adopted much from the whites, was this even a possible alternative? What were its strengths and weaknesses?

John Ridge (Source 5) was a Cherokee leader who eventually joined the "Treaty Party" and moved west, where he was murdered by Cherokees who thought he had betrayed them. In 1826, however, Ridge still was looking for a way for Cherokees to remain in the East. If many whites defended the Cherokees' right to stay because they had become "civilized" and others believed they should be allowed to retain their own traditional culture, what was Ridge's position? Was one alternative to allow the Cherokees to mix aspects of white culture with their own traditions and culture? What can you infer that the Cherokee women who petitioned their men (Source 6) might have thought of that?

Theoretically there were two additional alternatives that are not contained in the Evidence section. The first of these options (horrific, to be sure) was extermination of the Native Americans. Decades later, General Philip Sheridan was supposed to have remarked that the "only good Indians I ever saw were dead." Yet during the time period we are considering, no one openly expressed such an opinion, perhaps because, as historian Theda Perdue has noted, racial attitudes toward Native Americans had not reached the extremes that they would later.

A second theoretical alternative, one advocated by a few people at the time, was a more humane removal policy. Historian Mary Young has asserted, however, that, given the circumstances, General Winfield Scott's troops performed with a great deal of restraint.[17] Too, that would be exercising hindsight, which is always perfect.

What alternatives did President Andrew Jackson have other than Cherokee removal? What were the strengths and weaknesses of each option? Could removal have been avoided?

⚭ EPILOGUE ⚭

The war between the older immigrants and the newer arrivals to Indian territory went on for seven years, until peace between the two factions of Cherokees finally was made in 1846. During that period, some Cherokees reversed their trek and returned to North Carolina. When the Civil War broke out in 1861, factionalism once again emerged, with some Cherokees supporting the Confederacy and others backing the Union. Fighting between these factions (a "mini–Civil War") claimed the lives of as many as 25 percent of the Cherokee population.

In 1868, Congress recognized the obvious fact that the Cherokees who remained in the East had become a distinct group, named the Eastern Band of the Cherokees (as opposed to the migrating group, which was called the Cherokee Nation). In 1875 the federal government began to acquire land in North Carolina for a reservation, named the Qualla Boundary, which ultimately contained around 56,000 acres. In 1889, the Eastern Band received a charter from North Carolina granting the Cherokees what amounted to home rule in the Qualla Boundary. Then the federal government began an intensive program to "civilize" the eastern Cherokees, an effort that was ultimately unsuccessful. Cherokees clung stubbornly to their own language and traditions, and by 1900 fewer than one-fourth of the population could speak English— approximately half of them young people in white-administered boarding

17. See Mary E. Young, "Conflict Resolution on the Indian Frontier," *Journal of the Early Republic* 16 (Spring 1996): 18.

CHAPTER 6

ASSESSING
HISTORICAL
ALTERNATIVES:
THE REMOVAL
OF THE
CHEROKEES,
1838–1839

schools. Because they consistently voted Republican, after 1900 the Democratic majority in North Carolina disfranchised the Cherokees by passing a law requiring literacy tests prior to voting.

Meanwhile the Cherokee Nation (in the West) was experiencing its own difficulties. In spite of the fact that the 1830 Indian Removal Act guaranteed that Native Americans would always hold the land onto which they were placed, land grants to railroad companies and a territorial land rush stripped a good deal of land away from the Cherokees. In 1891 the Cherokee Nation owned 19.5 million acres. By 1971 it owned but 146,598.

In North Carolina, the creation of the Great Smoky Mountains National Park in 1934 offered the Eastern Band a way out of its economic quagmire. In November 1934, the council appropriated $50,000 for tourist facilities, and in 1937 the first Cherokee-owned motel (Newfound Lodge) was open for business. In 1939 an estimated 169,000 people visited the national park and purchased around $30,000 worth of Cherokee crafts.

The development of tourism undoubtedly helped alleviate a severe economic crisis for the Eastern Band. In 1932, at the low point of the Great Depression, it was estimated that 200 of the 496 Cherokee families in North Carolina needed public assistance. The New Deal did provide some jobs, through the Indian Emergency Conservation Work Program, a separate version of the Civilian Conservation Corps. But tourism also presented the Eastern Band with the problem of whether Cherokees could retain their cultural identity while at the same time catering to the desires of visitors with money.[18] In the 1990s, the Eastern Band turned to casino gambling to increase their revenues, although income from tourism and gambling is not evenly dispersed and many Cherokees still live extremely modestly.

The removal of most of the Cherokees in 1838–1839 (and in a second forced migration in 1841–1844) is a terrible chapter in the history of the United States. An analysis of the alternatives to removal that were available to the U.S. government, however, makes the subject of Cherokee removal not only a tragic one, but an exceedingly complex one as well.

18. Because tourists expected to see Native Americans with ornate feathered headdresses (typical of Plains Indians but never worn by Cherokees), Cherokees accommodatingly wore them.

QUESTIONS TO CONSIDER

Why did Brownson (Source 1) believe that slaves were better off than free laborers? What did he imply about women who worked? What major advantages did Reverend Mills observe in the Lowell system (Source 2)? In what important ways did the system (the factories and the boardinghouses) regulate the girls' lives? How did it protect the morals of its female employees? Of course, not all girls lived up to these standards. What did they do? How were they punished? Do you think Reverend Mills presented a relatively unbiased view? Why or why not? In what ways did the author of the article in *Voice of Industry* (Source 4) believe factory girls were being exploited?

Look carefully at the title page (Source 5) and the first editorial of the *Lowell Offering* (Source 6). What do they tell you about the factory girls, their interests, and their concerns? Was C.B. (Source 7) upholding the cult of true womanhood in her article about the dignity of labor? How did "home" in the boardinghouse (Source 8) differ from the girls' real homes? Based on what you read in Reverend Mills's account, in what ways might a boardinghouse have been similar to the girls' real homes?

The next three letters were written by girls who were rather angry. How did "a factory girl" (Source 9) try to disprove Brownson's view? What fears and anxieties do this letter and the one from Dorothea (Source 10) reveal? What were these two girls trying to prove? The third letter writer (Source 11) retained her sense of humor, but she also was upset. In this case, the

offensive remark to which she referred appeared in *Godey's Lady's Book,* the most popular American women's magazine of the period, and was written by the highly respected Sarah Josepha Hale, the magazine's editor and author of "Mary Had a Little Lamb." What had Mrs. Hale written? What was the factory girl's response? What advice did she give her coworkers about fashion? About being a true woman? Both the editor's valedictory and the editorial about the ten-hour-day petitions (Sources 12 and 13) want changes. What were they? How does the editor believe these changes can be achieved? Even "Song of the Spinners" (Source 14) contains a message. What do the lyrics tell you about the spinners' values and attitudes toward work?

What were the other realities of factory girls' lives? What does the bell schedule (Source 3) tell you? How would you describe the image that the pictures of the mill girls present (Sources 16 and 17)? What hopes (and fears) does the correspondence between the mill girls and their families (Sources 18 through 22) express? Why did Lucy Larcom (Source 15) have to go to work in the mills when she was so young? How did she feel about the work when she was a child? What contrast did she draw between young boys' and young girls' upbringing in the early nineteenth century? Did she and the other girls always obey the factory rules? What advantages did she discover in her factory experience? What were the disadvantages?

Now that you are thoroughly familiar with the ideas about how the working girls of Lowell were supposed to behave and the realities of the system under which they lived, you are ready to frame an answer to the central question: How did people react when the needs of a modernizing economy came into conflict with the ideas about women's place in society?

⌘ EPILOGUE ⌘

The Lowell system was a very real attempt to prevent the spread of the evils associated with the factory system and to make work in the textile mills "respectable" for young New England women. Working conditions in Lowell were considerably better than in most other New England mill towns. However, several major strikes (or "turnouts," as they were called) occurred in the Lowell mills in the mid-1830s, and by the mid-1840s Lowell began to experience serious labor problems. To remain competitive yet at the same time maximize profits, companies introduced the "speedup" (a much faster work pace) and the "stretch-out" (one worker was put in charge of more machinery—sometimes as many as four looms). The mills also cut wages, even though boardinghouse rents were rising. In Lowell, workers first tried to have the length of the workday reduced and, as did many other American workers, united in support of the Ten-Hour Movement. When women workers joined such protests, they further challenged the ideas embodied in the cult of true womanhood, especially that of submissiveness.

Even before the strikes, the Lowell system was breaking down, as more and more mills, far larger than their predecessors, were built. Construction of private housing (especially tenements) expanded, and a much smaller proportion of mill hands lived in boardinghouses. Both housing and neighborhoods became badly overcrowded. By 1850, mill owners were looking for still other ways besides the speedup and stretch-out to reduce the cost of labor. They found their answer in the waves of Irish immigrating to America to escape the economic hardships so widespread in their own country. Fewer and fewer "Yankee girls" were recruited for work in the textile mills. At one Lowell company, the number of native-born girls declined from 737 in 1836 to 324 in 1860, although the total number of female workers remained constant. Irish men, women, and increasing numbers of children filled the gap, because as wages declined, a family income became a necessity.

By 1860, what Reverend Mills had characterized as "the moral and intellectual advantages" of the Lowell system had come to an end. Indeed, many Americans could see little or no difference between our own factory towns and those of Europe.

CHAPTER 8

THE "PECULIAR INSTITUTION": SLAVES TELL THEIR OWN STORY

∽ THE PROBLEM ∽

With the establishment of its new government in 1789, the United States became a virtual magnet for foreign travelers, perhaps never more so than during the three decades immediately preceding our Civil War. Middle to upper class, interested in everything from politics to prison reform to botanical specimens to the position of women in American society, these curious travelers fanned out across the United States, and almost all wrote about their observations in letters, pamphlets, and books widely read on both sides of the ocean. Regardless of their special interests, however, few travelers failed to notice—and comment on—the "peculiar institution" of African American slavery.

As were many nineteenth-century women writers, English author Harriet Martineau was especially interested in those aspects of American society that affected women and children. She was appalled by the slave system, believing it degraded marriage by allowing southern white men to exploit female slaves sexually, a practice that often produced mulatto children born into slavery.

The young Frenchman Alexis de Tocqueville came to study the American penitentiary system and stayed to investigate politics and society. In his book *Democracy in America* (1842), Tocqueville expressed his belief that American slaves had completely lost their African culture—their customs, languages, religions, and even the memories of their countries. An English novelist who was enormously popular in the United States, the crusty Charles Dickens, also visited in 1842. He spent very little time in the

CHAPTER 8

THE "PECULIAR
INSTITUTION":
SLAVES TELL
THEIR OWN
STORY

South but collected (and published) advertisements for runaway slaves that contained gruesome descriptions of their burns, brandings, scars, and iron cuffs and collars. As Dickens departed for a steamboat trip to the West, he wrote that he left "with a grateful heart that I was not doomed to live where slavery was, and had never had my senses blunted to its wrongs and horrors in a slave-rocked cradle."[1]

In the turbulent 1850s, Fredrika Bremer, a Swedish novelist, traveled throughout the United States for two years and spent considerable time in South Carolina, Georgia, and Louisiana. After her first encounters with African Americans in Charleston, Bremer wrote to her sister that "they are ugly, but appear for the most part cheerful and well-fed."[2] Her subsequent trips to the plantations of the backcountry, however, increased her sympathy for slaves and her distrust of white southerners' assertions that "slaves are the happiest people in the world."[3] In fact, by the end of her stay, Bremer was praising the slaves' morality, patience, talents, and religious practices.

These travelers—and many more—added their opinions to the growing literature about the nature of American slavery and its effects. But the overwhelming majority of this literature was written by white people. What did the slaves themselves think? How did they express their feelings about the peculiar institution of slavery?

 BACKGROUND

By the time of the American Revolution, what had begun in 1619 as a trickle of Africans intended to supplement the farm labor of indentured servants from England had swelled to a slave population of approximately 500,000 people, the majority concentrated on tobacco, rice, and cotton plantations in the South. Moreover, as the African American population grew, what apparently had been a fairly loose and unregimented labor system gradually evolved into an increasingly harsh, rigid, and complete system of chattel slavery that tried to control nearly every aspect of the slaves' lives. By 1775, African American slavery had become a significant (some would have said indispensable) part of southern life.

The American Revolution did not reverse those trends. Although northern states in which African American slavery was not so deeply rooted began instituting gradual emancipation, after the Revolution, the slave system—as well as its harshness—increased in the South. The invention of the cotton gin, which enabled seeds to be removed from the easily grown short staple cotton, permitted southerners

1. Charles Dickens, *American Notes and Pictures from Italy* (London: Oxford University Press, 1957), p. 137.

2. Fredrika Bremer, *America of the Fifties: Letters of Fredrika Bremer,* ed. Adolph B. Benson (New York: American Scandinavian Foundation, 1924), p. 96.
3. Ibid., p. 100.

to cultivate cotton on the uplands, thereby spurring the westward movement of the plantation system and slavery. As a result, slavery expanded along with settlement into nearly every area of the South: the Gulf region, Tennessee, Kentucky, and ultimately Texas. Simultaneously, the slave population burgeoned, roughly doubling every thirty years (from approximately 700,000 in 1790 to 1.5 million in 1820 to more than 3.2 million in 1850). Because importation of slaves from Africa was banned in 1808 (although there was some illegal slave smuggling), most further gains in the slave population were from natural increase.

But as the slave population grew, the fears and anxieties of southern whites grew correspondingly. In 1793, a slave rebellion in the Caribbean caused tremendous consternation in the white South. Rumors of uprisings plotted by slaves were numerous. And the actual rebellion of Nat Turner in Virginia in 1831 (in which fifty-five whites were killed, many of them while asleep) only increased white insecurities and dread. In response, southern states passed a series of laws that made the system of slavery even more restrictive. Toward the end of his life, Thomas Jefferson (who did not live to see Nat Turner's uprising) agonized:

> But as it is, we have the wolf by the ears, and we can neither hold him, nor safely let him go. Justice is in one scale, and self-preservation in the other. . . . I regret that I am now to die in the belief, that the useless sacrifice of themselves by the generation of 1776, to acquire self-government

and happiness to their country, is to be thrown away by the unwise and unworthy passions of their sons.

By this time, however, Jefferson was nearly alone among white southerners. Most did not question the assertion that slavery was a necessity, that it was good for both the slave and the owner, and that it must be preserved at any cost.

It often has been pointed out that the majority of white southerners did not own slaves. In fact, the proportion of white southern families who did own slaves was actually declining in the nineteenth century, from one-third in 1830 to roughly one-fourth by 1860. Moreover, nearly three-fourths of these slaveholders owned fewer than ten slaves. Slaveholders, then, were a distinct minority of the white southern population, and those slaveholders with large plantations and hundreds of slaves were an exceedingly small group.

How, then, did the peculiar institution of slavery, as one southerner called it, become so embedded in the Old South? First, even though only a minority of southern whites owned slaves, nearly all southern whites were somehow touched by the institution of slavery. Fear of black uprisings prompted many nonslaveholders to support an increasingly rigid slave system that included night patrols, written passes for slaves away from plantations, supervised religious services for slaves, a law prohibiting teaching slaves to read or write, and other measures to keep slaves ignorant, dependent, and always under the eyes of whites. Many nonslaveholders also were afraid that emancipation would

CHAPTER 8

THE "PECULIAR
INSTITUTION":
SLAVES TELL
THEIR OWN
STORY

bring them into direct economic competition with blacks, who, it was assumed, would drive down wages. Finally, although large planters represented only a fraction of the white population, they virtually controlled the economic, social, and political institutions and were not about to injure either themselves or their status by eliminating the slave system that essentially supported them.

To defend their peculiar institution, white southerners constructed a remarkably complete and diverse set of arguments. Slavery, they maintained, was actually a far more humane system than northern capitalism. After all, slaves were fed, clothed, sheltered, cared for when they were ill, and supported in their old age, whereas northern factory workers were paid pitifully low wages, used, and then discarded when no longer useful. Furthermore, many white southerners maintained that slavery was a positive good because it had introduced the "barbarous" Africans to civilized American ways and, more importantly, to Christianity. Other southern whites stressed what they believed was the childlike, dependent nature of African Americans, insisting that they could never cope with life outside the paternalistic and "benevolent" institution of slavery. In such an atmosphere, in which many of the white southern intellectual efforts went into the defense of slavery, dissent and freedom of thought were not welcome. Hence those white southerners who disagreed and might have challenged the South's dependence on slavery remained silent, were hushed up, or decided to leave the region. In many

ways, then, the enslavement of African Americans partly rested on the limitation of rights and freedoms for southern whites as well.

But how did the slaves react to an economic and social system that meant that neither they nor their children would ever experience freedom? Most white southerners assumed that slaves were happy and content. Northern abolitionists (a minority of the white population) believed that slaves continually yearned for freedom. Both groups used oceans of ink to justify and support their claims. But evidence of how the slaves felt and thought is woefully sparse. Given the restrictive nature of the slave system (which included enforced illiteracy among slaves), this pitiful lack of evidence is hardly surprising.

How, then, can we learn how slaves felt and thought about the peculiar institution? Slave uprisings were almost nonexistent, but does that mean most slaves were happy with their lot? Runaways were common, and some, such as Frederick Douglass and Harriet Jacobs, actually reached the North and wrote about their experiences as slaves. Yet how typical were their experiences? Most slaves were born, lived, and died in servitude, did not participate in organized revolts, and did not run away. How did they feel about the system of slavery?

Although most slaves did not read or write, did not participate in organized revolts, and did not attempt to run away, they did leave a remarkable amount of evidence that can help us understand their thoughts and feelings. Yet we must be imaginative in how we approach and use that evidence.

In an earlier chapter, you discovered that statistical information (about births, deaths, age at marriage, farm size, inheritance, tax rolls, and so forth) can reveal a great deal about ordinary people, such as the New Englanders on the eve of the American Revolution. Such demographic evidence can help the historian form a picture of who these people were and the socioeconomic trends of the time, even if the people themselves were not aware of those trends. In this exercise, you will be using another kind of evidence and asking different questions. Your evidence will not come from white southerners (whose stake in maintaining slavery was enormous), foreign travelers (whose own cultural biases often influenced what they reported), or even white abolitionists in the North (whose urgent need to eradicate the "sin" of slavery sometimes led them to gross exaggerations for propaganda purposes). You will be using anecdotes, stories, and songs from the rich oral tradition of African American slaves, supplemented by the narratives of two runaway slaves, to investigate the human dimensions of the peculiar institution.

Some of the oral evidence was collected and transcribed by people soon after emancipation. However, much of the evidence did not come to light until many years later, when the former slaves who were still alive were very old men and women. In fact, not until the 1920s did concerted efforts to preserve the reminiscences of these people begin. In the 1920s, Fisk University collected a good deal of evidence. In the 1930s, the government-financed Federal Writers' Project accumulated more than two thousand narratives from ex-slaves in every southern state except Louisiana and deposited them in the Library of Congress in Washington, D.C.

Much of the evidence, however, is in the form of songs and stories that slaves created and told to one another. Like the narratives of former slaves, these sources also must be used with imagination and care.

The central question you are to answer is this: How did the slaves themselves view the peculiar institution? How did they endure under a labor system that, at its very best, was still based on the total ownership of one human being by another?

∞ THE METHOD ∞

Historians must always try to be aware of the limitations of their evidence. In the Federal Writers' Project, most of the former slaves were in their eighties or nineties (quite a few were older than one hundred) at the time they were interviewed. In other words, most of the interviewees had been children or young people in 1860. It is also important to know that although some of the interviewers were black, the overwhelming majority were white. Last, although many of the former slaves had moved to another location or a different state after the Civil War, many others were still

CHAPTER 8

THE "PECULIAR
INSTITUTION":
SLAVES TELL
THEIR OWN
STORY

living in the same county (sometimes even on the same land) where they had been slaves. In what ways might the age of the former slave, the race of the interviewer, or the place where the former slave was living have affected the narratives?

These narratives reveal much about these people's thoughts and feelings about slavery. What direct reactions did the ex-slaves give? Why did many of them choose to be indirect? Some chose to answer questions by telling stories. Why? Remember that although some of the stories or anecdotes may not actually be true, they can be taken as representative of what the former slaves wished had happened or what they really thought about an incident. Therefore, often you must pull the true meaning from a narrative, inferring what the interviewee meant as well as what he or she said.

As for slave songs and other contemporary evidence, most slaves could never have spoken their thoughts or vented their feelings directly. Instead, they often hid their true meanings through the use of symbols, metaphors, and allegories. Here again, you must be able to read between the lines, extracting thoughts, attitudes, and feelings that were purposely hidden or concealed from all but other slaves.

Included in the evidence are two accounts of runaway slaves who escaped to the North before the Civil War.

Frederick Bailey (who later changed his name to Douglass) ran away when he was about nineteen years old, but he was captured and returned. Two years later, he was able to escape, and he moved to Massachusetts, where he worked as a laborer. After joining an antislavery society and becoming a successful speaker, he published his autobiography (1845) and edited his own abolitionist newspaper, the *North Star*. Harriet Jacobs (who used the pen name Linda Brent) was twenty-seven years old when she ran away in 1845, but her narrative was not published until the beginning of the Civil War. Throughout her story, Jacobs used fictitious names and places to protect those who had helped her and to conceal the escape route she had used. Both Douglass and Jacobs were self-educated people who wrote their own books, although the abolitionist writer Lydia Maria Child made minor editorial revisions in Jacobs's manuscript.

As you examine each piece of evidence, jot down enough notes to allow you to recall that piece of evidence later. But also (perhaps in a separate column) write down the *attitude* that each piece of evidence communicates about the peculiar institution of slavery. What is the hidden message?

After you have examined each piece of evidence, look back over your notes. What attitudes about slavery stand out? What did the slaves think about the slave system?

∽ THE EVIDENCE ∽

Sources 1 through 16 from B. A. Botkin, Federal Writers' Project, *Lay My Burden Down: A Folk History of Slavery* (Chicago: University of Chicago Press, 1945).

1. Hog-Killing Time.

. . . I remember Mammy told me about one master who almost starved his slaves. Mighty stingy, I reckon he was.

Some of them slaves was so poorly thin they ribs would kinda rustle against each other like corn stalks a-drying in the hot winds. But they gets even one hog-killing time, and it was funny, too, Mammy said.

They was seven hogs, fat and ready for fall hog-killing time. Just the day before Old Master told off they was to be killed, something happened to all them porkers. One of the field boys found them and come a-telling the master: "The hogs is all died, now they won't be any meats for the winter."

When the master gets to where at the hogs is laying, they's a lot of Negroes standing round looking sorrow-eyed at the wasted meat. The master asks: "What's the illness with 'em?"

"Malitis," they tells him, and they acts like they don't want to touch the hogs. Master says to dress them anyway for they ain't no more meat on the place.

He says to keep all the meat for the slave families, but that's because he's afraid to eat it hisself account of the hogs' got malitis.

"Don't you all know what is malitis?" Mammy would ask the children when she was telling of the seven fat hogs and seventy lean slaves. And she would laugh, remembering how they fooled Old Master so's to get all them good meats.

"One of the strongest Negroes got up early in the morning," Mammy would explain, "long 'fore the rising horn called the slaves from their cabins. He skitted to the hog pen with a heavy mallet in his hand. When he tapped Mister Hog 'tween the eyes with the mallet, 'malitis' set in mighty quick, but it was a uncommon 'disease,' even with hungry Negroes around all the time."

2. The Old Parrot.

The mistress had an old parrot, and one day I was in the kitchen making cookies, and I decided I wanted some of them, so I tooks me out some and put them on a chair; and when I did this the mistress entered the door. I

CHAPTER 8

THE "PECULIAR
INSTITUTION":
SLAVES TELL
THEIR OWN
STORY

picks up a cushion and throws [it] over the pile of cookies on the chair, and Mistress came near the chair and the old parrot cries out, "Mistress burn, Mistress burn." Then the mistress looks under the cushion, and she had me whupped, but the next day I killed the parrot, and she often wondered who or what killed the bird.

3. The Coon and the Dog.

Every time I think of slavery and if it done the race any good, I think of the story of the coon and dog who met. The coon said to the dog, "Why is it you're so fat and I am so poor, and we is both animals?" The dog said: "I lay round Master's house and let him kick me and he gives me a piece of bread right on." Said the coon to the dog: "Better, then, that I stay poor." Them's my sentiment. I'm like the coon, I don't believe in 'buse.

4. The Partridge and the Fox.

. . . A partridge and a fox 'greed to kill a beef. They kilt and skinned it. Before they divide it, the fox said, "My wife says send her some beef for soup." So he took a piece of it and carried it down the hill, then come back and said, "My wife wants more beef for soup." He kept this up till all the beef was gone 'cept the liver. The fox come back, and the partridge says, "Now let's cook this liver and both of us eat it." The partridge cooked the liver, et its parts right quick, and then fell over like it was sick. The fox got scared and said that beef is pizen, and he ran down the hill and started bringing the beef back. And when he brought it all back, he left, and the partridge had all the beef.

5. The Rabbit and the Tortoise.

I want to tell you one story 'bout the rabbit. The rabbit and the tortoise had a race. The tortoise git a lot of tortoises and put 'em 'long the way. Ever' now and then a tortoise crawl 'long the way, and the rabbit say, "How you now, Br'er Tortoise?" And he say, "Slow and sure, but my legs very short." When they git tired, the tortoise win 'cause he there, but he never run the race, 'cause he had tortoises strowed out all 'long the way. The tortoise had other tortoises help him.

6. Same Old Thing.

The niggers didn't go to the church building; the preacher came and preached to them in their quarters. He'd just say, "Serve your masters. Don't steal your master's turkey. Don't steal your master's chickens. Don't steal your master's hogs. Don't steal your master's meat. Do whatsomever your master tells you to do." Same old thing all the time.

7. Freedom.

I been preaching the gospel and farming since slavery time. I jined the church 'most 83 years ago when I was Major Gaud's slave, and they baptizes me in the spring branch close to where I finds the Lord. When I starts preaching I couldn't read or write and had to preach what Master told me, and he say tell them niggers iffen they obeys the master they goes to Heaven; but I knowed there's something better for them, but daren't tell them 'cept on the sly. That I done lots. I tells 'em iffen they keeps praying, the Lord will set 'em free.

8. Prayers.

My master used to ask us children, "Do your folks pray at night?" We said "No," 'cause our folks had told us what to say. But the Lord have mercy, there was plenty of that going on. They'd pray, "Lord, deliver us from under bondage."

9. Hoodoo Doctor.

My wife was sick, down, couldn't do nothing. Someone got to telling her about Cain Robertson. Cain Robertson was a hoodoo doctor in Georgia. They [say] there wasn't nothing Cain couldn't do. She says, "Go and see Cain and have him come up here."

I says, "There ain't no use to send for Cain. Cain ain't coming up here because they say he is a 'two-head' nigger." (They called all them hoodoo men "two-head" niggers; I don't know why they called them two-head.) "And you know he knows the white folks will put him in jail if he comes to town."

But she says, "You go and get him."

CHAPTER 8

THE "PECULIAR
INSTITUTION":
SLAVES TELL
THEIR OWN
STORY

So I went.

I left him at the house, and when I came back in, he said, "I looked at your wife and she had one of them spells while I was there. I'm afraid to tackle this thing because she has been poisoned, and it's been going on a long time. And if she dies, they'll say I killed her, and they already don't like me and looking for an excuse to do something to me."

My wife overheard him and says, "You go on, you got to do something."

So he made me go to town and get a pint of corn whiskey. When I brought it back he drunk a half of it at one gulp, and I started to knock him down. I'd thought he'd get drunk with my wife lying there sick.

Then he said, "I'll have to see your wife's stomach." Then he scratched it, and put three little horns on the place he scratched. Then he took another drink of whiskey and waited about ten minutes. When he took them off her stomach, they were full of blood. He put them in the basin in some water and sprinkled some powder on them, and in about ten minutes more he made me get them and they were full of clear water and there was a lot of little things that looked like wiggle tails swimming around it.

He told me when my wife got well to walk in a certain direction a certain distance, and the woman that caused all the trouble would come to my house and start a fuss with me.

I said, "Can't you put this same thing back on her?"

He said, "Yes, but it would kill my hand." He meant that he had a curing hand and that if he made anybody sick or killed them, all his power to cure would go from him.

I showed the stuff he took out of my wife's stomach to old Doc Matthews, and he said, "You can get anything into a person by putting it in them." He asked me how I found out about it, and how it was taken out, and who did it.

I told him all about it, and he said, "I'm going to see that that nigger practices anywhere in this town he wants to and nobody bothers him." And he did.

10. Buck Brasefield.

They was pretty good to us, but old Mr. Buck Brasefield, what had a plantation 'jining us'n, was so mean to his'n that 'twa'n't nothing for 'em to run away. One nigger, Rich Parker, runned off one time, and whilst he gone he seed a hoodoo man, so when he got back Mr. Brasefield took sick and stayed sick two or three weeks. Some of the darkies told him, "Rich been to the hoodoo doctor." So Mr. Brasefield got up outen that bed and come a-yelling in the field, "You thought you had old Buck, but by God he rose again." Them niggers was so scared they squatted in the field just like partridges, and some of 'em whispered, "I wish to God he had-a died."

11. The White Lady's Quilts.

Now I'll tell you another incident. This was in slave times. My mother was a great hand for nice quilts. There was a white lady had died, and they were going to have a sale. Now this is true stuff. They had the sale, and Mother went and bought two quilts. And let me tell you, we couldn't sleep under 'em. What happened? Well, they'd pinch your toes till you couldn't stand it. I was just a boy and I was sleeping with my mother when it happened. Now that's straight stuff. What do I think was the cause? Well, I think that white lady didn't want no nigger to have them quilts. I don't know what Mother did with 'em, but that white lady just wouldn't let her have 'em.

12. Papa's Death.

My papa was strong. He never had a licking in his life. He helped the master, but one day the master says, "Si, you got to have a whopping," and my poppa says, "I never had a whopping and you can't whop me." And the master says, "But I can kill you," and he shot my papa down. My mama took him in the cabin and put him on a pallet. He died.

13. Forbidden Knowledge.

None of us was 'lowed to see a book or try to learn. They say we git smarter than they was if we learn anything, but we slips around and gits hold of that Webster's old blue-back speller and we hides it till 'way in the night and then we lights a little pine torch, and studies that spelling book. We learn it too. I can read some now and write a little too.

They wasn't no church for the slaves, but we goes to the white folks' arbor on Sunday evening, and a white man he gits up there to preach to the niggers. He say, "Now I takes my text, which is, Nigger obey your master and your mistress, 'cause what you git from them here in this world am all you ever going to git, 'cause you just like the hogs and the other animals—when you dies you ain't no more, after you been throwed in that hole." I guess we believed that for a while 'cause we didn't have no way finding out different. We didn't see no Bibles.

[183]

CHAPTER 8

THE "PECULIAR
INSTITUTION":
SLAVES TELL
THEIR OWN
STORY

14. Broken Families.

I seen children sold off and the mammy not sold, and sometimes the mammy sold and a little baby kept on the place and give to another woman to raise. Them white folks didn't care nothing 'bout how the slaves grieved when they tore up a family.

15. Burning in Hell.

We was scared of Solomon and his whip, though, and he didn't like frolicking. He didn't like for us niggers to pray, either. We never heard of no church, but us have praying in the cabins. We'd set on the floor and pray with our heads down low and sing low, but if Solomon heared he'd come and beat on the wall with the stock of his whip. He'd say, "I'll come in there and tear the hide off you backs." But some the old niggers tell us we got to pray to God that He don't think different of the blacks and the whites. I know that Solomon is burning in hell today, and it pleasures me to know it.

16. Marriage.

After while I taken a notion to marry and Massa and Missy marries us same as all the niggers. They stands inside the house with a broom held crosswise of the door and we stands outside. Missy puts a little wreath on my head they kept there, and we steps over the broom into the house. Now, that's all they was to the marrying. After freedom I gits married and has it put in the book by a preacher.

Sources 17 and 18 from Gilbert Osofsky, comp., *Puttin' on Ole Massa* (New York: Harper & Row, 1969), p. 22.

17. Pompey.

Pompey, how do I look?
O, massa, mighty.
What do you mean "mighty," Pompey?
Why, massa, you look noble.

What do you mean by "noble"?
Why, sar, you just look like one *lion.*
Why, Pompey, where have you ever seen a lion?
I see one down in yonder field the other day, massa.
Pompey, you foolish fellow, that was a *jackass.*
Was it, massa? Well you look just like him.

18. A Grave for Old Master.

Two slaves were sent out to dig a grave for old master. They dug it very deep. As I passed by I asked Jess and Bob what in the world they dug it so deep for. It was down six or seven feet. I told them there would be a fuss about it, and they had better fill it up some. Jess said it suited him exactly. Bob said he would not fill it up; he wanted to get the old man as near *home* as possible. When we got a stone to put on his grave, we hauled the largest we could find, so as to fasten him down as strong as possible.

Sources 19 through 21 from Lawrence W. Levine, "Slave Songs and Slave Consciousness: An Exploration in Neglected Sources," in *Anonymous Americans: Explorations in Nineteenth Century Social History,* ed. Tamara K. Hareven (Englewood Cliffs, N.J.: Prentice Hall, 1971), pp. 112, 113, 121.

19.

We raise de wheat,
Dey gib us de corn;
We bake de bread,
Dey gib us de crust;
We sif de meal,
Dey gib us de huss;
We [peel] de meat,
Dey gib us de skin;
And dat's de way
Dey take us in;
We skim de pot,
Dey gib us de liquor,
And say dat's good enough for nigger.

CHAPTER 8

THE "PECULIAR
INSTITUTION":
SLAVES TELL
THEIR OWN
STORY

20.

My old Mistiss promise me,
W'en she died, she'd set me free,
She lived so long dat 'er head got bal',
An, she give out'n de notion a dyin' at all.

21.

He delivered Daniel from the lion's den,
Jonah from de belly ob de whale,
And de Hebrew children from de fiery furnace,
And why not every man?

Sources 22 and 23 from Sterling Stuckey, "Through the Prism of Folklore: The Black Ethos in Slavery," *Massachusetts Review* 9 (1968): 421, 422.

22.

When I get to heaven, gwine be at ease,
Me and my God gonna do as we please.
Gonna chatter with the Father, argue with the Son,
Tell um 'bout the world I just come from.

23.

[*A song about Samson and Delilah*]

He said, 'An' if I had-'n my way,'
He said, 'An' if I had-'n my way,'
He said, 'An' if I had-'n my way,
I'd tear the build-in' down!'

Source 24 from Frederick Douglass, *Narrative of the Life of Frederick Douglass* (New York: Anchor Books, Doubleday, 1963), pp. 1–3, 13–15, 36–37, 40–41, 44–46, 74–75.

24. Autobiography of Frederick Douglass.

I was born in Tuckahoe, near Hillsborough, and about twelve miles from Easton, in Talbot county, Maryland. I have no accurate knowledge of my age, never having seen any authentic record containing it. By far the larger part of the slaves know as little of their ages as horses know of theirs, and it is the wish of most masters within my knowledge to keep their slaves thus ignorant. I do not remember to have ever met a slave who could tell of his birthday. They seldom come nearer to it than planting-time, harvesting-time, cherry-time, spring-time, or fall-time. A want of information concerning my own was a source of unhappiness to me even during childhood. The white children could tell their ages. I could not tell why I ought to be deprived of the same privilege. I was not allowed to make any inquiries of my master concerning it. He deemed all such inquiries on the part of a slave improper and impertinent, and evidence of a restless spirit. The nearest estimate I can give makes me now between twenty-seven and twenty-eight years of age. I come to this, from hearing my master say, some time during 1835, I was about seventeen years old.

My mother was named Harriet Bailey. She was the daughter of Isaac and Betsey Bailey, both colored, and quite dark. My mother was a darker complexion than either my grandmother or grandfather.

My father was a white man. He was admitted to be such by all I ever heard speak of my parentage. The opinion was also whispered that my master was my father; but of the correctness of this opinion, I know nothing; the means of knowing was withheld from me. . . .

[*His mother, a field hand, lived twelve miles away and could visit him only at night.*]

. . . I do not recollect of ever seeing my mother by the light of day. She was with me in the night. She would lie down with me, and get me to sleep, but long before I waked she was gone. Very little communication ever took place between us. Death soon ended what little we could have while she lived, and with it her hardships and suffering. She died when I was about seven years old, on one of my master's farms, near Lee's Mill. I was not allowed to be present during her illness, at her death, or burial. She was gone long before I knew any thing about it. Never having enjoyed, to any considerable extent, her soothing presence, her tender and watchful care, I received the tidings of her death with much the same emotions I should have probably felt at the death of a stranger. . . .

The slaves selected to go to the Great House Farm,[4] for the monthly allowance for themselves and their fellow-slaves, were peculiarly enthusiastic. While on their way, they would make the dense old woods, for miles around, reverberate with their wild songs, revealing at once the highest joy and the deepest sadness. They would compose and sing as they went along,

4. Great House Farm was the huge "home plantation" that belonged to Douglass's owner.

CHAPTER 8

THE "PECULIAR
INSTITUTION":
SLAVES TELL
THEIR OWN
STORY

consulting neither time nor tune. The thought that came up, came out—if not in the word, in the sound;—and as frequently in the one as in the other. . . .

I did not, when a slave, understand the deep meaning of those rude and apparently incoherent songs. I was myself within the circle; so that I neither saw nor heard as those without might see and hear. They told a tale of woe which was then altogether beyond my feeble comprehension; they were tones loud, long, and deep; they breathed the prayer and complaint of souls boiling over with the bitterest anguish. Every tone was a testimony against slavery, and a prayer to God for deliverance from chains.

I have often been utterly astonished, since I came to the north, to find persons who could speak of the singing, among slaves, as evidence of their contentment and happiness. It is impossible to conceive of a greater mistake. Slaves sing most when they are most unhappy. The songs of the slave represent the sorrows of his heart; and he is relieved by them, only as an aching heart is relieved by its tears. At least, such is my experience. I have often sung to drown my sorrow, but seldom to express my happiness. Crying for joy, and singing for joy, were alike uncommon to me while in the jaws of slavery. . . .

[Douglass was hired out as a young boy and went to live in Baltimore.]

Very soon after I went to live with Mr. and Mrs. Auld, she very kindly commenced to teach me the A, B, C. After I had learned this, she assisted me in learning to spell words of three or four letters. Just at this point of my progress, Mr. Auld found out what was going on, and at once forbade Mrs. Auld to instruct me further, telling her, among other things, that it was unlawful, as well as unsafe, to teach a slave to read. To use his own words, further, he said, "If you give a nigger an inch, he will take an ell.[5] A nigger should know nothing but to obey his master—to do as he is told to do. Learning would *spoil* the best nigger in the world. Now," said he, "if you teach that nigger (speaking of myself) how to read, there would be no keeping him. It would forever unfit him to be a slave. He would at once become unmanageable, and of no value to his master. As to himself, it could do him no good, but a great deal of harm. It would make him discontented and unhappy." These words sank deep into my heart, stirred up sentiments within that lay slumbering, and called into existence an entirely new train of thought. . . .

5. An ell was an English unit of measure for cloth, approximately 45 inches.

[Douglass came to believe that education could help him gain his freedom.]

The plan which I adopted, and the one by which I was most successful, was that of making friends of all the little white boys whom I met in the street. As many of these as I could, I converted into teachers. With their kindly aid, obtained at different times and in different places, I finally succeeded in learning to read. When I was sent on errands, I always took my book with me, and by doing one part of my errand quickly, I found time to get a lesson before my return. I used also to carry bread with me, enough of which was always in the house, and to which I was always welcome; for I was much better off in this regard than many of the poor white children in our neighborhood. This bread I used to bestow upon hungry little urchins, who, in return, would give me that more valuable bread of knowledge. I am strongly tempted to give the names of two or three of those little boys, as a testimonial of the gratitude and affection I bear them; but prudence forbids;—not that it would injure me, but it might embarrass them; for it is almost an unpardonable offence to teach slaves to read in this Christian country. . . .

I was now about twelve years old, and the thought of being a *slave for life* began to bear heavily upon my heart. . . . After a patient waiting, I got one of our city papers, containing an account of the number of petitions from the north, praying for the abolition of slavery in the District of Columbia, and of the slave trade between the States. From this time I understood the words *abolition* and *abolitionist,* and always drew near when that word was spoken, expecting to hear something of importance to myself and fellow-slaves. The light broke in upon me by degrees. . . .

[After talking with two Irish laborers who advised him to run away, Douglass determined to do so.]

. . . I looked forward to a time at which it would be safe for me to escape. I was too young to think of doing so immediately; besides, I wished to learn how to write, as I might have occasion to write my own pass.[6] I consoled myself with the hope that I should one day find a good chance. Meanwhile, I would learn to write.

The idea as to how I might learn to write was suggested to me by being in Durgin and Bailey's ship-yard, and frequently seeing the ship carpenters, after hewing, and getting a piece of timber ready for use, write on the timber the name of that part of the ship for which it was intended. When a piece of timber was intended for the larboard side, it would be marked

6. In many areas, slaves were required to carry written passes stating that they had permission from their owners to travel to a certain place.

CHAPTER 8

THE "PECULIAR
INSTITUTION":
SLAVES TELL
THEIR OWN
STORY

thus—"L." When a piece was for the starboard side, it would be marked thus—"S." A piece for the larboard side forward, would be marked thus— "L. F." When a piece was for starboard side forward, it would be marked thus—"S. F." For larboard aft, it would be marked thus—"L. A." For starboard aft, it would be marked thus—"S. A." I soon learned the names of these letters, and for what they were intended when placed upon a piece of timber in the ship-yard. I immediately commenced copying them, and in a short time was able to make the four letters named. After that, when I met with any boy who I knew could write, I would tell him I could write as well as he. The next word would be, "I don't believe you. Let me see you try it." I would then make the letters which I had been so fortunate as to learn, and ask him to beat that. In this way I got a good many lessons in writing, which it is quite possible I should never have gotten in any other way. During this time, my copy-book was the board fence, brick wall, and pavement; my pen and ink was a lump of chalk. With these, I learned mainly how to write. I then commenced and continued copying the Italics in Webster's Spelling Book, until I could make them all without looking on the book. By this time, my little Master Thomas had gone to school, and learned how to write, and had written over a number of copy-books. These had been brought home, and shown to some of our near neighbors, and then laid aside. My mistress used to go to class meeting at the Wilk Street meeting-house every Monday afternoon, and leave me to take care of the house. When left thus, I used to spend the time in writing in the spaces left in Master Thomas's copy-book, copying what he had written. I continued to do this until I could write a hand very similar to that of Master Thomas. Thus, after a long, tedious effort for years, I finally succeeded in learning how to write. . . .

[*After the death of his owner, Douglass was recalled to the plantation and put to work as a field hand. Because of his rebellious attitude, he was then sent to work for a notorious "slave-breaker" named Covey. When Covey tried to whip Douglass, who was then about sixteen years old, Douglass fought back.*]

We were at it for nearly two hours. Covey at length let me go, puffing and blowing at a great rate, saying that if I had not resisted, he would not have whipped me half so much. The truth was, that he had not whipped me at all. I considered him as getting entirely the worst end of the bargain; for he had drawn no blood from me, but I had from him. The whole six months afterwards, that I spent with Mr. Covey, he never laid the weight of his finger upon me in anger. He would occasionally say, he didn't want to get hold of me again. "No," thought I, "you need not; for you will come off worse than you did before."

This battle with Mr. Covey was the turning point in my career as a slave. It rekindled the few expiring embers of freedom, and revived within me a sense of my own manhood. It recalled the departed self-confidence, and inspired me again with a determination to be free. The gratification afforded by the triumph was a full compensation for whatever else might follow, even death itself. He only can understand the deep satisfaction which I experienced, who has himself repelled by force the bloody arm of slavery. I felt as I never felt before. It was a glorious resurrection, from the tomb of slavery, to the heaven of freedom. My long-crushed spirit rose, cowardice departed, bold defiance took its place; and I now resolved that, however long I might remain a slave in form, the day had passed forever when I could be a slave in fact. I did not hesitate to let it be known of me, that the white man who expected to succeed in whipping, must also succeed in killing me.

From this time I was never again what might be called fairly whipped, though I remained a slave four years afterwards. I had several fights, but was never whipped.

It was for a long time a matter of surprise to me why Mr. Covey did not immediately have me taken by the constable to the whipping-post, and there regularly whipped for the crime of raising my hand against a white man in defense of myself. And the only explanation I can now think of does not entirely satisfy me; but such as it is, I will give it. Mr. Covey enjoyed the most unbounded reputation for being a first-rate overseer and negro-breaker. It was of considerable importance to him. That reputation was at stake; and had he sent me—a boy about sixteen years old—to the public whipping-post, his reputation would have been lost; so, to save his reputation, he suffered me to go unpunished. . . .

[*During the Civil War, Douglass actively recruited African American soldiers for the Union, and he worked steadfastly after the war for African American civil rights. Douglass also held a series of federal jobs that culminated in his appointment as the U.S. minister to Haiti in 1888. He died in 1895 at the age of seventy-eight.*]

Source 25 from Linda Brent, *Incidents in the Life of a Slave Girl* (New York: Harcourt Brace Jovanovich, 1973), pp. xiii–xiv, 7, 9–10, 26–28, 48–49, 54–55, 179, 201–203, 207.

25. Autobiography of Linda Brent (Harriet Jacobs).

I wish I were more competent to the task I have undertaken. But I trust my readers will excuse deficiencies in consideration of circumstances. I was

CHAPTER 8

THE "PECULIAR
INSTITUTION":
SLAVES TELL
THEIR OWN
STORY

born and reared in Slavery; and I remained in a Slave State twenty-seven years. Since I have been at the North, it has been necessary for me to work diligently for my own support, and the education of my children. This has not left me much leisure to make up for the loss of early opportunities to improve myself; and it has compelled me to write these pages at irregular intervals, whenever I could snatch an hour from household duties. . . .

[*Brent explains that she hopes her story will help northern women realize the suffering of southern slave women.*]

I was born a slave; but I never knew it till six years of happy childhood had passed away. My father was a carpenter, and considered so intelligent and skilful in his trade, that when buildings out of the common line were to be erected, he was sent for from long distances, to be head workman. On condition of paying his mistress two hundred dollars a year, and supporting himself, he was allowed to work at his trade, and manage his own affairs. His strongest wish was to purchase his children; but, though he several times offered his hard earnings for that purpose, he never succeeded. In complexion my parents were a light shade of brownish yellow, and were termed mulattoes. They lived together in a comfortable home; and, though we were all slaves, I was so fondly shielded that I never dreamed I was a piece of merchandise, trusted to them for safe keeping, and liable to be demanded of them at any moment. I had one brother, William, who was two years younger than myself—a bright, affectionate child. I had also a great treasure in my maternal grandmother, who was a remarkable woman in many respects. . . .

[*When Linda Brent was six years old, her mother died, and six years later the kind mistress to whom Brent's family belonged also died. In the will, Brent was be-queathed to the mistress's five-year-old niece, Miss Emily Flint.*]

Dr. Flint, a physician in the neighborhood, had married the sister of my mistress, and I was now the property of their little daughter. It was not without murmuring that I prepared for my new home; and what added to my unhappiness, was the fact that my brother William was purchased by the same family. My father, by his nature, as well as by the habit of transacting business as a skilful mechanic, had more of the feelings of a freeman than is common among slaves. My brother was a spirited boy; and being brought up under such influences, he early detested the name of master and mistress. One day, when his father and his mistress both happened to call him at the same time, he hesitated between the two; being perplexed to know which had the strongest claim upon his obedience. He finally concluded to go to his mistress. When my father reproved him for it, he said, "You both called me, and I didn't know which I ought to go to first."

"You are *my* child," replied our father, "and when I call you, you should come immediately, if you have to pass through fire and water."

Poor Willie! He was now to learn his first lesson of obedience to a master. Grandmother tried to cheer us with hopeful words, and they found an echo in the credulous hearts of youth. . . .

My grandmother's mistress had always promised her that, at her death, she would be free; and it was said that in her will she made good the promise. But when the estate was settled, Dr. Flint told the faithful old servant that, under existing circumstances, it was necessary she should be sold. . . .

[*Brent's grandmother, widely respected in the community, was put up for sale at a local auction.*]

. . . Without saying a word, she quietly awaited her fate. No one bid for her. At last, a feeble voice said, "Fifty dollars." It came from a maiden lady, seventy years old, the sister of my grandmother's deceased mistress. She had lived forty years under the same roof with my grandmother; she knew how faithfully she had served her owners, and how cruelly she had been defrauded of her rights; and she resolved to protect her. The auctioneer waited for a higher bid; but her wishes were respected; no one bid above her. She could neither read nor write; and when the bill of sale was made out, she signed it with a cross. But what consequence was that, when she had a big heart overflowing with human kindness? She gave the old servant her freedom. . . .

During the first years of my service in Dr. Flint's family, I was accustomed to share some indulgences with the children of my mistress. Though this seemed to me no more than right, I was grateful for it, and tried to merit the kindness by the faithful discharge of my duties. But I now entered on my fifteenth year—a sad epoch in the life of a slave girl. My master began to whisper foul words in my ear. Young as I was, I could not remain ignorant of their import. I tried to treat them with indifference or contempt. The master's age, my extreme youth, and the fear that his conduct would be reported to my grandmother, made him bear this treatment for many months. He was a crafty man, and resorted to many means to accomplish his purposes. . . . The mistress, who ought to protect the helpless victim, has no other feelings towards her but those of jealousy and rage. . . . Even the little child, who is accustomed to wait on her mistress and her children,

CHAPTER 8

THE "PECULIAR
INSTITUTION":
SLAVES TELL
THEIR OWN
STORY

will learn, before she is twelve years old, why it is that her mistress hates such and such a one among the slaves. . . . She listens to violent outbreaks of jealous passion, and cannot help understanding what is the cause. She will become prematurely knowing in evil things. Soon she will learn to tremble when she hears her master's footfall. She will be compelled to realize that she is no longer a child. If God has bestowed beauty upon her, it will prove her greatest curse. That which commands admiration in the white woman only hastens the degradation of the female slave. . . .

[*Afraid to tell her grandmother about Dr. Flint's advances, Brent kept silent. But Flint was enraged when he found out that Brent had fallen in love with a young, free, African American carpenter. The doctor redoubled his efforts to seduce Brent and told her terrible stories about what happened to slaves who tried to run away. For a long time, she was afraid to try to escape because of stories such as the one she recounts here.*]

In my childhood I knew a valuable slave, named Charity, and loved her, as all children did. Her young mistress married, and took her to Louisiana. Her little boy, James, was sold to a good sort of master. He became involved in debt, and James was sold again to a wealthy slaveholder, noted for his cruelty. With this man he grew up to manhood, receiving the treatment of a dog. After a severe whipping, to save himself from further infliction of the lash, with which he was threatened, he took to the woods. He was in a most miserable condition—cut by the cowskin, half naked, half starved, and without the means of procuring a crust of bread.

Some weeks after his escape, he was captured, tied, and carried back to his master's plantation. This man considered punishment in his jail, on bread and water, after receiving hundreds of lashes, too mild for the poor slave's offence. Therefore he decided, after the overseer should have whipped him to his satisfaction, to have him placed between the screws of the cotton gin, to stay as long as he had been in the woods. This wretched creature was cut with the whip from his head to his feet, then washed with strong brine, to prevent the flesh from mortifying. . . . He was then put into the cotton gin, which was screwed down, only allowing him room to turn on his side when he could not lie on his back. Every morning a slave was sent with a piece of bread and bowl of water, which were placed within reach of the poor fellow. The slave was charged, under penalty of severe punishment, not to speak to him.

Four days passed, and the slave continued to carry the bread and water. On the second morning, he found the bread gone, but the water untouched. When he had been in the press four days and five nights, the slave informed his master that the water had not been used for four mornings, and that a horrible stench came from the gin house. The overseer was sent to examine into it. When the press was unscrewed, the dead body was found partly eaten by rats and vermin. . . .

[*Dr. Flint's jealous wife watched his behavior very closely, so Flint decided to build a small cabin out in the woods for Brent, who was now sixteen years old. Still afraid to run away, she became desperate.*]

And now, reader, I come to a period in my unhappy life, which I would gladly forget if I could. The remembrance fills me with sorrow and shame. It pains me to tell you of it; but I have promised to tell you the truth, and I will do it honestly, let it cost me what it may. I will not try to screen myself behind the plea of compulsion from a master; for it was not so. Neither can I plead ignorance or thoughtlessness. For years, my master had done his utmost to pollute my mind with foul images, and to destroy the pure principles inculcated by my grandmother, and the good mistress of my childhood. The influences of slavery had had the same effect on me that they had on other young girls; they had made me prematurely knowing, concerning the evil ways of the world. I knew what I did, and I did it with deliberate calculation. . . .

I have told you that Dr. Flint's persecutions and his wife's jealousy had given rise to some gossip in the neighborhood. Among others, it chanced that a white unmarried gentleman had obtained some knowledge of the circumstances in which I was placed. He knew my grandmother, and often spoke to me in the street. He became interested for me, and asked questions about my master, which I answered in part. He expressed a great deal of sympathy, and a wish to aid me. He constantly sought opportunities to see me, and wrote to me frequently. I was a poor slave girl, only fifteen years old.

So much attention from a superior person was, of course, flattering; for human nature is the same in all. I also felt grateful for his sympathy, and encouraged by his kind words. It seemed to me a great thing to have such a friend. By degrees, a more tender feeling crept into my heart. He was an educated and eloquent gentleman; too eloquent, alas, for the poor slave girl who trusted in him. Of course I saw whither all this was tending. I knew the impassable gulf between us; but to be an object of interest to a man who is not married, and who is not her master, is agreeable to the pride and feelings of a slave, if her miserable situation has left her any pride or sentiment. It seems less degrading to give one's self, than to submit to compulsion. There is something akin to freedom in having a lover who has no control over you, except that which he gains by kindness and attach-

CHAPTER 8

THE "PECULIAR
INSTITUTION":
SLAVES TELL
THEIR OWN
STORY

ment. A master may treat you as rudely as he pleases, and you dare not speak; moreover, the wrong does not seem so great with an unmarried man, as with one who has a wife to be made unhappy. There may be sophistry in all this; but the condition of a slave confuses all principles of morality, and, in fact, renders the practice of them impossible.

[Brent had two children, Benjy and Ellen, as a result of her relationship with Mr. Sands, the white "gentleman." Sands and Brent's grandmother tried to buy Brent, but Dr. Flint rejected all their offers. However, Sands was able (through a trick) to buy his two children and Brent's brother, William. After he was elected to Congress, Sands married a white woman. William escaped to the North, and Brent spent seven years hiding in the tiny attic of a shed attached to her grandmother's house. Finally, Brent and a friend escaped via ship to Philadelphia. She then went to New York City, where she found work as a nursemaid for a kind family, the Bruces, and was reunited with her two children. However, as a fugitive slave, she was not really safe, and she used to read the newspapers every day to see whether Dr. Flint or any of his relatives were visiting New York.]

But when summer came, the old feeling of insecurity haunted me. It was necessary for me to take little Mary[7] out daily, for exercise and fresh air, and the city was swarming with Southerners, some of whom might recognize me. Hot weather brings out snakes and slaveholders, and I like one class of the venomous creatures as little as I do the other. What a comfort it is, to be free to *say* so! . . .

I kept close watch of the newspapers for arrivals; but one Saturday night, being much occupied, I forgot to examine the Evening Express as usual. I went down into the parlor for it, early in the morning, and found the boy about to kindle a fire with it. I took it from him and examined the list of arrivals. Reader, if you have never been a slave, you cannot imagine the acute sensation at my heart, when I read the names of Mr. and Mrs. Dodge,[8] at a hotel in Courtland Street. It was a third-rate hotel, and that circumstance convinced me of the truth of what I had heard, that they were short of funds and had need of my value, as *they* valued me; and that was by dollar and cents. I hastened with the paper to Mrs. Bruce. Her heart and hand were always open to every one in distress, and she always warmly sympathized with mine. It was impossible to tell how near the enemy was. He might have passed and repassed the house while we were sleeping. He might at that moment be waiting to pounce upon me if I ventured out of doors. I had never seen the husband of my young mistress, and therefore I could not distinguish him from any other stranger. A carriage was hastily ordered; and, closely veiled, I followed Mrs. Bruce, taking the baby again

7. Mary was the Bruces' baby.
8. Emily Flint and her husband.

with me into exile. After various turnings and crossings, and returnings, the carriage stopped at the house of one of Mrs. Bruce's friends, where I was kindly received. Mrs. Bruce returned immediately, to instruct the domestics what to say if any one came to inquire for me.

It was lucky for me that the evening paper was not burned up before I had a chance to examine the list of arrivals. It was not long after Mrs. Bruce's return to her house, before several people came to inquire for me. One inquired for me, another asked for my daughter Ellen, and another said he had a letter from my grandmother, which he was requested to deliver in person.

They were told, "She *has* lived here, but she has left."

"How long ago?"

"I don't know, sir."

"Do you know where she went?"

"I do not, sir." And the door was closed. . . .

[*Mrs. Bruce was finally able to buy Brent from Mr. Dodge, and she immediately gave Brent her freedom.*]

Reader, my story ends with freedom; not in the usual way, with marriage. I and my children are now free! We are as free from the power of slaveholders as are the white people of the north; and though that, according to my ideas, is not saying a great deal, it is a vast improvement in *my* condition. The dream of my life is not yet realized. I do not sit with my children in a home of my own. I still long for a hearthstone of my own, however humble. I wish it for my children's sake far more than for my own. But God so orders circumstances as to keep me with my friend Mrs. Bruce. Love, duty, gratitude, also bind me to her side. It is a privilege to serve her who pities my oppressed people, and who has bestowed the inestimable boon of freedom on me and my children. . . .

[*Harriet Jacobs's story was published in 1861, and during the Civil War she did relief work with the newly freed slaves behind the Union army lines. For several years after the war ended, she worked tirelessly in Georgia to organize orphanages, schools, and nursing homes. Finally, she returned to the North, where she died in 1897 at the age of eighty-four.*]

∽ QUESTIONS TO CONSIDER ∽

The evidence in this chapter falls into three categories: reminiscences from former slaves, culled from interviews conducted in the 1930s (Sources 1

CHAPTER 8

THE "PECULIAR
INSTITUTION":
SLAVES TELL
THEIR OWN
STORY

through 18); songs transcribed soon after the Civil War, recalled by runaway slaves, or remembered years after (Sources 19 through 23); and the autobiographies of two slaves who escaped to the North: Frederick Douglass and Harriet Jacobs (Sources 24 and 25).

These categories are artificial at best, and you might want to rearrange the evidence in a way that may suit your purposes better.

The evidence contains a number of subtopics, and arrangement into those subtopics may be profitable. For example:

1. How did slaves feel about their masters and/or mistresses?
2. How did slaves feel about their work? Their families? Their religion?
3. How did they feel about freedom?
4. How did slaves feel about themselves?

By regrouping the evidence into subtopics and then using each piece of evidence to answer the question for that subtopic, you should be able to answer the central question: What did slaves (or former slaves) think and feel about the peculiar institution of slavery?

As mentioned, some of the slaves and former slaves chose to be direct in their messages (see, for example, Source 19), but many more chose to communicate their thoughts and feelings more indirectly or obliquely. Several of the symbols and metaphors used are easy to figure out (see Source 23), but others will take considerably more care. The messages are there, however.

Frederick Douglass and Harriet Jacobs wrote their autobiographies for northern readers. Furthermore, both of these runaway slaves were active in abolitionist work. Do these facts mean that this evidence is worthless? Not at all, but the historian must be very careful when analyzing such obviously biased sources. Which parts of Douglass's and Jacobs's stories seem to be exaggerated or unlikely to be true? What do these writers say about topics such as their work, religious beliefs, and families? Does any other evidence from the interviews, tales, or songs corroborate what Douglass and Jacobs wrote?

One last point you might want to consider: Why have historians neglected this kind of evidence for so long?

 EPILOGUE

Even before the Civil War formally ended, thousands of African Americans began casting off the shackles of slavery. Some ran away to meet the advancing Union armies (who often treated them no better than their former masters and mistresses). Others drifted into cities, where they hoped to find work opportunities for themselves and their families. Still others stayed on the land, perhaps hoping to become free farmers. At the end of the war, African Americans were quick to establish their own churches and enrolled in schools established by the Freedmen's Bureau. For most former slaves, the impulse seems to have been to look forward and not backward into the agonizing past of slavery.

Yet memories of slavery were not forgotten and often were passed down orally, from generation to generation. In 1976, Alex Haley's book *Roots* and the twelve-part television miniseries based on it stunned an American public that had assumed that blacks' memories of their origins and of slavery had been for the most part either forgotten or obliterated.[9] Although much of Haley's work contains the author's artistic license, the skeleton of the book was the oral tradition transmitted by his family since the capture of his ancestor Kunta Kinte in West Africa in the late eighteenth century. Not only had Haley's family remembered its African origins, but stories about slavery had not been lost; they had been passed down through the generations.

While Haley was engaged in his twelve years of research and writing, historian Henry Irving Tragle proposed to compile a documentary history of the Nat Turner rebellion of 1831. Talking to black people in 1968 and 1969 in Southampton County, Virginia, where the rebellion occurred, Tragle discovered that in spite of numerous attempts to obliterate Turner from the area's historical memory, Turner's action had become part of the oral history of the region. As the surprised Tragle wrote, "I believe it possible to say with certainty that Nat Turner did exist as a folk-hero to several generations of black men and women who have lived and died in Southampton County since 1831."[10] Again, oral history had persisted and triumphed over time, and professional historians began looking with a new eye on what in the past many had dismissed as unworthy of their attention.

Folk music, customs, religious practices, stories, and artifacts also received new attention. Increasingly, students of history have been able to reconstruct the lives, thoughts, and feelings of people once considered inarticulate. Of course, these people were not inarticulate, but it took imagination to let their evidence speak.

Many people have argued about the impact of slavery on blacks and whites alike, and that question may never be answered fully. What we *do* know is that an enormous amount of historical evidence about slavery exists, from the perspectives of both African Americans and whites. And the memory of that institution lingers. It is part of what one southern white professional historian calls the "burden of southern history," a burden to be overcome but never completely forgotten.

9. A condensed version of *Roots* appeared in 1974 in *Reader's Digest*.

10. Henry Irving Tragle, *The Southampton Slave Revolt of 1831: A Compilation of Source Material* (Amherst: University of Massachusetts Press, 1971), p. 12.

CHAPTER 9

THE COMPROMISE OF 1850:
THE RHETORIC OF THE
SLAVERY QUESTION

 THE PROBLEM

In February 1851, an African American waiter at the Cornhill Coffee House in Boston was arrested by a federal marshal and taken directly to court for a hearing. Frederick Jenkins, also called Shadrach, was accused of being a slave who had escaped from Virginia the previous year. Before the proceedings could continue, Jenkins was rescued by a large crowd that included other African Americans and sent to safety in Canada. Six months later, a more violent confrontation occurred at Christiana in Lancaster County, Pennsylvania. When slave catchers arrived with a marshal to arrest two fugitive slaves, fighting broke out. Two of the slave catchers and three African Americans were killed, and almost fifty people who had

taken part in the "riot" were charged with treason. No one was convicted.

In the same month as the Christiana riot, a barrel maker named William "Jerry" Henry was arrested by a federal marshal in Syracuse, New York. Handcuffed and in leg irons, he was marched through a large, astonished crowd to the courthouse for a hearing. Accused of being an escaped slave from Missouri, Jerry was rescued by the crowd, recaptured by the city police, and rescued again by a group of abolitionists and African Americans. Like Frederick Jenkins, Jerry Henry was sent to Canada, where he lived in freedom for the rest of his life. Every year afterward until the Civil War, the citizens of Syracuse celebrated the anniversary of Jerry's escape.

In each of these incidents, antislavery northerners had refused to obey the provisions of the new Fugitive Slave Act, an important part of the Compromise of 1850. Southerners were outraged because, like many other Americans, they had hoped that the compromise would fulfill the promises of its advocates—that is, that it would ease the sectional tensions over the slavery question.

What were these disagreements? How were they supposed to be resolved by the compromise? In this chapter, you will analyze the rhetoric of the debates over the Compromise of 1850 in order to understand the issues, the compromises made, and the major southern and northern objections to these compromises.

☙ BACKGROUND ❧

The Mexican War (1846–1848) and the vast new territories acquired at its conclusion precipitated a major crisis in the United States. Even during the war, the nation was far from united behind the Democratic president, James K. Polk. Political opposition was strong, particularly among Whigs such as Abraham Lincoln, who criticized Polk in a speech in the House of Representatives, and in the Northeast, which feared a further erosion of its power by the admission of more western states.

Newspapers in New York City, Charleston, Cincinnati, Boston, and other cities condemned the conflict. Abolitionists, of course, were convinced that the war was a slaveholders' plot to expand the peculiar institution of slavery. And although there is no evidence that President Polk ever heard of him, in the small town of Concord, Massachusetts, Henry David Thoreau spent a night in jail for refusing to pay his poll taxes. Later, in response to questions, Thoreau published "Civil Disobedience," an essay in which he explained that part of his reason for not paying his taxes was his opposition to the Mexican War.

More troubling to President Polk than Whig and antislavery opposition was the opposition within his own Democratic party. In the summer of 1846, a young Pennsylvania congressman, David Wilmot, introduced an amendment to a war appropriations bill. The Wilmot Proviso, as this amendment came to be known, demanded that there should be no extension of slavery into the territories gained by the Mexican War. Although abolitionists were delighted and quickly supported this idea, the proviso really reflected the "free-soil" sentiment of those who could accept slavery where it already existed, such as in Texas, but who opposed its expansion into California or New Mexico. Without meaning to split his party, Wilmot had given antislavery

CHAPTER 9

THE COMPROMISE
OF 1850: THE
RHETORIC OF THE
SLAVERY
QUESTION

proponents and free-soilers a weapon that they could use against the South in the struggle over the newly acquired territories.

At stake were California, Nevada, New Mexico, parts of Wyoming and Colorado, and most of Arizona. The discovery of gold in 1849 in California and the subsequent gold rush meant that the question of California's statehood could not be put off for very long. In fact, California's population grew so rapidly that it skipped the usual progression from unorganized to organized territory; it called a convention, drew up a constitution, and applied for admission to the Union as a free state.

The admission of California and the fate of the other western territories were not the only issues that divided the North and the South. For years, an active slave market had existed in the nation's capitol, Washington, D.C. Characterized by slaveholding "pens" and "depots," the market and its traffic in human beings deeply offended many northern and western congressmen, who wished to see this trade outlawed. In addition, debt-ridden Texas, which already had slavery, was engaged in a boundary dispute, claiming a large chunk of New Mexico territory to which, presumably, slavery could spread. And finally southerners, particularly those from the border states, had been complaining about the ease with which runaway slaves were escaping to the North and the ineffectiveness of the existing fugitive slave law.

During the debates over the Compromise of 1850, these issues were discussed again and again. Slavery was not a new concern, of course; it had been raised by the central government's acquisition of the states' western land claims as early as the American Revolution. The resulting Northwest Ordinance of 1787 established a process by which territories could become states and banned slavery in the area that became the states of Ohio, Indiana, Illinois, Michigan, and Wisconsin.

The Northwest Ordinance was passed without much sectional disagreement, but that was not to be the case when delegates met to form the new Constitution. Probably because the delegates shared a national outlook, they were able to compromise on the slavery question, which was regarded as primarily a political and economic issue. Delegates agreed that three-fifths of the slaves would be counted for purposes of representation and taxation. The Constitution also stipulated that Congress could not ban the importation of new slaves until 1808. And in Article IV, the Constitution provided: "No person held to service or labor in one State, under the laws thereof, escaping into another, will, in consequence of any law or regulation therein, be discharged from such service or labor, but shall be delivered up on claim of the party to whom such service or labor may be due."

In spite of the strong feelings of nationalism and patriotism stemming from the American Revolution and the War of 1812, the West, Northeast, and South were frequently divided over such policies as the tariff, the continuation of the national bank, government support for internal improvements such as roads and canals, and the use of government force against the Indians. By the late 1820s, slavery had become the most divisive of these sectional interests.

As the admission of Missouri as a slave state was being considered in the House of Representatives in 1820, a New York congressman proposed an amendment prohibiting the transfer of any more slaves to Missouri and providing for gradual emancipation of the slaves already there. Passed by the House after acrimonious debate, the amendment was defeated in the Senate by a sharply sectional vote. The elderly Thomas Jefferson recognized the significance of what had happened, writing that it "filled me with terror."

In many ways, the issue of slavery was still a political one. The balance of eleven free states and eleven slave states would be tipped in favor of the South if Missouri were to be admitted as a slave state. But there was far more hostility between the North and South over slavery than there had been previously, with some southerners believing that the North wanted to destroy slavery and some northerners insisting that the South was purposefully working to expand slavery. Eventually a compromise was worked out that both sides could support. Missouri entered the Union a slave state, balanced by Maine, which entered as a free state. More important, to prevent further problems with western territories the compromise drew a line along Missouri's southern border (36°30′) north of which slavery was prohibited. Most contemporaries thought that the South had gained the most from the Missouri Compromise, although a few noted that for the second time Congress had prohibited slavery in the western territories.

Meanwhile, abolitionist thought was turning in a new direction. As many historians have pointed out, there was not just a single abolitionist movement seeking to eliminate slavery. Rather, there were many different abolitionist movements, ranging from the humanitarianism of the early Quakers to the gradual emancipation schemes of such men as Lewis Tappan of New York. Yet another kind of abolitionist hoped to buy slaves' freedom and resettle, or colonize, them in Africa. By the early 1830s, however, a new kind of abolitionism, represented by William Lloyd Garrison and his newspaper, the *Liberator,* was quickly gaining converts, especially among women and African Americans. Slavery was a sin that must be ended immediately, Garrison argued, and the freed slaves should be equal to whites in the eyes of the law. Since slavery was now a moral issue, those who did not work to emancipate the slaves were implicitly sinners themselves, even if they had never seen a slave. Although abolitionists were always in the minority, the immediatists were persistent, vocal, and committed. Through their literature, speeches, and petition campaigns, they kept the issue of slavery constantly in the public view.

By the late 1840s, then, the slavery question had become heated. With regard to the settlement of the western territories, there seemed to be four alternatives:

CHAPTER 9

THE COMPROMISE
OF 1850: THE
RHETORIC OF THE
SLAVERY
QUESTION

1. The old Missouri Compromise line should simply be extended westward.
2. Congress should not permit the extension of slavery into any new territories gained by the Mexican War, the position of the Wilmot Proviso, and the free-soilers.
3. The people of a territory should decide for themselves whether to have slavery, a concept known as popular sovereignty.
4. Congress had no constitutional power to regulate slavery in the territories, an idea articulated by John C. Calhoun and many other southerners.

When California applied for statehood, the stage was set for a major sectional clash over slavery—one that could endanger the very foundations of the Union. The major protagonists in the debate over the Compromise of 1850 would be three elder statesmen—Henry Clay of Kentucky, Daniel Webster of Massachusetts, and John C. Calhoun of South Carolina—and a relative newcomer to Congress, William Seward of New York. All four men were lawyers; Calhoun was a Democrat, and the other three were Whigs. Clay, Webster, and Calhoun had all begun their public service in Congress prior to the War of 1812; Seward had just been elected to Congress in 1848.

Henry Clay was known for his nationalism, perhaps best represented by the "American System" he proposed in the 1820s that would have provided government support for both eastern and western economic interests. Opposed to Andrew Jackson in the disputed election of 1824, Clay was a consistent supporter of the Bank of the United States. Although he was nominated and ran for president, Clay was never elected to that office. Daniel Webster was also a nationalist with unsuccessful presidential aspirations. As secretary of state, however, he was able to settle the northeastern boundary dispute with England. Although Webster was personally opposed to slavery, he believed that since the Constitution had recognized its existence, it could not be interfered with where it already existed. John C. Calhoun also began his public career as a nationalist, a "war hawk" who favored war with England in 1812, and in general he supported the same ideas as Henry Clay. Elected vice president under Andrew Jackson, Calhoun resigned in a dispute over the protective tariff. By the 1840s, he had become the spokesman and defender of southern sectional interests. Only eleven years old at the outbreak of the War of 1812, William Seward had been governor of New York before being elected to Congress. As governor, he had supported internal improvements and strongly opposed slavery.

The Senate debates over the Compromise of 1850 began in January and did not conclude until a form of the compromise was finally approved in September. In this chapter, you will be reading excerpts and analyzing the rhetoric of the speeches of Clay, Calhoun, Webster, and Seward. What were the issues? How were they supposed to be resolved by the compromise? What were the major southern and northern objections to the compromise?

⚮ THE METHOD ⚮

As David Zarefsky and James Andrews have pointed out in *American Voices,*[1] their study of historically significant speeches, it is important to understand how our forebears came to grips with the major political, economic, and social questions of their day. One way to understand these issues is through the study of *rhetoric,* the process of selecting and utilizing language in order to convince or persuade others. An analysis of rhetoric allows us to identify the various beliefs, values, and goals surrounding an issue.

The study of rhetoric requires the student to cultivate a critical attitude toward what is being said. Scholars like Zarefsky and Andrews have isolated certain similarities in all rhetorical situations. All rhetoric has a *context,* that is, some outcome that the speaker wants to alter or influence. The *character of the speaker* (perceived by the audience as either positive or negative) will always influence the audience's response to the speaker. Moreover, the *audience itself*—both the people actually hearing the speech and the broader, invisible audience for whom the speech may be intended—will influence the speaker. All rhetoric also utilizes a kind of *logical argument,* intended to convince the audience of a particular belief or course of action. The role of *language and style* is much more difficult to determine. At times, language may be opaque and get in the way of our understanding. Yet we live in a world of words and also communicate through language. Thus, an analysis of the language of public discourse, such as speeches and debates, yields important clues to the intent of the speaker and the emotional content and underlying ideas of the issue being debated.

In this chapter, we know that the *context* of the debate involved a series of compromises intended to eliminate sectional disagreements about issues directly related to slavery. We also know the *audience* for the speeches: The debates took place in the U.S. Senate, but almost all Americans avidly followed them in the newspapers. We even know a good deal about the background of the speakers themselves. But we do not know exactly what compromises were proposed, the ways in which the speakers attempted to persuade the audience to accept or reject these compromises, or the reasoning behind the speakers' positions on these issues. This is the focus of your analysis.

1. David Zarefsky and James Andrews, *American Voices* (White Plains, N.Y.: Longman, 1989).

CHAPTER 9

THE COMPROMISE
OF 1850: THE
RHETORIC OF THE
SLAVERY
QUESTION

⚭ **THE EVIDENCE** ⚭

Sources 1 through 4 from *Congressional Globe,* 31st Cong., 1st sess., Appendix, pp. 115–127, 262–265, 451–455, 476–484.

1. Speech of Mr. Clay, of Kentucky, in the Senate of the United States, February 5–6, 1850.

Mr. President, never, on any former occasion, have I risen under feelings of such deep solicitude. I have witnessed many periods of great anxiety, of peril, and of danger, even to the country; but I have never before arisen to address any assembly so oppressed, so appalled, so anxious. . . .

[Clay discusses the disruptive influence of the abolitionists, the disagreements affecting the work of Congress, and the animosity between the political parties. He has come out of retirement, he says, to try to design a compromise that will return peace and harmony to the country.]

When I came to consider this subject, there were two or three general purposes which seemed to me most desirable, if possible, to accomplish. The one was to settle all the controverted questions arising out of the subject of slavery; and it seemed to me to be doing very little if we settled one question and left other disturbing questions unadjusted. . . .

Another principal object which attracted my attention was, to endeavor to frame such a scheme of accommodation as that neither of the two classes of States into which our country is unhappily divided should make a sacrifice of any great principle. . . .

Another purpose, sir, which I had in view was this: I was aware of the difference of opinion prevailing between these two classes of States. I was aware that while a portion of the Union was pushing matters, as it seemed to me, to a dangerous extremity, another portion of the Union was pushing them to an opposite, and perhaps to a no less dangerous extremity. It appeared to me, then, that if any arrangement, any satisfactory adjustment could be made of the controverted questions between the two classes of States, that adjustment, that arrangement, could only be successful and effectual by exacting from both parties some concession—not of principle, not of principle at all, but of feeling, of opinion, in relation to the matters in controversy between them. I believe that the resolutions which I have prepared fulfill that object. . . .

The first resolution, Mr. President, as you are aware, relates to California; and it declares that California, with suitable limits, ought to be admitted as a member of this Union, without the imposition of any restriction, either to interdict or to introduce slavery within her limits. Now is there any concession in this resolution by either party to the other? I know that gentlemen who come from the slave holding States say that the North gets all that it desires; but by whom does it get it? Does it get it by any action of Congress? If slavery be interdicted in California, is it done by this Government? No, sir; the interdiction is imposed by California herself. And has it not been the doctrine of all parties, that when a State is about to be admitted into the Union, that State has a right to decide for itself whether it will or will not have within its limits slavery? . . .

[*After reminding the other senators that the Wilmot Proviso prohibiting slavery in the area gained from the Mexican War applied only to territories, not states, Clay reviews the history of the Northwest Ordinance of 1787 and the Missouri Compromise. He pleads with the free states to give up their insistence on the Wilmot Proviso and notes that in their statehood convention Californians voted to exclude slavery.*]

. . . What do you want?—what do you want?—you who reside in the free States. Do you want that there shall be no slavery introduced into the territories acquired by the war with Mexico? Have you not your desire in California? And in all human probability you will have it in New Mexico also. What more do you want? You have got what is worth more than a thousand Wilmot provisos. You have nature on your side—facts upon your side—and this truth staring you in the face, that there is no slavery in those territories. . . .

[*Clay suggests that Texas give up some of its land claims to New Mexico in return for the U.S. government payment of some of Texas's debts. Turning to the question of slavery in Washington, D.C., Clay argues that it would not be fair to the adjoining slave states of Virginia and Maryland to eliminate slavery in Washington without their permission. Instead, he suggests leaving slavery but eliminating the notorious slave markets and slave depots or "pens."*]

Well, then, I really do not think that this resolution, which proposes to abolish that trade, ought to be considered as a concession by either class of States to the other class. I think it should be regarded as an object, acceptable to both, conformable to the wishes and feelings of both; and yet, sir, in these times of fearful and alarming excitement—in these times when every night that I go to sleep, and every morning when I awake, it is with the apprehension of some new and terrible tidings upon this agitating subject. . . .

[*After expressing his concern that the Nashville Convention of southern states may discuss secession, Clay introduces his resolution for a stronger, more effective fugi-*

CHAPTER 9

THE COMPROMISE
OF 1850: THE
RHETORIC OF THE
SLAVERY
QUESTION

tive slave law. He begins by reviewing the constitutional provision for the return of bound laborers who escape from one state to another and the responsibility of citizens, as well as government officials, to uphold this provision.]

. . . I do not say that a private individual is obliged to make the tour of his whole State, in order to assist the owner of a slave to recover his property; but I do say, if he is present when the owner of a slave is about to assert his rights and regain possession of his property, that he, that every man present, whether officer or agent of the State Governments, or private individual, is bound to assist in the execution of the laws of their country. . . .

[*Clay talks at length about the so-called personal liberty laws passed by free states in order to ensure such protections as a trial by jury for captured runaway slaves.*]

. . . Then, Mr. President, I think that the whole class of legislation, beginning in the northern States, and extending to some of the western States, by which obstructions and impediments have been thrown in the way of the recovery of fugitive slaves, are unconstitutional, and have originated in a spirit which I trust will correct itself when these States come to consider calmly upon the nature of their duty. . . . I know too well, and so do the honorable Senators from Ohio know, that it is at the utmost hazard and insecurity of life itself, that a Kentuckian can cross the river and go into the interior and take back the fugitive slave to the State from which he has fled. . . .

. . . Well, sir, I do not mean to contest the ground; I am not going to argue the question whether if a man voluntarily carries his slave into a free State, he is or is not entitled to his freedom. I am not going to argue that question. I know what its decision has been in the North. What I mean to say is, that it is unkind, unneighborly, it is not in the spirit of that fraternal connection existing between all parts of this Confederacy. But as to the exact and legal principle in the way suggested . . . it is but proper, when there is not purpose of a permanent abode . . . it is but the right of good neighborhood, and kind and friendly feeling, to allow the owner of the slave to pass with his property unmolested.

[*At this point Clay speaks against fanatics—southern fire-eaters and northern abolitionists—and relates specific instances of violence concerning fugitive slaves. He explains why he does not believe the Missouri Compromise line should be extended and pleads for the passage of his compromise and the preservation of the Union.*]

But, I must take the occasion to say that, in my opinion, there is no right on the part of one or more of the States to secede from the Union. War and the dissolution of the Union are identical and inseparable. . . . I think that the Constitution of the thirteen States was made, not merely for the generation which then existed, but for posterity, undefined, unlimited, permanent and perpetual—for their posterity, and for every subsequent State which might come into the Union, binding themselves by that indissoluble bond. It is to remain for that posterity now and forever.

[*Clay tries to imagine what a divided nation would be like, with two armies and navies, a long war, and terrible destruction.*]

And, finally, Mr. President, I implore, as the best blessing which Heaven can bestow upon me upon earth, that if the direful and sad event of the dissolution of the Union shall happen, I may not survive to behold the sad and heart-rending spectacle.

2. Speech of Mr. Calhoun, of South Carolina, in the Senate of the United States.
[*Read by Senator James Mason of Virginia, March 4, 1850.*[2]]

I have, Senators, believed from the first that the agitation of the subject of slavery would, if not prevented by some timely and effective measure, end in disunion. Entertaining this opinion, I have, on all proper occasions, endeavored to call the attention of each of the two great parties which divide the country to adopt some measure to prevent so great a disaster, but without success. The agitation has been permitted to proceed, with almost no attempt to resist it, until it has reached a period when it can no longer be disguised or denied that the Union is in danger. You have thus had forced upon you the greatest and the gravest question that can ever come under your consideration: How can the Union be preserved?

[*Calhoun asks what has endangered the Union.*]

To this question there can be but one answer: that the immediate cause is the almost universal discontent which pervades all the States composing the southern section of the Union. This widely extended discontent is not of recent origin. It commenced with the agitation of the slavery question, and has been increasing ever since. The next question, going one step further back, is: What has caused this widely diffused and almost universal discontent?

2. Calhoun was very ill and too weak to deliver his speech.

CHAPTER 9

THE COMPROMISE
OF 1850: THE
RHETORIC OF THE
SLAVERY
QUESTION

[Calhoun argues that it is not simply irresponsible party politics that puts the Union in danger.]

One of the causes, is undoubtedly, to be traced to the long-continued agitation of the slave question on the part of the North, and the many aggressions which they have made on the rights of the South during the time. . . .

There is another, lying back of it, with which this is intimately connected, that may be regarded as the great and primary cause. That is to be found in the fact that the equilibrium between the two sections in the Government, as it stood when the Constitution was ratified and the Government put in action, has been destroyed. At that time there was nearly a perfect equilibrium between the two, which afforded ample means to each to protect itself against the aggression of the other; but as it now stands, one section has the exclusive power of controlling the Government, which leaves the other without any adequate means of protecting itself against its encroachment and oppression. . . .

[Citing census statistics since 1790, Calhoun demonstrates that in spite of counting only three-fifths of the slaves, the slave states and free states were approximately equal in Congress at the time the Constitution was adopted. By 1840, however, the balance of population had shifted to northern states.]

The result of the whole is to give the northern section a predominance in every part of the Government, and thereby concentrate in it the two elements which constitute the Federal Government—a majority of their States and a majority of their population, estimated in federal numbers. Whatever section concentrates the two in itself possesses the control of the entire Government.

[Calhoun points out that the question of the vast territories gained from the Mexican War, along with the potential statehood of Oregon and Minnesota, has created a crisis. He concludes that the Northwest Ordinance of 1787 and the Missouri Compromise of 1820 have already wrongly denied southerners access to huge tracts of land.]

I have not included the territory recently acquired by the treaty with Mexico. The North is making the most strenuous efforts to appropriate the whole to herself, by excluding the South from every foot of it. If she should succeed, it will add to that from which the South has already been excluded 526,078 square miles, and would increase the whole which the North has appropriated to herself to 1,764,023, not including the portion that she may succeed in excluding us from in Texas. To sum up the whole, the United

States, since they declared their independence, have acquired 2,373,046 square miles of territory, from which the North will have excluded the South, if she should succeed in monopolizing the newly acquired territories, from about three-fourths of the whole, leaving to the South but about one-fourth.

Such is the first and great cause that has destroyed the equilibrium between the two sections of the Government. . . .

[*Calhoun complains that high tariffs benefit the North but hurt the South and says that the central government has become far too powerful compared with the state governments. In any difference of opinion, he argues, the North always dominates the South.*]

. . . There is a question of vital importance to the southern section, in reference to which the views and feeling of the two sections are as opposite and hostile as they can possibly be.

I refer to the relation between the two races in the southern section, which constitutes a vital portion of her social organization. Every portion of the North entertains views and feeling more or less hostile to it. Those most opposed and hostile regard it as a sin, and consider themselves under the most sacred obligation to use every effort to destroy it. Indeed to the extent that they conceive they have the power, they regard themselves as implicated in the sin, and responsible for suppressing it by the use of all and every means. Those less opposed and hostile, regard it as a crime—an offence against humanity, as they call it; and although not so fanatical, feel themselves bound to use all efforts to effect the same object; while those who are least opposed and hostile, regard it as a blot and a stain on the character of what they call the nation, and feel themselves accordingly bound to give it no countenance or support. On the contrary, the southern section regards the relation as one which cannot be destroyed without subjecting the two races to the greatest calamity, and the section to poverty, desolation and wretchedness; and accordingly they feel bound by every consideration of interest and safety, to defend it. . . .

[*Calhoun maintains that northern domination of the federal government gave the abolitionists their opportunity to try to "act for the purpose of destroying the existing relation between the two races in the South." They did this through antislavery petition campaigns and the passage of state personal liberty laws.*]

. . . Unless something decisive is done, I again ask what is to stop this agitation, before the great and final object at which it aims—the abolition of slavery in the South—is consummated? Is it, then, not certain that if

CHAPTER 9

THE COMPROMISE
OF 1850: THE
RHETORIC OF THE
SLAVERY
QUESTION

something decisive is not now done to arrest it, the South will be forced to choose between abolition and secession? Indeed, as events are now moving, it will not require the South to secede to dissolve the Union. Agitation will of itself effect it, of which its past history furnishes abundant proof. . . .

It is a great mistake to suppose that disunion can be effected by a single blow. The cords which bind these States together in one common Union are far too numerous and powerful for that. Disunion must be the work of time. It is only through a long process, and successively, that the cords can be snapped, until the whole fabric falls asunder. Already the agitation of the slavery question has snapped some of the most important, and has greatly weakened all the others. . . .

[*Here Calhoun discusses the North-South divisions in several major Protestant denominations and the political bad feelings between the sections. If this continues, he warns, only force will hold the Union together.*]

. . . How can the Union be saved? To this I answer there is but one way by which it can be, and that is, by adopting such measures as will satisfy the States belonging to the southern section that they can remain in the Union consistently with their honor and their safety. There is, again, only one way by which that can be effected, and that is, by removing the causes by which this belief has been produced. Do *that,* and discontent will cease, harmony and kind feelings between the sections be restored, and every apprehension of danger to the Union removed. The question then is, By what can this be done? But, before I undertake to answer this question, I propose to show by what the Union cannot be saved.

It cannot, then, be saved by eulogies on the Union, however splendid or numerous. The cry of "Union, Union, the glorious Union," can no more prevent disunion than the cry of "Health, health, glorious health!" on the part of the physician can save a patient lying dangerously ill. So long as the union, instead of being regarded as a protector, is regarded in the opposite character, by not much less than a majority of the States, it will be in vain to attempt to conciliate them by pronouncing eulogies on it. . . .

[*Calhoun maintains that the very people who claim they want to save the Union are those who violate the fugitive slave provisions of the Constitution. Pointing out that George Washington was both a slaveholder and a great patriot, Calhoun opposes California's admission as a free state.*]

Having now shown what cannot save the Union, I return to the question with which I commenced, How can the Union be saved? There is but one way by which it can with any certainty; and that is, by a full and final settlement, on the principle of justice, of all the questions at issue between the two sections. The South asks for justice, simple justice, and less she ought not to take. She has no compromise to offer but the Constitution, and no concession or surrender to make. She has already surrendered so much that she has little left to surrender. . . .

But can this be done? Yes, easily; not by the weaker party, for it can of itself do nothing—not even protect itself—but by the stronger. The North has only to will it to accomplish it—to do justice by conceding to the South an equal right in the acquired territory, and to do her duty by causing the stipulations relative to fugitive slaves to be faithfully fulfilled—to cease the agitation of the slave question, and to provide for the insertion of a provision in the Constitution, by an amendment, which will restore to the South in substance the power she possessed of protecting herself, before the equilibrium between the sections was destroyed by the action of this Government. . . .

[*Calhoun repeats that only the North, by giving up all its attempts to dominate the South, can save the Union.*]

It is time, Senators, that there should be an open and manly avowal on all sides, as to what is intended to be done. If the question is not now settled, it is uncertain whether it ever can hereafter be; and we . . . should come to a distinct understanding as to our respective views, in order to ascertain whether the great questions at issue can be settled or not. If you, who represent the stronger portion, cannot agree to settle them on the broad principle of justice and duty, say so; and let the States we both represent agree to separate and part in peace. If you are unwilling we should part in peace, tell us so, and we shall know what to do, when you reduce the question to submission or resistance. If you remain silent, you will compel us to infer by your acts what you intend. In that case, California will become the test question. If you admit her, under all the difficulties that oppose her admission, you compel us to infer that you intend to exclude us from the whole of the acquired territories, with the intention of destroying irretrievably the equilibrium between the two sections. We would be blind not to perceive, in that case, that your real objects are power and aggrandizement, and infatuated not to act accordingly.

[*Calhoun concludes by saying that he has expressed his opinions in the hope of saving the Union.*]

CHAPTER 9

THE COMPROMISE
OF 1850: THE
RHETORIC OF THE
SLAVERY
QUESTION

3. Speech of Mr. Webster, of Massachusetts, in the Senate of the United States, March 7, 1850.

Mr. President, I wish to speak today, not as a Massachusetts man, nor as a northern man, but as an American, and a member of the Senate of the United States. It is fortunate that there is a Senate of the United States; a body not yet moved from its propriety, not lost to a just sense of its own dignity, and its own high responsibilities, and a body to which the country looks with confidence, for wise, moderate, patriotic, and healing counsels. It is not to be denied that we live in the midst of strong agitations, and surrounded by very considerable dangers to our institutions of government. The imprisoned winds are let loose. The East, the West, the North, and the stormy South, all combine to throw the whole ocean into commotion, to toss its billows to the skies, and to disclose its profoundest depths. I do not expect, Mr. President, to hold, or to be fit to hold, the helm in combat of the political elements; but I have a duty to perform, and I mean to perform it with fidelity,—not without a sense of the surrounding dangers, but not without hope. I have a part to act, not for my own security or safety, for I am looking out for a fragment upon which to float away from the wreck, if wreck there must be, but for the good of the whole, and the preservation of the whole; and there is that which will keep me to my duty during this struggle, whether the sun and the stars shall appear, or shall not appear, for many days. I speak to-day for the preservation of the Union. "Hear me for my cause." I speak to-day, out of a solicitous and anxious heart, for the restoration to the country of that quiet and that harmony which make the blessings of this Union so rich and so dear to us all. These are the topics that I propose to myself to discuss; these are the motives, and the sole motives, that influence me in the wish to communicate my opinions to the Senate and the country; and if I can do anything, however little, for the promotion of these ends, I shall have accomplished all that I desire. . . .

[*Webster reviews the constitutional compromises about slavery and the events surrounding Texan independence. The U.S. government has pledged to create new states from the Texan territory, he notes, which will probably be slave states.*]

Now, as to California and New Mexico, I hold slavery to be excluded from those territories by a law even superior to that which admits and sanctions it in Texas—I mean the law of nature—of physical geography—the law of the formation of the earth. That law settles forever, with strength beyond all terms of human enactment, that slavery cannot exist in California or New Mexico. Understand me, sir—I mean slavery as we regard it; slaves in the gross, of the colored race, transferable by sale and delivery, like other property. . . .

I look upon it, therefore, as a fixed fact, to use an expression current to the day, that both California and New Mexico are destined to be free, so far as they are settled at all, which I believe, especially in regard to New Mexico, will be very little for a great length of time—free by the arrangement of things by the Power above us. . . .

. . . and I would not take pains to reaffirm an ordinance of nature, nor to re-enact the will of God. And I would put in no Wilmot proviso, for the purpose of a taunt or a reproach. I would put into it no evidence of the votes of superior power, to wound the pride, even whether a just pride, a rational pride, or an irrational pride—to wound the pride of the gentlemen who belong to the southern States. I have no such object—no such purpose. They would think it a taunt—an indignity. They would think it to be an act taking away from them what they regard a proper equality of privilege; and whether they expect to realize any benefit from it or not, they would think it a theoretic wrong—that something more or less derogatory to their character and their rights had taken place. I propose to inflict no such wound upon any body, unless something essentially important to the country, and efficient to the preservation of liberty and freedom, is to be effected. . . .

[*Webster reiterates his position on the Wilmot Proviso, noting that each side already has a long list of grievances against the other side.*]

These are disputed topics, and I have no inclination to enter into them. But I will state these complaints, especially one complaint of the South, which has in my opinion just foundation; and that is, that there has been found at the North, among individuals and among the Legislatures of the North, a disinclination to perform, fully, their constitutional duties, in regard to the return of persons bound to service, who have escaped into the free States. In that respect, it is my judgment that the South is right, and the North is wrong. . . .

[*Webster points out the court decisions in favor of giving up the fugitives to their owners and says he will support the new fugitive slave act.*]

. . . And I desire to call the attention of all sober-minded men, of all conscientious men, in the North, of all men who are not carried away by any fanatical idea, or by any false idea whatever, to their constitutional obligations. I put it to all the sober and sound minds at the North, as a question of morals and a question of conscience, What right have they, in

CHAPTER 9

THE COMPROMISE
OF 1850: THE
RHETORIC OF THE
SLAVERY
QUESTION

all their legislative capacity, or any other, to endeavor to get round this Constitution, to embarrass the free exercise of the rights secured by the Constitution, to the person whose slaves escape from them? None at all—none at all. . . .

[*Webster speaks against state resolutions about slavery, the extremism of some abolitionists, and the violent tone of newspapers. He then criticizes a speech in which a southern senator maintained that the situation of the southern slaves was better than that of northern workers.*]

. . . But does he know how remarks of that sort will be received by laboring people of the North? Why, who are the laboring people of the North? They are the North. They are the people who cultivate their own farms with their own hands—freeholders, educated men, independent men. Let me say, sir, that five sixths of the whole property of the North, is in the hands of the laborers of the North. . . . And what can these people think when so respectable and worthy a gentleman as the member from Louisiana, undertakes to prove that the absolute ignorance, and the abject slavery of the South, is more in conformity with the high purposes and destinies of immortal, rational, human beings, than the educated, the independent free laborers of the North? . . .

Mr. President, I should much prefer to have heard, from every member on this floor, declarations of opinion that this Union should never be dissolved, than the declaration of opinion that in any case, under the pressure of any circumstances, such a dissolution was possible. I hear with pain, and anguish, and distress, the word secession, especially when it falls from the lips of those who are eminently patriotic, and known to the country, and known all over the world, for their political services. Secession! Peaceable secession! Sir, your eyes and mine are never destined to see that miracle. The dismemberment of this vast country without convulsion! The breaking up of the fountains of the great deep without ruffling the surface! Who is so foolish—I beg everybody's pardon—as to expect to see any such thing? . . .

I would rather hear of natural blasts and mildews, war, pestilence, and famine, than to hear gentlemen talk of secession. To break up! to break up this great Government! to dismember this great country! to astonish Europe with an act of folly, such as Europe for two centuries has never beheld in any government! No, sir! no sir! There will be no secession. Gentlemen are not serious when they talk of secession. . . .

[*Webster urges the upcoming convention of southern states to be conciliatory, and he voices his willingness to allow the federal government to help southern states relocate free African Americans.*]

And now, Mr. President, instead of speaking of the possibility or utility of secession, instead of dwelling in these caverns of darkness, instead of groping with those ideas so full of all that is horrid and horrible, let us come out into the light of day; let us enjoy the fresh air of liberty and union: let us cherish those hopes which belong to us; let us devote us to those great objects that are fit for our consideration and our action; let us raise our conceptions to the magnitude and the importance of the duties that devolve upon us; let our comprehension be as broad as the country for which we act, our aspirations as high as its certain destiny; let us not be pigmies in a case that calls for men. Never did there devolve, on any generation of men, higher trusts than now devolve upon us for the preservation of this Constitution, for ages to come. It is a great popular Constitutional Government, guarded by legislation, by law, by judicature, and defended by the whole affections of the people. No monarchical throne presses these States together; no iron chain of despotic power encircles them; they live and stand upon a Government popular in its form, representative in its character, founded upon principles of equality, and calculated, we hope, to last forever. In all its history, it has been beneficent, it has trodden down no man's liberty; it has crushed no State. Its daily respiration is liberty and patriotism; its yet youthful veins are full of enterprise, courage, and honorable love of glory and renown. . . .

[*Concluding his speech in support of the compromise, Webster notes that the country has received vast new territories and likens the newly expanded America to the beautiful silver shield carried by the classical hero Achilles.*]

4. Speech of Mr. Seward, of New York, in the Senate of the United States, March 11, 1850.

. . . But it is insisted that the admission of California shall be attended by a COMPROMISE of questions which have arisen out of SLAVERY. I AM OPPOSED TO ANY SUCH COMPROMISE, IN ANY AND ALL THE FORMS IN WHICH IT HAS BEEN PROPOSED. . . .

[*Seward says he is opposed to all legislative compromises in general because they do not allow legislators to consider each separate question carefully.*]

Sir, it seems to me, as if slavery had laid its paralyzing hand upon myself, and the blood were coursing less freely than its wont through my veins, when I endeavor to suppose that such a compromise has been effected, and

CHAPTER 9

THE COMPROMISE
OF 1850: THE
RHETORIC OF THE
SLAVERY
QUESTION

my utterance forever is arrested upon all the great questions, social, moral, and political, arising out of a subject so important, and as yet so incomprehensible. What am I to receive in this compromise? freedom in California. It is well; it is a noble acquisition; it is worth a sacrifice. But what am I to give as an equivalent? a recognition of a claim to perpetuate slavery in the District of Columbia; forbearance towards more stringent laws concerning the arrest of persons suspected of being slaves found in the free States; forbearance from the *proviso* of freedom in the charters of new territories. None of the plans of compromise offered, demand less than two, and most of them insist on all of these conditions. The equivalent then is, some portion of liberty—some portion of human rights in one region, for liberty in another region. But California brings gold and commerce as well as freedom. I am, then, to surrender some portion of human freedom in the District of Columbia, and in East California and New Mexico, for the mixed consideration of liberty, gold, and power on the Pacific coast. . . .

[*Seward argues that California should be admitted as a free state. However, he objects to the underlying principle of the compromise: that of classifying the states as northern or southern.*]

. . . The argument is that the States are severally equal, and that these two classes were equal at the first, and that the Constitution was founded on that equilibrium—that the States being equal and the classes of states [Northern and Southern] being equal in rights, they are to be regarded as constituting an association, in which each State, and each of these classes of States, respectively, contribute in due proportions—that the new territories are a common acquisition, and the people of these several States and classes of States, have an equal right to participate in them respectively— that the right of the people of the slave States to emigrate to the territories with their slaves, as property, is necessary to afford such a participation on their part, inasmuch as the people of the free States emigrate into the same territories with their property. And the argument deduces from this right the principle, that if Congress exclude slavery from any part of this new domain, it would be only just to set off a portion of the domain—some say south of 36°30′, others south of 34°—which should be regarded at least as free to slavery, and be organized into slave States.

Argument, ingenious and subtle—declamation, earnest and bold—and persuasion gentle, and winning as the voice of the turtle-dove when it is heard in the land—all alike and altogether, have failed to convince me of the soundness of this principle of the compromise, or of any one of the propositions on which it is attempted to be established. . . .

. . . All men are equal by the law of nature and of nations. But States are only lawful aggregations of individual men, who severally are equal; therefore States are equal in natural rights. All this is just and sound; but assuming the same premises, to wit: that all men are equal by the law of nature and of nations, the rights of property in slaves fall to the ground; for one who is equal to the other, cannot be the owner or property of that other. But you answer that the Constitution recognizes property in slaves. It would be sufficient, then, to reply, that this constitutional recognition must be void, because it is repugnant to the law of nature and of nations. But I deny that the Constitution recognizes property in man. . . .

[*Seward argues that the Constitution alludes to slavery only with respect to counting slaves from taxation and representation and also as fugitive laborers. However, he notes, the Constitution refers to them as persons, not as slaves.*]

The right to *have* a slave, implies the right in some one to *make* the slave; that right must be equal and mutual, and this would resolve society into a state of perpetual war. But if we grant the original equality of the States, and grant also the constitutional recognition of slaves as property, still the argument we are considering fails; because the States are not parties to the Constitution as States; it is the Constitution of the people of the United States. . . .

[*Seward continues this argument, noting that slavery is only a temporary condition, while freedom is the basic institution of the Constitution.*]

But there is yet another aspect in which this principle must be examined. It regards the domain only as a possession, to be enjoyed, either in common or by partition, by the citizens of the old States. It is true, indeed, that the national domain is ours; it is true, it was acquired by the valor and with the wealth of the whole nation; but we hold, nevertheless, no arbitrary power over it. We hold no arbitrary authority over anything, whether acquired lawfully, or seized by usurpation. The Constitution regulates our stewardship; the Constitution devotes the domain to union, to justice, to defence, to welfare, and to liberty.

But there is a higher law than the Constitution, which regulates our authority over the domain, and devotes it to the same noble purposes. The territory is a part—no inconsiderable part—of the common heritage of mankind, bestowed upon them by the Creator of the universe. We are his stewards, and must so discharge our trust as to secure, in the highest attainable degree, their happiness. How momentous that trust is. . . .

CHAPTER 9

THE COMPROMISE
OF 1850: THE
RHETORIC OF THE
SLAVERY
QUESTION

And now the simple, bold, and even awful question which presents itself to us, is this: Shall we, who are founding institutions, social and political, for countless millions—shall we, who know by experience the wise and the just, and are free to choose them, and to reject the erroneous and unjust—shall we establish human bondage, or permit it, by our sufferance, to be established? Sir, our forefathers would not have hesitated an hour. They found slavery existing here, and they left it only because they could not remove it. There is not only no free State which would now establish it, but there is no slave State, which, if it had had the free alternative, as we now have, would have found slavery. Indeed, our revolutionary predecessors had precisely the same question before them in establishing an organic law, under which the States of Ohio, Michigan, Illinois, Wisconsin, and Iowa have since come into the Union; and they solemnly repudiated our excluded slavery from those States forever. I confess that the most alarming evidence of our degeneracy, which has yet been given is found in the fact that we even debate such a question.

Sir, there is no Christian nation, thus free to choose as we are, which would establish slavery. . . . We cannot establish slavery, because there are certain elements of the security, welfare, and greatness of nations, which we all admit, or ought to admit, and recognize as essential; and these are the security of natural rights, the diffusion of knowledge, and the freedom of industry. Slavery is incompatible with all of these, and just in proportion to the extent that it prevails and controls in any republican state, just to that extent it subverts the principle of democracy, and converts the State into an aristocracy or a despotism. . . .

∽ QUESTIONS TO CONSIDER ∽

It is probably easiest to begin by reading all four selections, which are arranged chronologically, to determine what each speaker thought and wanted. What does Henry Clay (Source 1) say that he is trying to do? What does he propose for California? Why? Why is he so opposed to the Wilmot Proviso? What solution does he propose for the problem of the Washington, D.C., slave trade? What does

he think the duties of individual citizens and states are with respect to runaway slaves? Why? What does he think about the idea that some states might secede from the nation?

The second major speech is that of John C. Calhoun (Source 2), representing the South. What does Calhoun believe is the real question underlying the debates? In what ways specifically does he believe the North has injured the South? How does he describe the difference of opinion between the North and the South about race? What does he believe will happen to the Union? Can the South save it? Why or why not? Can the North save it? Why or why not? What is his position on the admission of California as a free state?

Famous orator Daniel Webster's speech (Source 3) was widely anticipated, and the visitors' galleries were packed for hours before he was scheduled to appear. What does Webster say that he is going to do? Why does he believe California and New Mexico will be free states? Why does he oppose the Wilmot Proviso? What is his opinion about northern aid to fugitive slaves? What is his response to the southern comparison of the slave system to the free labor of the North? What is his response to the idea of secession?

The final piece of evidence is William Seward's speech (Source 4) against the compromise. Why does he specifically oppose the compromise about California, and what does he think generally about compromises dealing with slavery in the territories? Why? What does he mean when he refers to a "higher law" than the Constitution? How does he justify his unwavering opposition to slavery?

Now that you have extracted the major ideas and arguments from the speeches, you should examine them again, focusing on the rhetoric. This time you are looking for the ways in which the speakers use language and emotional appeals to persuade their listeners. How does Henry Clay describe his state of mind? How does he

plead with northerners about the Wilmot Proviso? Do his arguments about fugitive slaves seem fair and reasonable? Why or why not? How does he feel about the Union?

What is the tone of Calhoun's speech? Do you think he really believes that the Union can be saved? Why or why not? Why does he talk about what cannot save the Union? What is the implicit threat in his final conclusions? Webster's speech is justly famous, and for many years northern schoolchildren were required to memorize the first paragraph as an example of the best kind of oratory. What images does Webster present in this paragraph? What emotions does he hope to arouse in his listeners? Do his arguments about California and New Mexico seem reasonable? Why or why not? What kinds of men does he say he wants to reach through his appeal? What images does he evoke in response to the idea of secession? How does he characterize the Union? Seward also uses some powerful images, particularly when talking about slavery. What are these images? What kinds of logical arguments does he make against slavery? How persuasive are they? In his conclusion, what action does he want his hearers to take?

Finally, summarize the answers you have found to the following questions: What were the major compromises? What were the underlying arguments in favor of them? What were the principal northern and southern objections to the compromise? In what ways did each speaker use rhetoric to try to persuade others to support his position?

CHAPTER 9
THE COMPROMISE
OF 1850: THE
RHETORIC OF THE
SLAVERY
QUESTION

◠ **EPILOGUE** ◠

Although Clay's original omnibus bill did not pass, by the fall of 1850 Stephen Douglas was successful in obtaining passage of all the major parts as individual acts. California was admitted as a free state, the Texas–New Mexico boundary was settled, a new fugitive slave law was enacted, and the slave trade (but not slavery itself) was abolished in the District of Columbia.

A spokesman for the South throughout his life, John C. Calhoun died a few weeks after his speech opposing the Compromise of 1850 was read in Congress. Henry Clay, one of the greatest statesmen of his day, died two years later. The great orator Daniel Webster also died in 1852. His support for the compromise had cost him greatly among both his antislavery constituents in New England and his many other admirers. Accused of betraying his principles in hopes of southern support for his presidential aspirations, Webster concluded his public career as secretary of state under President Millard Fillmore. William Seward, not yet fifty years old when he opposed the compromise, went on to serve as secretary of state in the Lincoln and Johnson administrations.

The Compromise of 1850 that was supposed to settle all the vexing questions related to slavery was never able to accomplish that goal. Most troubling were the immediate incidents related to the new Fugitive Slave Act. Under its terms, accused runaways could be pursued in free states, could not testify on their own behalf, and were denied the right to a trial by jury. Furthermore, the courts appointed commissioners who received ten dollars for rulings in favor of the slaveholders and only five dollars for rulings in favor of the alleged runaways. Because of the often violent demonstrations and rescues of captured runaways, southern disunionists gained support, abolitionist societies increased their memberships, and the informal network of escape routes, the "underground railroad," spread. By the time of the initial serialization of Harriet Beecher Stowe's *Uncle Tom's Cabin* in 1851, which featured the terrible consequences of the pursuit of fugitive slaves as a central element in the plot, northern public opinion had been moving steadily in the antislavery direction.

Nor had the question of the westward expansion of slavery actually been settled by the compromise. Both the Whigs and the Democrats experienced severe tensions between the northern and southern wings of their respective parties over the new Fugitive Slave Act. But Stephen Douglas's introduction of the Kansas-Nebraska Act in 1854 completed the virtual destruction of the second political party system. Although the Kansas territory was north of the old 36°30′ Missouri Compromise line and thus should have been closed to slavery, the act assumed that the Compromise of 1850 had superseded the Missouri Compromise. By providing for popular sovereignty in Kansas, the act opened up the possibility of the expansion of slavery into a previously free territory. Barely passing the House of Representatives, the Kansas-Nebraska Act set off a competition between the North and the South to encourage settlement. The result was "bleeding Kansas," as proslavery and antislavery supporters battled for supremacy in the territory.

During the next six years, the nation experienced a series of violent confrontations related directly or indirectly to the slavery question, culminating in the election of Abraham Lincoln in 1860 and the outbreak of the Civil War in 1861. At best, the Compromise of 1850 had delayed the war only for a decade.

CHAPTER 10

THE PRICE FOR VICTORY: THE DECISION TO USE AFRICAN AMERICAN TROOPS

❦ THE PROBLEM ❦

With the outbreak of war at Fort Sumter in April 1861, many northern African Americans volunteered for service in the Union army. President Abraham Lincoln initially rejected black petitions to become soldiers. On April 29, Secretary of War Simon Cameron wrote one of many letters to African American volunteers; it curtly stated that "this Department has no intention at present to call into the service of the Government any colored soldiers."[1] Later, in July 1862, when Congress passed the Confiscation Act (part of which authorized the presi-

dent to use escaped slaves for the suppression of the rebellion "in such manner as he may judge best,") and the Militia Act (which authorized him to enroll African Americans for military service), Lincoln virtually ignored both laws, arguing that the two acts *authorized* him to recruit blacks but did not *require* him to do so.

Curiously, in the South, too, free blacks and some slaves petitioned to be included in the newly formed Confederate army, perhaps hoping that such service might improve their conditions or even win them freedom. Like Lincoln, Confederate president Jefferson Davis rejected African American volunteers for military service and consistently opposed their use. Yet ultimately both chief executives changed their minds and accepted Af-

1. The letter was addressed to "Jacob Dodson (colored)" and is in *The War of the Rebellion: A Compilation of the Official Records of the Union and Confederate Armies* (Washington, D.C.: U.S. Government Printing Office, 1899), Series III, Vol. I, p. 133.

rican Americans into the armed forces, although in Davis's case, the policy reversal came too late for black units to see action on the Confederate side. And although the recruitment of African American soldiers by the South might have prolonged the conflict, it probably would not have altered the ultimate outcome. In this chapter, you will examine the evidence so as to answer the following questions:

1. What were the arguments in the North and South against arming African Americans and using them as regular soldiers? What were the arguments in favor of this move? How did the reasons in the North and South differ? How were they similar?

2. What do you think were the principal reasons that both the United States and the Confederate States of America changed their policies? How did the reasons in the North and South differ? How were they similar?

 BACKGROUND

Although many leaders in both the North and South studiously tried to avoid public discussion of the issue, the institution of slavery unquestionably played a major role in bringing on the American Civil War. As slavery intruded into the important issues and events of the day (such as westward expansion, the Mexican War, the admission of new states to the Union, the course charted for the proposed transcontinental railroad, and the right of citizens to petition Congress), as well as into all the major institutions (churches and schools, for example), an increasing number of northerners and southerners came to feel that the question of slavery must be settled, and settled on the battlefield. Therefore, when news arrived of the firing on Fort Sumter, many greeted the announcement with relief. Lincoln's call for seventy-five thousand volunteers was answered with an enormous response. A wave of patriotic fervor swept across the northern states, as crowds greeted Union soldiers marching south to "lick the rebels." In the South, too, the outbreak of war was greeted with great enthusiasm. In Charleston, South Carolina, a day of celebration was followed by a night of parades and fireworks. Many southerners compared the upcoming war with the American Revolution, when, so the thinking went, an outnumbered but superior people had been victorious over the tyrant.

Yet for a number of reasons, most northern and southern leaders carefully avoided the slavery issue even after the war had begun. To Abraham Lincoln, the debate over the abolition of slavery threatened to divert northerners from what he considered the war's central aim: preserving the Union and denying the South's right to secede. In addition, Lincoln realized

CHAPTER 10

THE PRICE FOR
VICTORY: THE
DECISION TO
USE AFRICAN
AMERICAN
TROOPS

that a great number of northern whites, including himself, did not view African Americans as equals and might well oppose a war designed to liberate slaves from bondage. Finally, in large parts of Virginia, North Carolina, Kentucky, and Tennessee and in other pockets in the South, Union sentiment was strong, largely because of the antiplanter bias in these states. But anti-Negro sentiment also was strong in these same areas. With the border states so crucial to the Union both politically and militarily (as points of invasion into the South), it is not surprising that Lincoln purposely discouraged any notion that the war was for the purpose of emancipating slaves. Therefore, when influential editor Horace Greeley publicly called on Lincoln in August 1862 to make the Civil War a war for the emancipation of slaves, the president replied that the primary purpose of the war was to preserve the Union. "My paramount object in this struggle," Lincoln wrote, "is *not* either to save or destroy slavery" (italics added):

> If I could save the Union without freeing *any* slave I would do it, and if I could save it by freeing *all* the slaves I would do it; and if I could save it by freeing some and leaving others alone I would also do that. What I do about slavery, and the colored race, I do because I believe it helps to save the Union; and what I forbear, I forbear because I do *not* believe it would help to save the Union.[2]

Hence President Lincoln, in spite of his "*personal* wish that all men every where could be free" (italics added), strongly resisted all efforts to turn the Civil War into a moral crusade to, in his words, "destroy slavery."

On the Confederate side, President Jefferson Davis also had reasons to avoid making slavery (in this case, its preservation) a primary war aim. Davis feared, correctly, that foreign governments would be unwilling to recognize or aid the Confederacy if the preservation of slavery was the most important southern reason for fighting. In addition, the majority of white southerners did not own slaves, often disliked people who did, and, Davis feared, might not fight if the principal war aim was to defend the peculiar institution. Therefore, while Lincoln was explaining to northerners that the war was being fought to preserve the Union, Davis was trying to convince southerners that the struggle was for independence and the defense of constitutional rights.

Yet as it became increasingly clear that the Civil War was going to be a long and costly conflict, issues concerning slavery and the use of African Americans in the war effort continually came to the surface. In the North, reports of battle casualties in 1862 caused widespread shock and outrage, and some feared that the United States would be exhausted before the Confederacy was finally subdued—if it was to be subdued at all.[3] Also, many

2. Lincoln to Greeley, August 22, 1862, in Roy P. Basler, ed., *The Collected Works of Abraham Lincoln* (New Brunswick, N.J.: Rutgers University Press, 1953), Vol. V, pp. 388–389. Italics added.

3. The following is an estimate of Union casualties (the sum of those killed, wounded, and missing) for the principal engagements of 1862: Shiloh (April, 13,000 casualties), Seven Pines (May, 6,000), Seven Days (June, 16,000), Antietam (September, 12,400), Fredericksburg (December, 12,000).

northerners came to feel that emancipation could be used as both a political and a diplomatic weapon. Those European nations (especially England, which had ended slavery throughout its own empire in 1833) that had been technically neutral but were leaning toward the Confederacy might, northerners reasoned, be afraid to oppose a government committed to such a worthy cause as emancipation. Some northerners also hoped that a proclamation of emancipation would incite widespread slave rebellions in the South that would cripple the Confederacy. Not to be overlooked, however, are those northerners (a minority) who sincerely viewed slavery as a stain on American society and whose eradication was a moral imperative.

Gradually, President Lincoln came to favor the emancipation of slaves, although never to the extent that the abolitionists wanted. In early 1862, the president proposed the gradual emancipation of slaves by the states, with compensation for the slave owners and colonization of the former slaves outside the boundaries of the United States. When Congress mandated that Lincoln go further than that, by passing the Confiscation Act of 1862, which explicitly called for the permanent emancipation of all slaves in the Confederacy, the president simply ignored the law, choosing not to enforce it.[4] But political and diplomatic considerations prompted Lincoln to alter his course and support the issuing of the Preliminary Emancipation Proclamation in September 1862. So that his action would not be

interpreted as one of desperation, the president waited until after the Union "victory" at the Battle of Antietam. Although the proclamation (scheduled to take effect on January 1, 1863) actually freed slaves only in areas still under Confederate control (hence immediately freeing no one), the act was a significant one regarding a shift in war aims. The final Emancipation Proclamation was issued on January 1, 1863.[5]

The second important issue that Lincoln and other northern leaders had to face was whether to arm African Americans and make them regular soldiers in the Union army. Blacks had seen service in the American Revolution and the War of 1812, prompting abolitionist Frederick Douglass, a former slave, to criticize the United States' initial policy of excluding African Americans from the army in the Civil War, saying in February 1862,

> Colored men were good enough to fight under Washington. They are not good enough to fight under McClellan. They were good enough to fight under Andrew Jackson. They are not good enough to fight under Gen. Halleck. They were good enough to help win American Independence, but they are not good enough to help preserve that independence against treason and rebellion.[6]

4. It was this action by Lincoln that prompted the exchange between Greeley and the president in August 1862.

5. The Preliminary Emancipation Proclamation was issued to test public opinion in the North and to give southern states the opportunity to retain slavery by returning to the Union before January 1, 1863. No state in the Confederacy took advantage of Lincoln's offer, and the final proclamation was issued and took effect on January 1, 1863.

6. Quoted in James M. McPherson, *The Negro's Civil War: How American Negroes Felt*

CHAPTER 10

THE PRICE FOR
VICTORY: THE
DECISION TO
USE AFRICAN
AMERICAN
TROOPS

Emancipation of slaves in the South was one thing, but making blacks United States soldiers was another. Such a decision would imply that white northerners recognized African Americans as equals. Although most abolitionists preached the dual message of emancipation and racial equality, most northern whites did not look on African Americans as equals, a belief that they shared with their president. Would whites fight alongside blacks even in racially separated units? Were blacks, many northern whites asked, courageous enough to stand and hold their positions under fire? What would African Americans want as a price for their aid? Throughout 1862, northern leaders carried on an almost continual debate over whether to accept African Americans into the Union army, an issue that had a number of social, ideological, and moral implications.

In the Confederacy, the issue of arming African Americans for the southern war effort was also a divisive one. The northern superiority in population, supplemented by continued immigration from Europe, put the South at a terrific numerical disadvantage, a disadvantage that could be lessened by the enlistment of at least a portion of the approximately four million slaves. Southern battle casualties also had been fearfully high, in some battles higher than those of the Union.[7] How long could the Confederacy hold out as its numbers continually eroded? If the main goal of the war was southern independence, shouldn't Confederate leaders use all available means to secure that objective? It was known that some northern whites, shocked by Union casualty figures, were calling on Lincoln to let the South go in peace. If the Confederacy could hold out, many southerners hoped, northern peace sentiments might grow enough to force the Union to give up. If slaves could help in that effort, some reasoned, why not arm them? Yet, as in the North, the question of whether to arm African Americans had significance far beyond military considerations. Except for the promise of freedom, what would motivate the slaves to fight for their masters? If freedom was to be offered, then what, many surely would argue, was the war being fought over in the first place? Would southern whites fight with blacks? Would some African Americans, once armed, then turn against their masters? And finally, if southern whites were correct in their insistence that African Americans were essentially docile, childlike creatures, what conceivable support could they give to the war effort? Interestingly, there were some remarkable similarities in the points debated by the northern and southern policymakers and citizens.

and Acted During the War for the Union (New York: Pantheon Books, 1965), p. 163.

7. The following are estimates of Confederate casualties for the principal engagements of 1862–1863: Seven Days (June 1862, 20,000), Antietam (September 1862, 13,700), Fredericksburg (December 1862, 5,000), Gettysburg (July 1863, 28,000).

∽ THE METHOD ∽

In this chapter, you are confronted with two sets of evidence: private and official correspondence, reports, newspaper articles and editorials, and laws and proclamations. One set concerns the argument in the North over whether to arm blacks, and the other set deals with the same question in the South. Read and analyze each series separately. Take notes as you go along, always being careful not to lose track of your central objectives.

By now you should be easily able to identify and list the major points, pro and con, in a debate. Jotting down notes as you read the evidence is extremely helpful. Be careful, however, because some reports, articles, and letters contain more than one argument.

Several earlier chapters required that you read between the lines—that is, identify themes and issues that are implied though never directly stated.

What emotional factors can you identify on both sides of the question? How important would you say these factors were in the final decision? For example, you will see from the evidence that at no time in the debate being carried on in the North were battle casualties mentioned. Were casualties therefore of no importance in the debate? How would you go about answering this question?

In some cases, the identity of the author of a particular piece (if known) can give you several clues as to that person's emotions, fears, anxieties, and needs. Where the identity of the author is not known, you may have to exercise a little historical imagination. What might this person really have meant when he or she said (or failed to say) something? Can you infer from the context of the argument any emotions that are not explicitly stated?

∽ THE EVIDENCE ∽

NORTH

Source 1 from James M. McPherson, *The Negro's Civil War: How American Negroes Felt and Acted During the War for the Union* (New York: Pantheon Books, 1965), p. 33.

1. Petition of Some Northern Blacks to President Lincoln, October 1861.

We, the undersigned, respectfully represent to Your Excellency that we are native citizens of the United States, and that, notwithstanding much injustice and oppression which our race have suffered, we cherish a strong attachment for the land of our birth and for our Republican Government.

CHAPTER 10

THE PRICE FOR
VICTORY: THE
DECISION TO
USE AFRICAN
AMERICAN
TROOPS

We are filled with alarm at the formidable conspiracy for its overthrow, and lament the vast expense of blood and treasure which the present war involves. . . . We are anxious to use our power to give peace to our country and permanence to our Government.

We are strong in numbers, in courage, and in patriotism, and in behalf of our fellow countrymen of the colored race, we offer to you and to the nation a power and a will sufficient to conquer rebellion, and establish peace on a permanent basis. We pledge ourselves, upon receiving the sanction of Your Excellency, that we will immediately proceed to raise an efficient number of regiments, and so fast as arms and equipments shall be furnished, we will bring them into the field in good discipline, and ready for action.

Source 2 from Bell Irvin Wiley, *The Life of Billy Yank: The Common Soldier of the Union* (Baton Rouge: Louisiana State University Press, 1971), p. 109.

2. A. Davenport (a Union Soldier from New York) to His Home Folk, June 19, 1861.

I think that the best way to settle the question of what to do with the darkies would be to shoot them.

Source 3 from McPherson, *The Negro's Civil War,* p. 162.

3. Newspaper Editorial by Frederick Douglass, *Douglass' Monthly,* September 1861.

Our Presidents, Governors, Generals and Secretaries are calling, with almost frantic vehemence, for men—"Men! men! send us men!" they scream, or the cause of the Union is gone; . . . and yet these very officers, representing the people and Government, steadily and persistently refuse to receive the very class of men which have a deeper interest in the defeat and humiliation of the rebels, than all others. . . . What a spectacle of blind, unreasoning prejudice and pusillanimity[8] is this! The national edifice is on fire. Every man who can carry a bucket of water, or remove a brick, is wanted; but those who have the care of the building, having a profound respect for the feeling of the national burglars who set the building on fire,

8. Cowardice.

are determined that the flames shall only be extinguished by Indo-Caucasian[9] hands, and to have the building burnt rather than save it by means of any other. Such is the pride, the stupid prejudice and folly that rules the hour.

Why does the Government reject the negro? Is he not a man? Can he not wield a sword, fire a gun, march and countermarch, and obey orders like any other? . . . If persons so humble as we can be allowed to speak to the President of the United States, we should ask him if this dark and terrible hour of the nation's extremity is a time for consulting a mere vulgar and unnatural prejudice? . . . We would tell him that this is no time to fight with one hand, when both are needed; that this is no time to fight only with your white hand, and allow your black hand to remain tied. . . . While the Government continues to refuse the aid of colored men, thus alienating them from the national cause, and giving the rebels the advantage of them, it will not deserve better fortunes than it has thus far experienced.—Men in earnest don't fight with one hand, when they might fight with two, and a man drowning would not refuse to be saved even by a colored hand.

Source 4 from Roy P. Basler, ed., *The Collected Works of Abraham Lincoln* (New Brunswick, N.J.: Rutgers University Press, 1953), Vol. V, p. 222.

4. Lincoln's Proclamation Revoking General Hunter's Order of Military Emancipation of May 9, 1862.[10]

May 19, 1862

I, Abraham Lincoln, president of the United States, proclaim and declare, that the government of the United States, had no knowledge, information, or belief, of an intention on the part of General Hunter to issue such a proclamation; nor has it yet, any authentic information that the document is genuine. And further, that neither General Hunter, nor any other commander, or person, has been authorized by the Government of the United States, to make proclamations declaring the slaves of any State free; and that the supposed proclamation, now in question, whether genuine or false, is altogether void, so far as respects such declaration.

9. Douglass meant European American.
10. On April 12, 1862, General David Hunter organized the first official regiment of African American soldiers. On May 9, Hunter proclaimed that slaves in Georgia, Florida, and South Carolina were free. Lincoln overruled both proclamations, and the regiment was disbanded without pay. Observers reported that the regiment, composed of former slaves, was of poor quality. Do you think those reports influenced Lincoln's thinking? Lincoln also overruled similar proclamations by General John C. Frémont in Missouri.

CHAPTER 10

THE PRICE FOR
VICTORY: THE
DECISION TO
USE AFRICAN
AMERICAN
TROOPS

Sources 5 and 6 from *Diary and Correspondence of Salmon P. Chase*,[11] in *Annual Report of the American Historical Association for the Year 1902* (Washington, D.C.: U.S. Government Printing Office, 1903), Vol. II, pp. 45–46, 48–49.

5. Diary of Salmon P. Chase, Entry for July 21, 1862.

. . . I went at the appointed hour, and found that the President had been profoundly concerned at the present aspect of affairs, and had determined to take some definitive steps in respect to military action and slavery. He had prepared several Orders, the first of which contemplated authority to Commanders to subsist their troups in the hostile territory—the second, authority to employ negroes as laborers—the third requiring that both in the case of property taken and of negroes employed, accounts should be kept with such degrees of certainty as would enable compensation to be made in proper cases—another provided for the colonization of negroes in some tropical country.

A good deal of discussion took place upon these points. The first Order was universally approved. The second was approved entirely; and the third, by all except myself. I doubted the expediency of attempting to keep accounts for the benefit of the inhabitants of rebel States. The Colonization project was not much discussed.

The Secretary of War presented some letters from Genl. Hunter in which he advised the Department that the withdrawal of a large proportion of his troups to reinforce Genl. McClellan,[12] rendered it highly important that he should be immediately authorized to enlist all loyal persons without reference to complexion. Messrs. Stanton,[13] Seward[14] and myself, expressed ourselves in favor of this plan, and no one expressed himself against it. (Mr. Blair[15] was not present.) The President was not prepared to decide the question but expressed himself as averse to arming negroes. The whole matter was postponed until tomorrow. . . .

6. Diary of Salmon P. Chase, Entry for July 22, 1862.

. . . The question of arming slaves was then brought up and I advocated it warmly. The President was unwilling to adopt this measure, but proposed to issue a proclamation, on the basis of the Confiscation Bill, calling upon

11. Chase was Lincoln's secretary of the treasury from 1861 until 1864.
12. George McClellan (1826–1885) was commander of the Army of the Potomac in 1862. Lincoln removed him because of his excessive caution and lack of boldness.
13. Edwin Stanton (1814–1869), secretary of war.
14. William Seward (1801–1872), secretary of state.
15. Montgomery Blair (1813–1883), postmaster general.

the States to return to their allegiance—warning the rebels the provisions of the Act would have full force at the expiration of sixty days adding on his own part, a declaration of his intention to renew, at the next session of Congress, his recommendation of compensation to States adopting the gradual abolishment of slavery and proclaiming the emancipation of all slaves within States remaining in insurrection on the first of January, 1863.

I said that I should give to such a measure my cordial support: but I should prefer that no new expression on the subject of compensation should be made, and I thought that the measure of Emancipation could be much better and more quietly accomplished by allowing Generals to organize and arm the slaves (thus avoiding depredation and massacre on the one hand, and support to the insurrection on the other) and by directing the Commanders of Departments to proclaim emancipation within their Districts as soon as practicable; but I regarded this as so much better than inaction on the subject, that I should give it my entire support.

The President determined to publish the first three Orders forthwith, and to leave the other for some further consideration. The impression left upon my mind by the whole discussion was, that while the President thought that the organization, equipment and arming of negroes, like other soldiers, would be productive of more evil than good, he was not willing that Commanders should, at their discretion, arm, for purely defensive purposes, slaves coming within their lines.

Mr. Stanton brought forward a proposition to draft 50,000 men. Mr. Seward proposed that the number should be 100,000. The President directed that, whatever number were drafted, should be a part of the 3,000,000 already called for. No decision was reached, however.

Source 7 from Basler, ed., *The Collected Works of Abraham Lincoln,* Vol. V, p. 338.

7. Lincoln's Memorandum on Recruiting Negroes.

[July 22, 1862?]

To recruiting free negroes, no objection.
To recruiting slaves of disloyal owners, no objection.
To recruiting slaves of loyal owners, *with their consent,* no objection.
To recruiting slaves of loyal owners *without* consent, objection, *unless the necessity is urgent.*
To conducting offensively, while recruiting, and to carrying away slaves not suitable for recruits, objection.

CHAPTER 10

THE PRICE FOR
VICTORY: THE
DECISION TO
USE AFRICAN
AMERICAN
TROOPS

Source 8 from *Diary and Correspondence of Salmon P. Chase,* pp. 53–54.

8. Diary of Salmon P. Chase, Entry for August 3, 1862.

. . . There was a good deal of conversation on the connection of the Slavery question with the rebellion. I expressed my conviction for the tenth or twentieth time, that the time for the suppression of the rebellion without interference with slavery had passed; that it was possible, probably, at the outset, by striking the insurrectionists wherever found, strongly and decisively; but we had elected to act on the principles of a civil war, in which the whole population of every seceding state was engaged against the Federal Government, instead of treating the active secessionists as insurgents and exerting our utmost energies for their arrest and punishment;— that the bitternesses of the conflict had now substantially united the white population of the rebel states against us; that the loyal whites remaining, if they would not prefer the Union without Slavery, certainly would not prefer Slavery to the Union; that the blacks were really the only loyal population worth counting; and that, in the Gulf States at least, their right to Freedom ought to be at once recognized, while, in the Border States, the President's plan of Emancipation might be made the basis of the necessary measures for their ultimate enfranchisement;—that the practical mode of effecting this seemed to me quite simple;—that the President had already spoken of the importance of making of the freed blacks on the Mississippi, below Tennessee, a safeguard to the navigation of the river;—that Mitchell, with a few thousand soldiers, could take Vicksburgh;—assure the blacks freedom on condition of loyalty; organize the best of them in companies, regiments etc. and provide, as far as practicable for the cultivation of the plantations by the rest:—that Butler should signify to the slaveholders of Louisiana that they must recognize the freedom of their workpeople by paying them wages;—and that Hunter should do the same thing in South-Carolina.

Mr. Seward expressed himself as in favor of any measures likely to accomplish the results I contemplated, which could be carried into effect without Proclamations; and the President said he was pretty well cured of objections to any measure except want of adaptedness to put down the rebellion; but did not seem satisfied that the time had come for the adoption of such a plan as I proposed. . . .

Source 9 from Basler, ed., *The Collected Works of Abraham Lincoln*, Vol. V, pp. 356–357.

9. President Lincoln, "Remarks to Deputation of Western Gentlemen," August 4, 1862. From an article in the *New York Tribune*, August 5, 1862.

A deputation of Western gentlemen waited upon the President this morning to offer two colored regiments from the State of Indiana. Two members of Congress were of the party. The President received them courteously, but stated to them that he was not prepared to go the length of enlisting negroes as soldiers. He would employ all colored men offered as laborers, but would not promise to make soldiers of them.

The deputation came away satisfied that it is the determination of the Government not to arm negroes unless some new and more pressing emergency arises. The President argued that the nation could not afford to lose Kentucky at this crisis, and gave it as his opinion that to arm the negroes would turn 50,000 bayonets from the loyal Border States against us that were for us. . . .

Source 10 from McPherson, *The Negro's Civil War*, pp. 163–164.

10. Letter to the Editor, *New York Tribune*, August 16, 1862.[16]

I am quite sure there is not one man in ten but would feel himself degraded as a volunteer if negro equality is to be the order in the field of battle. . . . I take the liberty of warning the abettors of fraternizing with the blacks, that one negro regiment, in the present temper of things, put on equality with those who have the past year fought and suffered, will withdraw an amount of life and energy in our army equal to disbanding ten of the best regiments we can now raise.

16. This was a letter to the editor and did not reflect the opinion of Horace Greeley, editor of the *Tribune* and supporter of racial equality for African Americans.

CHAPTER 10

THE PRICE FOR
VICTORY: THE
DECISION TO
USE AFRICAN
AMERICAN
TROOPS

Source 11 from William Wells Brown,[17] *The Negro in the American Rebellion: His Heroism and His Fidelity* (Boston: Lee & Shepard, 1867), pp. 101–104.

11. Reminiscence of a Black Man of the Threat to Cincinnati, September 1862.[18]

The mayor's proclamation, under ordinary circumstances, would be explicit enough. "Every man, of every age, be he citizen or alien," surely meant the colored people. . . . Seeking to test the matter, a policeman was approached, as he strutted in his new dignity of provostguard. To the question, humbly, almost trembling, put, "Does the mayor desire colored men to report for service in the city's defence?" he replied, "You know d——d well he doesn't mean you. Niggers ain't citizens."—"But he calls on all, citizens and aliens. If he does not mean all, he should not say so."—"The mayor knows as well as you do what to write, and all he wants is for you niggers to keep quiet." This was at nine o'clock on the morning of the second. The military authorities had determined, however, to impress the colored men for work upon the fortifications. The privilege of volunteering, extended to others, was to be denied to them. Permission to volunteer would imply some freedom, some dignity, some independent manhood. . . .

If the guard appointed to the duty of collecting the colored people had gone to their houses, and notified them to report for duty on the fortifications, the order would have been cheerfully obeyed. But the brutal ruffians who composed the regular and special police took every opportunity to inflict abuse and insult upon the men whom they arrested. . . .

The captain of these conscripting squads was one William Homer, and in him organized ruffianism had its fitting head. He exhibited the brutal malignity of his nature in a continued series of petty tyrannies. Among the first squads marched into the yard was one which had to wait several hours before being ordered across the river. Seeking to make themselves as comfortable as possible, they had collected blocks of wood, and piled up bricks, upon which they seated themselves on the shaded side of the yard. Coming into the yard, he ordered all to rise, marched them to another part, then issued the order, "D—n you, squat." Turning to the guard, he added, "Shoot the first one who rises." Reaching the opposite side of the river, the same squad were marched from the sidewalk into the middle of the dusty road, and again the order, "D—n you, squat," and the command to shoot the first one who should rise. . . .

17. Brown was an African American who ultimately served in the Union army and recorded his experiences.
18. In early September 1862, the citizens of Cincinnati, Ohio, feared a raid on the city by Confederates. Mayor George Hatch issued a proclamation calling on "every man of every age" to take part in the defense of the city.

Calling up his men, he would address them thus: "Now, you fellows, hold up your heads. Pat, hold your musket straight; don't put your tongue out so far; keep your eyes open: I believe you are drunk. Now, then, I want you fellows to go out of this pen, and bring all the niggers you can catch. Don't come back here without niggers: if you do, you shall not have a bit of grog. Now be off, you shabby cusses, and come back in forty minutes, and bring me niggers; that's what I want." This barbarous and inhuman treatment of the colored citizens of Cincinnati continued for four days, without a single word of remonstrance, except from the "Gazette."

Source 12 from John G. Nicolay and John Hay, eds., *Abraham Lincoln—Complete Works* (New York: Century Co., 1894), Vol. II, pp. 234–235, 242–243.

12. Lincoln's Reply to a Committee from the Religious Denominations of Chicago, Asking the President to Issue a Proclamation of Emancipation, September 13, 1862.

The subject presented in the memorial is one upon which I have thought much for weeks past, and I may even say for months. I am approached with the most opposite opinions and advice, and that by religious men who are equally certain that they represent the divine will. I am sure that either the one or the other class is mistaken in that belief, and perhaps in some respects both. I hope it will not be irreverent for me to say that if it is probable that God would reveal his will to others on a point so connected with my duty, it might be supposed he would reveal it directly to me; for, unless I am more deceived in myself than I often am, it is my earnest desire to know the will of Providence in this matter. And if I can learn what it is, I will do it. These are not, however, the days of miracles, and I suppose it will be granted that I am not to expect a direct revelation. I must study the plain physical facts of the case, ascertain what is possible, and learn what appears to be wise and right. . . .

I admit that slavery is the root of the rebellion, or at least its *sine qua non*.[19] The ambition of politicians may have instigated them to act, but they would have been impotent without slavery as their instrument. I will also concede that emancipation would help us in Europe, and convince them that we are incited by something more than ambition. I grant, further, that it would help somewhat at the North, though not so much, I fear, as you

19. An essential element or condition; a necessary ingredient.

CHAPTER 10

THE PRICE FOR
VICTORY: THE
DECISION TO
USE AFRICAN
AMERICAN
TROOPS

and those you represent imagine. Still, some additional strength would be added in that way to the war, and then, unquestionably, it would weaken the rebels by drawing off their laborers, which is of great importance; but I am not so sure we could do much with the blacks. If we were to arm them, I fear that in a few weeks the arms would be in the hands of the rebels; and, indeed, thus far we have not had arms enough to equip our white troops. I will mention another thing, though it meet only your scorn and contempt. There are fifty thousand bayonets in the Union armies from the border slave States. It would be a serious matter if, in consequence of a proclamation such as you desire, they should go over to the rebels. I do not think they all would—not so many, indeed, as a year ago, or as six months ago—not so many to-day as yesterday. Every day increases their Union feeling. They are also getting their pride enlisted, and want to beat the rebels.

Sources 13 through 15 from Basler, ed., *The Collected Works of Abraham Lincoln,* Vol. V, pp. 444, 509, 28–30.

13. Lincoln to Vice President Hannibal Hamlin.

(Strictly private.)   Executive Mansion,
                                  Washington, September 28, 1862.

My Dear Sir:

   Your kind letter of the 25th is just received. It is known to some that while I hope something from the proclamation,[20] my expectations are not as sanguine as are those of some friends. The time for its effect southward has not come; but northward the effect should be instantaneous.

   It is six days old, and while commendation in newspapers and by distinguished individuals is all that a vain man could wish, the stocks have declined, and troops came forward more slowly than ever. This, looked soberly in the face, is not very satisfactory. We have fewer troops in the field at the end of six days than we had at the beginning—the attrition among the old outnumbering the addition of the new. The North responds to the proclamation sufficiently in breath; but breath alone kills no rebels.

   I wish I could write more cheerfully; nor do I thank you the less for the kindness of your letter. Yours very truly,

                                                          A. LINCOLN

20. Lincoln was referring to his Preliminary Emancipation Proclamation, which he issued on September 22, 1862. Lincoln's hope was that the threat of emancipation would cause the South to surrender so as to keep slavery intact. See again Lincoln's letter to Horace Greeley, August 22, 1862, on page 226.

14. Lincoln to Carl Schurz.

Gen. Carl Schurz   Executive Mansion,
                                                    Washington, Nov. 24, 1862.

My dear Sir

   I have just received, and read your letter of the 20th. The purport of it
is that we lost the late elections,[21] and the administration is failing, because
the war is unsuccessful; and that I must not flatter myself that I am not
justly to blame for it. I certainly know that if the war fails, the administration fails, and that I *will* be blamed for it, whether I deserve it or not. And
I ought to be blamed, if I could do better. You think I could do better;
therefore you blame me already. I think I could not do better; therefore I
blame you for blaming me. . . .

15. The Emancipation Proclamation.

                                                            January 1, 1863
                        By the President of the United States of America:
                                A Proclamation. . . .

   Now, therefore I, Abraham Lincoln, President of the United States, by
virtue of the power in me vested as Commander-in-Chief, of the Army and
Navy of the United States in time of actual armed rebellion against authority and government of the United States, and as a fit and necessary war
measure for suppressing said rebellion, do, on this first day of January, in
the year of our Lord one thousand eight hundred and sixty three, and in
accordance with my purpose so to do publicly proclaimed for the full period
of one hundred days, from the day first above mentioned, order and desig-
nate as the States and parts of States wherein the people thereof respectively, are this day in rebellion against the United States, the following,
to wit: . . .

[*Here Lincoln identified the geographic areas of the South still under the control of
the Confederacy.*]

   And by virtue of the power, and for the purpose aforesaid, I do order and
declare that all persons held as slaves within said designated States, and

21. In the congressional elections of 1862, the Republicans lost three seats in the House of
Representatives, although they were still the majority party. Senators were not elected by the
people until the Seventeenth Amendment to the Constitution was ratified in 1913.

CHAPTER 10

THE PRICE FOR
VICTORY: THE
DECISION TO
USE AFRICAN
AMERICAN
TROOPS

parts of States, are, and henceforward shall be free; and that the Executive government of the United States, including the military and naval authorities thereof, will recognize and maintain the freedom of said persons.

And I hereby enjoin upon the people so declared to be free to abstain from all violence, unless in necessary self-defence; and I recommend to them that, in all cases when allowed, they labor faithfully for reasonable wages.

And I further declare and make known, that such persons of suitable condition, will be received into the armed services of the United States to garrison forts, positions, stations, and other places, and to man vessels of all sorts in said service.[22]

And upon this act, sincerely believed to be an act of justice, warranted by the Constitution, upon military necessity, I invoke the considerate judgment of mankind, and the gracious favor of Almighty God.

In witness whereof, I have hereunto set my hand and caused the seal of the United States to be affixed.

Done at the City of Washington, this first day of January, in the year of our Lord one thousand eight hundred and sixty three, and of the Independence of the United States of America the eighty-seventh. By the President:

ABRAHAM LINCOLN

Source 16 from George Washington Williams, *A History of the Negro Troops in the War of the Rebellion, 1861–65* (New York: Harper and Brothers, 1888), pp. 66–67, 90–91.

16. Reminiscence of a Former Black Soldier in the Union Army.

At first the faintest intimation that Negroes should be employed as soldiers in the Union Army was met with derision. By many it was regarded as a joke. The idea of arming the ex-slaves seemed ridiculous to most civil and military officers. . . .

Most observing and thoughtful people concluded that centuries of servitude had rendered the Negro slave incapable of any civil or military service. . . . Some officers talked of resigning if Negroes were to be called upon to fight the battles of a free republic. The privates in regiments from large cities and border States were bitter and demonstrative in their opposition. The Negro volunteers themselves were subjected to indignities from rebel civilians within the Union lines, and obtained no protection from the white troops. . . .

22. This paragraph was not part of the preliminary proclamation issued by Lincoln on September 22, 1862. See Basler, ed., *The Collected Works of Abraham Lincoln*, Vol. V, pp. 433–436.

Source 17 from Lawrence Frederick Kohl and Margaret Cosse Richard, eds., *Irish Green and Union Blue: The Civil War Letters of Peter Welsh, Color Sergeant, 28th Regiment, Massachusetts Volunteers* (New York: Fordham University Press, 1986), p. 62.

17. Fragment of a Letter from a Union Soldier, Early 1863.

I see by late papers that the governor of Massachusetts has been autheured to raise nigar regiments. i hope he may succeed but i doubt it very much if they can raise a few thousand and sent them out here i can assure you that whether they have the grit to go into battle or not if they are placed in front and any brigade of this army behind them they will have to go in or they will meet as hot a reception in their retreat as in their advance[.] The feeling against nigars is intensly strong in this army as is plainly to be seen wherever and whenever they meet them[.] They are looked upon as the principal cause of this war and this feeling is especially strong in the Irish regiments[.]

Source 18 from *The War of the Rebellion,* Series III, Vol. III, p. 16.

18. L. Thomas to Governor of Rhode Island, January 15, 1863.

ADJUTANT-GENERAL'S OFFICE,
Washington, D.C., January 15, 1863.

GOVERNOR OF RHODE ISLAND
Providence, R. I.:
SIR: I am directed to say that the President will accept into the service of the United States an infantry regiment of volunteers of African descent, if offered by your State and organized according to the rules and regulations of the service.
I am, very respectfully,

L. THOMAS,
Adjutant-General.

CHAPTER 10

THE PRICE FOR
VICTORY: THE
DECISION TO
USE AFRICAN
AMERICAN
TROOPS

Source 19 from Glenn W. Sunderland, *Five Days to Glory* (South Brunswick, N.J.: A. S. Barnes & Co., 1970), pp. 97–98.

19. Letter from Tighlman Jones (a Union Soldier) to Brother Zillman Jones, October 6, 1863.

You have heard of Negroes being enlisted to fight for Uncle Sam. If you would like to know what the soldiers think about the idea I can almost tell you. Why, that is just what they desire. There is some soldiers who curse and blow and make a great noise about it but we set him as a convalescent who is like a man who is afraid of the smallpox who curses the works of a power he can in no way avoid, but will kick and rail and act the part of a fool, but of no avail, nature will have its own course, or to say that this war will free the Negroes and that they will enlist and fight to sustain the Government. I think more of a Negro Union soldier than I do of all the cowardly Copperhead trash of the north[23] and there is no soldier but what approves of the course of the present administration and will fight till the Rebels unconditionally surrender and return to their allegiance.

Source 20 from Dudley Cornish, *The Sable Arm: Negro Troops in the Union Army, 1861–1865* (New York: W. W. Norton, 1966), pp. ix–x.

20. Editorial, *New York Times,* March 7, 1864.

There has been no more striking manifestation of the marvelous times that are upon us than the scene in our streets at the departure of the first of our colored regiments. Had any man predicted it last year he would have been thought a fool, even by the wisest and most discerning. History abounds with strange contrasts. It always has been an ever-shifting melodrama. But never, in this land at least, has it presented a transition so extreme and yet so speedy as what our eyes have just beheld.

Eight months ago the African race in this City were literally hunted down like wild beasts.[24] They fled for their lives. When caught, they were shot down in cold blood, or stoned to death, or hung to the trees or the lampposts. Their homes were pillaged; the asylum which Christian charity had

23. Copperheads were northerners who opposed the war and advocated peace at any price.
24. In mid-1863, demonstrations against conscription in New York City turned into an ugly mob action against African Americans, partly because of their connection, through the Emancipation Proclamation of January 1, 1863, to the war and partly because of economic competition with the poorer whites who constituted most of the rioters.

provided for their orphaned children was burned; and there was no limit to the persecution but in the physical impossibility of finding further material on which the mob could wreak its ruthless hate. Nor was it solely the raging horde in the streets that visited upon the black man the nefarious wrong. Thousands and tens of thousands of men of higher social grade, of better education, cherished precisely the same spirit. . . .

How astonishingly has all this been changed. The same men who could not have shown themselves in the most obscure street in the City without peril of instant death, even though in the most suppliant attitude, now march in solid platoons, with shouldered muskets, slung knapsacks, and buckled cartridge boxes down through our gayest avenues and our busiest thoroughfares to the pealing strains of martial music and are everywhere saluted with waving handkerchiefs, with descending flowers, and with the acclamations and plaudits of countless beholders. They are halted at our most beautiful square, and amid an admiring crowd, in the presence of many of our most prominent citizens, are addressed in an eloquent and most complimentary speech by the President of our chief literary institution, and are presented with a gorgeous stand of colors in the names of a large number of the first ladies of the City, who attest on parchment, signed by their own fair hands, that they "will anxiously watch your career, glorifying in your heroism, ministering to you when wounded and ill, and honoring your martyrdom with benedictions and with tears."

It is only by such occasions that we can at all realize the prodigious revolution which the public mind everywhere is experiencing. Such developments are infallible tokens of a new epoch.

SOUTH

Sources 21 and 22 from *The War of the Rebellion,* Series IV, Vol. I, pp. 482, 529.

21. Correspondence Between W. S. Turner and the Confederate War Department, July 17, 1861.

HELENA, ARK., *July 17, 1861.*

Hon. L. P. WALKER[25]:

DEAR SIR: I wrote you a few days since for myself and many others in this district to ascertain if we could get negro regiments received for Confederate service, officered, of course, by white men. All we ask is arms, clothing, and provisions, and usual pay for officers and not one cent pay for negroes.

25. Walker was the Confederate secretary of war from February to September 1861.

CHAPTER 10

THE PRICE FOR
VICTORY: THE
DECISION TO
USE AFRICAN
AMERICAN
TROOPS

Our negroes are too good to fight Lincoln hirelings, but as they pretend to love negroes so much we want to show them how much the true Southern cotton-patch negro loves them in return. The North cannot complain at this. They proclaim negro equality from the Senate Chamber to the pulpit, teach it in their schools, and are doing all they can to turn the slaves upon master, mistress, and children. And now, sir, if you can receive the negroes that can be raised we will soon give the Northern thieves a gorge of the negroes' love for them that will never be forgotten. As you well know, I have had long experience with negro character. I am satisfied they are easy disciplined and less trouble than whites in camp, and will fight desperately as long as they have a single white officer living. I know one man that will furnish and arm 100 of his own and his son for their captain. The sooner we bring a strong negro force against the hirelings the sooner we shall have peace, in my humble judgment. Let me hear from you.

Your old friend,

W. S. TURNER

22. Correspondence Between W. S. Turner and the Confederate War Department, August 2, 1861.

CONFEDERATE STATES OF AMERICA, WAR DEPARTMENT,

Richmond, August 2, 1861.

W. S. TURNER,

Helena, Ark.:

SIR: In reply to your letter of the 17th of July I am directed by the Secretary of War to say that this Department is not prepared to accept the negro regiment tendered by you, and yet it is not doubted that almost every slave would cheerfully aid his master in the work of hurling back the fanatical invader. Moreover, if the necessity were apparent there is high authority for the employment of such forces. Washington himself recommended the enlistment of two negro regiments in Georgia, and the Congress sanctioned the measure. But now there is a superabundance of our own color tendering their services to the Government in its day of peril and ruthless invasion, a superabundance of men when we are bound to admit the inadequate supply of arms at present at the disposal of the Government.

Respectfully,

A. T. BLEDSOE
Chief of Bureau of War.

Sources 23 through 26 from Robert F. Durden, *The Gray and the Black: The Confederate Debate on Emancipation* (Baton Rouge: Louisiana State University Press, 1972), pp. 30–31, 54–58, 61, 66–67.

23. *Montgomery* (Ala.) *Weekly Mail*, "Employment of Negroes in the Army," September 9, 1863.

. . . We must either employ the negroes ourselves, or the enemy will employ them against us. While the enemy retains so much of our territory, they are, in their present avocation and status, a dangerous element, a source of weakness. They are no longer negative characters, but subjects of volition as other people. They must be taught to know that this is peculiarly the country of the black man—that in no other is the climate and soil so well adapted to his nature and capacity. He must further be taught that it is his duty, as well as the white man's, to defend his home with arms, if need be.

We are aware that there are persons who shudder at the idea of placing arms in the hands of negroes, and who are not willing to trust them under any circumstances. The negro, however, is proverbial for his faithfulness under kind treatment. He is an affectionate, grateful being, and we are persuaded that the fears of such persons are groundless.

There are in the slaveholding States four millions of negroes, and out of this number at least six hundred thousand able-bodied men capable of bearing arms can be found. Lincoln proposes to free and arm them against us. There are already fifty thousand of them in the Federal ranks. Lincoln's scheme has worked well so far, and if no[t] checkmated, will most assuredly be carried out. The Confederate Government must adopt a counter policy. It must thwart the enemy in this gigantic scheme, at all hazards, and if nothing else will do it—if the negroes cannot be made effective and trustworthy to the Southern cause in no other way, we solemnly believe it is the duty of this Government to forestall Lincoln and proceed at once to take steps for the emancipation or liberation of the negroes itself. Let them be declared free, placed in the ranks, and told to fight for their homes and country. . . .

Such action on the part of our Government would place our people in a purer and better light before the world. It would disabuse the European mind of a grave error in regard to the cause of our separation. It would prove to them that there were higher and holier motives which actuated our people than the mere love of property. It would show that, although slavery is one of the principles that we started to fight for, yet it falls far short of being the chief one; that, for the sake of our liberty, we are capable

CHAPTER 10

THE PRICE FOR
VICTORY: THE
DECISION TO
USE AFRICAN
AMERICAN
TROOPS

of any personal sacrifice; that we regard the emancipation of slaves, and the consequent loss of property as an evil infinitely less than the subjugation and enslavement of ourselves; that it is not a war exclusively for the privilege of holding negroes in bondage. It would prove to our soldiers, three-fourths of whom never owned a negro, that it is not "the rich man's war and the poor man's fight," but a war for the most sacred of all principles, for the dearest of all rights—the right to govern ourselves. It would show them that the rich man who owned slaves was not willing to jeopardize the precious liberty of the country by his eagerness to hold on to his slaves, but that he was ready to give them up and sacrifice his interest in them whenever the cause demanded it. It would lend a new impetus, a new enthusiasm, a new and powerful strength to the cause, and place our success beyond a peradventure. It would at once remove all the odium which attached to us on account of slavery, and bring us speedy recognition, and, if necessary, intervention.

24. General Patrick Cleburne to General Joseph Johnston, January 2, 1864.

We have now been fighting for nearly three years, have spilled much of our best blood, and lost, consumed, or thrown to the flames an amount of property equal in value to the specie currency of the world. . . . Our soldiers can see no end to this state of affairs except in our own exhaustion; hence, instead of rising to the occasion, they are sinking into a fatal apathy, growing weary of hardships and slaughters which promise no results. In this state of things it is easy to understand why there is a growing belief that some black catastrophe is not far ahead of us, and that unless some extraordinary change is soon made in our condition we must overtake it. . . .

In view of the state of affairs what does our country propose to do? In the words of President Davis "no effort must be spared to add largely to our effective force as promptly as possible. The sources of supply are to be found in restoring to the army all who are improperly absent, putting an end to substitution, modifying the exemption law, restricting details, and placing in the ranks such of the able-bodied men now employed as wagoners, nurses, cooks, and other employees, as are doing service for which the negroes may be found competent.". . . [W]e propose, in addition to a modification of the President's plans, that we retain in service for the war all troops now in service, and that we immediately commence training a large reserve of the most courageous of our slaves, and further that we guarantee freedom within a reasonable time to every slave in the South who shall remain true to the Confederacy in this war. As between the loss of independence and the loss of slavery, we assume that every patriot will freely give up the latter—give up the negro slave rather than be a slave himself. If we are correct in this assumption it only remains to show how this great national sacrifice is, in all human probabilities, to change the current of success and sweep the invader from our country.

Our country has already some friends in England and France, and there are strong motives to induce these nations to recognize and assist us, but they cannot assist us without helping slavery, and to do this would be in conflict with their policy for the last quarter of a century. . . . But this barrier once removed, the sympathy and the interests of these and other nations will accord with their own, and we may expect from them both moral support and material aid. . . .

Will the slaves fight? . . . The negro slaves of Saint Domingo, fighting for freedom, defeated their white masters and the French troops sent against them.[26] The negro slaves of Jamaica revolted, and under the name of Maroons held the mountains against their masters for 150 years; and the experience of this war has been so far that half-trained negroes have fought as bravely as many other half-trained Yankees. If, contrary to the training of a lifetime, they can be made to face and fight bravely against their former masters, how much more probable is it that with the allurement of a higher reward, and led by those masters, they would submit to discipline and face dangers.

25. President Jefferson Davis to General Walker, January 13, 1864—Reaction to Cleburne's Proposal.

I have received your letter, with its inclosure, informing me of the propositions [Cleburne's proposal] submitted to a meeting of the general officers on the 2d instant, and thank you for the information. Deeming it to be injurious to the public service that such a subject should be mooted, or even known to be entertained by persons possessed of the confidence and

26. On August 23, 1791, thousands of slaves in the French colony of Saint Dominigue (in Spanish, Santo Domingo; now Haiti) revolted against their white masters. Ultimately led by Toussaint Louverture (often spelled L'Ouverture), the slaves overthrew their masters, beat back invasions from both Britain and France, and declared Haiti an independent republic in 1804. Whites who fled from Haiti to the United States reported atrocities that filled white southerners with alarm for years after. See especially Alfred N. Hunt, *Haiti's Influence on Antebellum America* (Baton Rouge: Louisiana State University Press, 1988).

CHAPTER 10

THE PRICE FOR
VICTORY: THE
DECISION TO
USE AFRICAN
AMERICAN
TROOPS

respect of the people, I have concluded that the best policy under the circumstances will be to avoid all publicity, and the Secretary of War has therefore written to General Johnston requesting him to convey to those concerned my desire that it should be kept private. If it be kept out of public journals its ill effect will be much lessened.

26. General Joseph Johnston to General Hardee et al., January 31, 1864—Reaction to Cleburne's Proposal.

Lieutenant-General Hardee, Major-Generals Cheatham, Hindman, Cleburne, Stewart, Walker, Brigadier-Generals Bate and P. Anderson:
GENERAL:

I have just received a letter from the Secretary of War in reference to Major-General Cleburne's memoir read in my quarters about the 2d instant. In this letter the Honorable Secretary expresses the earnest conviction of the President "that the dissemination or even promulgation of such opinions under the present circumstances of the Confederacy, whether in the Army or among the people, can be productive only of discouragement, distraction, and dissension." The agitation and controversy which must spring from the presentation of such views by officers high in the public confidence are to be deeply deprecated, and while no doubt or mistrust is for a moment entertained of the patriotic intents of the gallant author of the memorial, and such of his brother officers as may have favored his opinions, it is requested that you communicate to them, as well as all others present on the occasion, the opinions, as herein expressed, of the President, and urge on them the suppression, not only of the memorial itself, but likewise of all discussion and controversy respecting or growing out of it. . . .

Source 27 from Bell Irvin Wiley, ed., *Letters of Warren Akin, Confederate Congressman* (Athens: University of Georgia Press, 1959), pp. 32–33.

27. Letter from Warren Akin to Nathan Land, October 31, 1864.

As to calling out the negro men and placing them in the army, with the promise that they shall be free at the end of the war, I can only say it is a question of fearful magnitude. Can we prevent subjugation, confiscation, degradation and slavery without it? If not, will our condition or that of the negro, be any worse by calling them into service?

On the other hand: Can we feed our soldiers and their families if the negro men are taken from the plantations? Will our soldiers submit to having our negroes along side them in the ditches, or in line of battle? When the negro is taught the use of arms and the art of war, can we live in safety with them afterwards? Or if it be contemplated to send them off to another country, when peace is made, will it be right to force them to a new, distant and strange land, after they have fought for and won the independence of this? Would they go without having another war? Involving, perhaps a general insurrection of all the negroes? To call forth the negroes into the army, with the promise of freedom, will it not be giving up the great question involved by doing the very thing Lincoln is now doing? The Confederate States may take private property for public use, by paying for it; but can we ever pay for 300,000 negro men at present prices, in addition to our other indebtedness? The Confederate Government may buy the private negro property of the Citizens, but can it set them free among us, to corrupt our slaves, and place in peril our existence? These are some of the thoughts that have passed th[r]ough my mind on the subject. But I can not say that I have a definite and fixed opinion. If I were convinced that we will be subjugated, with the long train of horrors that will follow it, unless the negroes be placed in the army, I would not hesitate to enrol our slaves and put them to fighting. Subjugation will give us free negroes in abundance— enemies at that—while white slaves will be more numerous than free negroes. We and our children will be slaves, while our freed negroes will lord it over us. It is impossible for the evils resulting from placing our slaves in the army to be greater than those that will follow subjugation. We may (if necessary) put our slaves in the army, win our independence, and have liberty and homes for ourselves and children. But subjugation will deprive us of our homes, houses, property, liberty, honor, and every thing worth living for, leaving for us and our posterity only the chains of slavery, tenfold more galling and degrading than that now felt by our negroes. But I will not enlarge, I have made suggestions merely for your reflection.

Source 28 from McPherson, *The Negro's Civil War,* pp. 243–244.

28. Judah P. Benjamin (Secretary of War, Confederacy) to Fred A. Porcher (an Old Friend and Former Classmate), December 21, 1864.

For a year past I have seen that the period was fast approaching when we should be compelled to use every resource of our command for the defense of our liberties. . . . The negroes will certainly be made to fight against us

CHAPTER 10

THE PRICE FOR
VICTORY: THE
DECISION TO
USE AFRICAN
AMERICAN
TROOPS

if not armed for our defense. The drain of that source of our strength is steadily fatal, and irreversible by any other expedient than that of arming the slaves as an auxiliary force.

I further agree with you that if they are to fight for our freedom they are entitled to their own. Public opinion is fast ripening on the subject, and ere the close of the winter the conviction on this point will become so widespread that the Government will have no difficulty in inaugurating the policy [of recruiting Negro soldiers].

. . . It is well known that General Lee, who commands so largely the confidence of the people, is strongly in favor of our using the negroes for defense, and emancipating them, if necessary, for that purpose. Can you not yourself write a series of articles in your papers, always urging this point as the true issue, viz, is it better for the negro to fight for us or against us?

Source 29 from Durden, *The Gray and the Black,* pp. 89–91.

29. *Richmond Enquirer,* November 4, 1864, Letter to the Editor in Reply to the Editorial of October 6, 1864.

Can it be possible that you are serious and earnest in proposing such a step to be taken by our Government? Or were you merely discussing the matter as a something which might be done? An element of power which might be used—meaning thereby to intimidate or threaten our enemy with it as a weapon of offence which they may drive us to use? Can it be possible that a Southern man—editor of a Southern journal—recognizing the right of property in slaves, admitting their inferiority in the scale of being and also their social inferiority, would recommend the passage of a law which at one blow levels all distinctions, deprives the master of a right to his property, and elevates the negro to an equality with the white man?—for, disguise it as you may, those who fight together in a common cause, and by success win the *same* freedom, enjoy equal rights and equal position, and in this case, are distinguished only by color. Are we prepared for this? Is it for this we are contending? Is it for this we would seek the aid of our slaves? . . . When President Davis said: "We are not fighting for slavery, but independence," he meant that the question and subject of slavery was a matter settled amongst ourselves and one that admitted of no dispute—that he intended to be independent of all foreign influences on this as well as on other matters—free to own slaves if he pleased—free to lay our own taxes—free to govern ourselves. He never intended to ignore the question of slavery or to do aught else but express the determination to be *independent* in this as well as in all other matters. What has embittered the feelings of the two sections of the old Union? What has gradually driven them to the final separation? What is it that has made two nationalities of them, if it is not slavery?

The Yankee *steals* my slave, and makes a soldier and freeman of him to *destroy* me. You *take* my slave, and make a soldier and freeman of him to *defend* me. The difference in your intention is very great; but is not the practice of both equally pernicious to the slave and destruction to the country? And at the expiration of ten years after peace what would be the relative difference between my negro *stolen* and freed by the Yankee and my negro taken and freed by you? Would they not be equally worthless and vicious? How would you distinguish between them? How prevent the return of him whose hand is red with his master's blood, and his enjoyment of those privileges which you so lavishly bestow upon the faithful freedman?

Have you thought of the influence to be exerted by these half or quarter million of free negroes in the midst of slaves as you propose to leave them at the end of the war; these men constitute the bone and sinew of our slaves, the able-bodied between 18 and 45. They will be men who know the value and power of combination; they will be well disciplined, trained to the use of arms, with the power and ability of command; at the same time they will be grossly and miserably ignorant, without any fixed principle of life or the ability of acquiring one. . . .

Sources 30 and 31 from McPherson, *The Negro's Civil War*, p. 244.

30. Howell Cobb, Speech in the Confederate Senate, 1864.

. . . If slaves will make good soldiers our whole theory of slavery is wrong. . . . The day you make soldiers of them is the beginning of the end of the revolution.

31. Robert Toombs, Speech in the Confederate Senate, 1864.

. . . The worst calamity that could befall us would be to gain our independence by the valor of our slaves. . . . The day that the army of Virginia allows a negro regiment to enter their lines as soldiers they will be degraded, ruined, and disgraced.

CHAPTER 10

THE PRICE FOR
VICTORY: THE
DECISION TO
USE AFRICAN
AMERICAN
TROOPS

Source 32 from Durden, *The Gray and the Black,* pp. 93–94.

32. *Lynchburg* (Va.) *Republican,* November 2, 1864.

The proposition is so strange—so unconstitutional—so directly in conflict with all of our former practices and teachings—so entirely subversive of our social and political institutions—and so completely destructive of our liberties, that we stand completely appalled [and] dumfounded [*sic*] at its promulgation.

They propose that Congress shall conscribe two hundred and fifty thousand slaves, arm, equip and fight them in the field. As an inducement of them to be faithful, it is proposed that, at the end of the war, they shall have their freedom and live amongst us. "The conscription of negroes," says the *Enquirer,* "should be accompanied with freedom and the privilege of remaining in the States." This is the monstrous proposition. The South went to war to defeat the designs of the abolitionists, and behold! in the midst of the war, we turn abolitionists ourselves! We went to war because the Federal Congress kept eternally meddling with our domestic institutions, with which we contended they had nothing to do, and now we propose to end the war by asking the Confederate Congress to do precisely what Lincoln proposes to do—free our negroes and make them the equals of the white man! We have always been taught to believe that slaves are property, and under the exclusive control of the States and the courts. This new doctrine teaches us that Congress has a right to free our negroes and make them the equals of their masters. . . .

Source 33 from Wiley, ed., *Letters of Warren Akin,* p. 117.

33. Mary V. Akin to Warren Akin, January 8, 1865.

. . . Every one I talk to is in favor of putting negros in the army and that *immediately.* Major Jones speaks very strongly in favor of it. I think slavery is now gone and what little there is left of it should be rendered as serviceable as possible and for that reason the negro men ought to be put to fighting and where some of them will be killed, if it is not done there will soon be more negroes than whites in the country and they will be the free race. I want to see them *got rid of soon.* . . .

Sources 34 through 36 from Durden, *The Gray and the Black,* pp. 163, 195, 202–203.

34. *Macon* (Ga.) *Telegraph and Confederate,* January 11, 1865.

Mr. Editor:

A lady's opinion may not be worth much in such an hour as this, but I cannot resist the temptation of expressing my approbation of "The crisis— the Remedy," copied from the Mobile Register. Would to God our Government would act upon its suggestions at once. The women of the South are not so in love with their negro property, as to wish to see husbands, fathers, sons, brothers, slain to protect it; nor would they submit to Yankee rule, could it secure to them a thousand waiting maids, whence now they possess one. . . .

35. *Richmond Whig,* February 28, 1865.

Mobile, Feb. 14—One of the largest meetings ever assembled in Mobile was held at the Theatre last night, which was presided over by Hon. Judge Forsyth.

Resolutions were unanimously adopted declaring our unalterable purpose to sustain the civil and military authorities to achieve independence— that our battle-cry henceforth should be—"Victory or Death"—that there is now no middle-ground between treachery and patriotism—that we still have an abiding confidence in our ability to achieve our independence—that the Government should immediately place one hundred thousand negroes in the field—that reconstruction is no longer an open question.

36. Confederate Congress, "An Act to Increase the Military Force of the Confederate States," March 13, 1865.

The Congress of the Confederate States of America do enact, That in order to provide additional forces to repel invasion, maintain the rightful possession of the Confederate States, secure their independence, and preserve their institutions, the President be, and he is hereby, authorized to ask for and accept from the owners of slaves, the services of such number of able-bodied negro men as he may deem expedient, for and during the war, to perform military service in whatever capacity he may direct.

CHAPTER 10

THE PRICE FOR
VICTORY: THE
DECISION TO
USE AFRICAN
AMERICAN
TROOPS

Sec. 2. That the General-in-Chief be authorized to organize the said slaves into companies, battalions, regiments and brigades, under such rules and regulations as the Secretary of War may prescribe, and to be commanded by such officers as the President may appoint.

Sec. 3. That while employed in the service the said troops shall receive the same rations, clothing and compensation as are allowed to other troops in the same branch of the service.

Sec. 4. That if, under the previous sections of this act, the President shall not be able to raise a sufficient number of troops to prosecute the war successfully and maintain the sovereignty of the States and the independence of the Confederate States, then he is hereby authorized to call on each State, whenever he thinks it expedient, for her quota of 300,000 troops, in addition to those subject to military service under existing laws, or so many thereof as the President may deem necessary to be raised from such classes of the population, irrespective of color, in each State, as the proper authorities thereof may determine: *Provided,* that no more than twenty-five per cent of the male slaves between the ages of eighteen and forty-five, in any State, shall be called for under the provisions of this act.

Sec. 5. That nothing in this act shall be construed to authorize a change in the relation which the said slaves shall bear toward their owners, except by consent of the owners and of the States in which they may reside, and in pursuance of the laws thereof.

Approved March 13, 1865.

QUESTIONS TO CONSIDER

Begin by examining the evidence from the North. For each piece of evidence, answer the following questions:

1. Is the writer for or against using African Americans as soldiers?
2. What are the principal reasons for taking this position? (A piece of evidence may have more than one reason, as does Lincoln's September 13, 1862, reply to a delegation of Chicago Christians, Source 12.)

At this point, you will confront your first problem. Some pieces of evidence do not speak directly to the issue of enlisting African Americans as soldiers (two such examples are A. Davenport's letter and William Wells Brown's recollections, Sources 2 and 11, respectively). Yet are there implied reasons for or against arming African Americans? Included in these reasons may be unstated racial feelings (look again at Lincoln's September 13, 1862, remarks in Source 12), casualty figures (note when the casualties were suffered and consult the evidence for any shifts in the argument at that time), or political considerations.

The central figure in the decision of whether the United States should arm African Americans was Abraham Lincoln. In July 1862, Congress gave the president the authority to do so, yet Lincoln hesitated. How did members of Lincoln's cabinet attempt to influence his opinion in July–August 1862? What was Lincoln's reply?

President Lincoln's memorandum (Source 7), probably written after the July 22 cabinet meeting, appears to show a shift in his opinion. How does this compare with his remarks on August 4, 1862 (Source 9), and September 13, 1862? How would you explain this shift?

By January 1, 1863, the president had changed his public stance completely and was on record as favoring taking African Americans into the United States Army (Source 15). Because President Lincoln did not live to write his memoirs and kept no diary,

we are not sure what arguments or circumstances were responsible for the shift in his position. Yet a close examination of the evidence and some educated guesswork will allow you to come very close to the truth. Do Lincoln's letters to Hamlin and Schurz (Sources 13 and 14) provide any clues?

The remaining evidence from the North deals with northern reactions to Lincoln's decision (Sources 16 through 20). Was the decision a popular one in the army? Among private citizens? Can you detect a shift in northern white public opinion? Can you explain this shift?

Now repeat the same steps for the South (Sources 21 through 36). In what ways was the debate in the South similar to that in the North? In what ways was it different? Which reasons do you think were most influential in the Confederacy's change of mind about arming African Americans? How would you prove this?

⧌ EPILOGUE ⧍

Even after northern leaders adopted the policy that blacks would be recruited as soldiers in the Union army, many white northerners still doubted whether blacks would volunteer and, if they did, whether they would fight. Yet the evidence overwhelmingly demonstrates that African Americans rushed to the colors and were an effective part of the Union war effort. By the end of the Civil War, approximately 190,000 African American men had served in the United States army

and navy, a figure that represents roughly 10 percent of all the North's fighting men throughout the war. Former slaves who had come within the Union lines during the war made up the majority of African American soldiers, and Louisiana, Kentucky, and Tennessee contributed the most African American soldiers to the Union cause (approximately 37 percent of the total), probably because these states had been occupied the longest by Union troops.

CHAPTER 10

THE PRICE FOR
VICTORY: THE
DECISION TO
USE AFRICAN
AMERICAN
TROOPS

Although, as we have seen, Lincoln initially opposed the use of black soldiers, once he changed his mind, he pursued the new policy with vigor. Moreover, the president was determined to be fair to those African Americans who had volunteered to serve the Union. In an August 19, 1864, interview, Lincoln said, "There have been men who have proposed to me to return to slavery the black warriors . . . to their masters to conciliate the South. I should be damned in time & in eternity for so doing. The world shall know that I will keep my faith."[27]

Black soldiers were employed by the Union largely in noncombat roles (to garrison forts, protect supply dumps and wagons, load and unload equipment and supplies, guard prison camps, and so on). Nevertheless, a number of black regiments saw combat, participating in approximately four hundred engagements, including thirty-nine major battles. One of the most famous battles was the ill-fated assault on Fort Wagner (near Charleston, South Carolina), led by the 54th Massachusetts Infantry, the first black regiment recruited in the North. Almost half the regiment, including its commander, Colonel Robert Gould Shaw, was lost in the frontal attack, but the troops fought valiantly in the losing effort. The *Atlantic Monthly* reported, "Through the cannon smoke of that dark night, the manhood of the colored race shines before many eyes." Over a century later, the regiment was immortalized in the film *Glory*.[28]

27. Basler, ed., *The Collected Works of Abraham Lincoln,* Vol. VII, pp. 506–508.
28. The Confederates refused to return Shaw's body to his parents for burial, saying, "We have buried him with his niggers."

Overall, African American casualties were high: more than one-third of the African American soldiers were killed or wounded, although the majority of deaths, as with white soldiers, came from disease rather than battle wounds. The percentage of desertions among African Americans was lower than for the army as a whole. Moreover, twenty-one black soldiers and sailors were awarded the Congressional Medal of Honor, the nation's most distinguished award to military personnel.

Yet there is another side to the story of African American service in the Union army and navy. African American volunteers were rigidly segregated, serving in all-black regiments, usually under white officers. At first, black troops received less pay than their white counterparts. However, after many petitions and protests by African American soldiers, Congress at last established the principle of equal pay for African American soldiers in June 1864. Unfortunately, racial incidents within the Union army and navy were common.

Confederate reaction to the Union's recruitment of African American troops was predictably harsh. The Confederate government announced that any blacks taken as prisoners of war would be either shot on the spot or returned to slavery. In retaliation, Lincoln stated that he would order a Confederate prisoner of war executed for every African American prisoner shot by the South and would order a southern prisoner to do hard labor for every African American prisoner returned to slavery. Most Confederates treated black prisoners of war the same as they did whites. Nevertheless, in several instances, surrendering African Americans were murdered, the most notable instance occurring at Fort Pillow, Tennessee, where apparently several dozen African American prisoners of war and their white commander, Major William Bradford, were shot "while attempting to escape." After another engagement, one Confederate colonel bragged, "I then ordered every one shot, and with my Six Shooter I assisted in the execution of the order." Yet in spite of his warning, Lincoln did not retaliate, even though a United States Senate investigating committee charged that about three hundred African American Union soldiers had been murdered. The president probably felt that any action on his part would only further inflame the Confederates.

Within the Confederacy, the adoption of the policy to recruit African American soldiers came too late, the last gasp of a dying nation that had debated too long between principle and survival. In the month between the approval of the policy and the end of the war at Appomattox Court House, some black companies were organized, but there is no record that they ever saw action. For a conflict that had raged for four agonizingly long years, the end came relatively quickly.

The debate over the use of African American troops points out what many abolitionists had maintained for years: Although slavery was a moral concern that consumed all who touched it, the institution of slavery was but part of the problem facing black—and white—Americans. More insidious and less easily eradicated was racism, a set of assumptions, feelings, and emotions that has survived long after slavery was destroyed. The debate in both the North and the South over the use of African American troops clearly demonstrates that the true problem confronting many people of the Civil War era was their own feelings, anxieties, and fears.

CHAPTER 11

THE PROBLEMS OF RECONSTRUCTION: ANDREW JOHNSON, CONGRESS, AND SOUTHERN SUFFRAGE

∽ THE PROBLEM ∽

After four years of bloody warfare, the end came quickly. On April 2, 1865, General Ulysses Grant's Army of the Potomac crashed through Confederate lines at Petersburg, Virginia, leaving the Confederate capital, Richmond, vulnerable. Confederate president Jefferson Davis's government scattered, while General Robert E. Lee, commander of the Army of Northern Virginia, tried to escape westward. But Lee was stopped near Appomattox Court House and on April 9 surrendered to his adversary in a modest farmhouse.[1] After accepting Lee's surrender, Grant told his troops, "The war is over. The rebels are our countrymen again."[2]

And yet Grant's promises were not so easily kept. With the end of the fighting, the North had to decide how it would deal with the South. On what terms would the southern states be allowed to take up their proper places in the Union? How should former Confederates be treated? And, most important, who should be allowed to vote in setting up state governments and electing people to state and national offices?

Five days after Lee's surrender at Appomattox, President Abraham Lincoln was shot while attending the theater (he died at 7:22 A.M. the next day, on April 15). The new president,

1. Confederate general Joseph E. Johnston's troops were still in the field, but they surrendered to Union general William Tecumseh Sherman at Durham Station, North Carolina, on April 26.

2. Bruce Catton, *Grant Takes Command* (Boston: Little, Brown, 1969), p. 468.

Andrew Johnson of Tennessee, was faced with these crucially important questions. Earlier, he had said, "Treason must be made odious, and the traitors must be punished and impoverished," a sentence that he had used in many speeches, including his 1864 acceptance of the vice presidency.

Yet almost immediately after his assumption of the presidency, President Andrew Johnson changed course. At first appearing to side with Radical Republicans[3] in Congress, Johnson soon took a different path, granting numerous pardons to ex-Confederates (thus allowing them to reclaim their former property, hold office, and vote) and not supporting the right to vote for the freedmen. In his last public speech (April 11, 1865), Lincoln had endorsed a limited suffrage for African Americans, so Johnson could not claim to be merely following the policies of his predecessor.[4]

Your task in this chapter will not be an easy one. By examining and analyzing the evidence, determine why President Johnson chose the path he did with regard to who would vote in the postwar South. Why did he pardon so many former Confederates? Why did he oppose African American suffrage? Who should be allowed to vote in a free society, and who should determine the requirements for voting (residency, citizenship, property, literacy, etc.)? Most important, how would the United States secure its victory in the American Civil War?

❧ BACKGROUND ❧

From the outset of the Civil War, President Abraham Lincoln pursued a dual policy. On one hand, he attempted to crush the rebellion with armed might; on the other, he almost ceaselessly tried to get the South to give up its rebellion voluntarily and return to the Union.[5] Thus on September 22, 1862, he issued a Preliminary Emancipation Proclamation, promising that any southern states that gave up the struggle prior to January 1, 1863, would be allowed to take up their normal places in the Union with slavery intact. After that date, Lincoln warned, he would act to free the slaves in those states still in rebellion. It was an invitation that no Confederate state accepted. Thus, keeping his promise, Lincoln issued the Emanci-

3. The Radical Republicans were the left wing of the Republican party. They favored the abolition of slavery, a harsher policy against the defeated South, and full equality for African Americans.

4. On Lincoln's endorsement of limited African American suffrage, see Roy P. Basler, ed., *The Collected Works of Abraham Lincoln* (New Brunswick, N.J.: Rutgers University Press, 1953), Vol. VIII, pp. 399–405, esp. p. 403.

5. Lincoln continuously maintained that the southern states had not left the Union and had no right to secede, although he did admit that their normal relations with the rest of the states had been "suspended" or "disturbed"—hence the name "civil" war.

CHAPTER 11

THE PROBLEMS OF
RECONSTRUCTION:
ANDREW JOHNSON,
CONGRESS, AND
SOUTHERN
SUFFRAGE

pation Proclamation on January 1, 1863.[6]

In a similar vein, on December 8, 1863, President Lincoln issued his Proclamation of Amnesty and Reconstruction. In it he set forth the way in which a state could resume normal relations within the Union. A lenient plan, it offered full pardon and restoration of all rights ("except as to slaves") to all persons who took an oath of loyalty to the Union and promised to accept emancipation, the lone exceptions being high-ranking civil and military officers of the Confederate government. When 10 percent of the number of people who had cast votes in the state in 1860 had taken the oath, a new state government could be established and the state was permitted to take its regular place in the Union. Nothing was said about black suffrage.[7] In July 1864, Radical Republicans in Congress passed a considerably harsher plan (the Wade-Davis bill), but Lincoln pocket-vetoed it.

All of these proclamations as well as other efforts were wartime measures designed to sap the Confederacy of white support by offering the mildest of surrender, amnesty, and reconstruction terms. Since President Lincoln was trying to lure white southerners away from their loyalty to the Confederacy while at the same time pursuing the war vigorously on the field, one would have been surprised had his terms been more stringent.

What the president's plans actually were, especially with regard to who would be able to vote in the postwar South, will never be known, for he died less than a week after Lee's surrender. His last public speech nevertheless hinted that he was moving toward embracing limited African American suffrage.

Although they outdid each other in oratorical eulogies to the fallen president, secretly Radical Republicans were not altogether displeased by Lincoln's death. For one thing, Lincoln could be used as a martyr for their own cause, which included building a Republican party in the South by disfranchising pro-Confederate whites and instituting African American suffrage. Surely this was the reason they tried to concoct the notion that Lincoln's assassination had been part of a pro-southern plot, behind which were former Confederate president Jefferson Davis and other leading "rebels." More important, however, was the Radical Republicans' belief that Andrew Johnson would be more sympathetic to their cause, which included a thorough reconstruction of the southern economy, society, and life. After all, hadn't Johnson been a harsh military governor of Tennessee (1862–1864) and hadn't he said many times that treason "must be made odious, and the traitors must be punished and impoverished"?[8] Black abolitionist Frederick Douglass had said that slavery "is not abolished until the black man has the ballot," and the American

6. For the Preliminary Emancipation Proclamation, see Basler, *Lincoln Works,* Vol. V, pp. 433–436. For the Emancipation Proclamation, see ibid., Vol. VI, pp. 28–30.
7. For the Proclamation of Amnesty and Reconstruction, see ibid., Vol. VII, pp. 53–56.

8. Johnson had included this phrase in many of his speeches, including his acceptance of the Union party's vice-presidential nomination in 1864.

Anti-Slavery Society (with its new president, Wendell Phillips) took up the motto, "No Reconstruction Without Negro Suffrage."[9] Radical Republicans believed Johnson was more sympathetic to these entreaties than Lincoln had been.

And yet the Radical Republicans seriously misjudged President Andrew Johnson. Although many of his initial statements and speeches as president had given Radicals the impression that he supported a more thoroughgoing reconstruction of the South than Lincoln had (on the issue of African American suffrage, he told Radical Republican senator Charles Sumner that there was "no difference between us"),[10] by the end of May 1865, Radicals were increasingly alarmed that the president either had misled them or had changed his mind with regard to the reconstruction of the South.

Andrew Johnson was an exceedingly complex individual—virtually a bundle of contradictions. Born to a very poor family in Raleigh, North Carolina, in 1808 (his father was a janitor, and his mother worked as a servant in a local inn), young Andrew was bound out as an apprentice to learn the tailor's trade. Moving to Greeneville, Tennessee, in 1826, Johnson married the daughter of a shoemaker, became comparatively well off by speculating in real estate, and discovered a taste for politics. Elected as a Greeneville

alderman in 1829, he worked his way up the Democratic party political ladder: mayor, state representative, state senator, U.S. congressman, governor of Tennessee, and U.S. senator. His political power base was the white yeoman farmer, and for years he fought against Tennessee's planter aristocracy, which on one occasion he had called an "illegitimate, swaggering, bastard, scrub aristocracy."[11] Yet at the same time he defended the institution of slavery and in the 1840s delivered a speech in Congress in which he stated that the "black race of Africa were inferior to the white man in point of intellect—better calculated in physical structure to undergo drudgery and hardship."[12]

Johnson had harbored presidential ambitions as early as 1852. When the Democratic convention met in Charleston in 1860, he hoped that he would emerge as a compromise candidate and secure the party's nomination. The convention, however, broke up without nominating a candidate; delegates from the lower South walked out when a platform guaranteeing federal protection of slavery in the territories was rejected. When the convention reconvened in Baltimore, Johnson hoped he would secure the vice-presidential nomination behind Illinois senator Stephen Douglas, but he withdrew his name when that prospect appeared unlikely. During the 1860 campaign, Johnson supported

9. William Lloyd Garrison had resigned the presidency of the society at the end of the Civil War.

10. See Sumner to Wendell Phillips, May 1, 1865, in Beverly Wilson Palmer, ed., *The Selected Letters of Charles Sumner* (Boston: Northeastern University Press, 1990), Vol. II, p. 298.

11. See Hans L. Trefousse, *Andrew Johnson, A Biography* (New York: W. W. Norton, 1989), p. 64.

12. *Congressional Globe,* 28th Cong., 1st sess., 1843–1844, appendix 95–98.

CHAPTER 11

THE PROBLEMS OF
RECONSTRUCTION:
ANDREW JOHNSON,
CONGRESS, AND
SOUTHERN
SUFFRAGE

southern Democrat John C. Breckinridge.

When senators from the seceding states walked out of Congress in 1861, Johnson was the only southern senator who refused to leave; he continued to occupy a seat until Lincoln appointed him military governor of Tennessee on March 3, 1862. By late August 1863, he had reversed his position on emancipation, energetically aided in the recruitment of twenty thousand African American soldiers for the Union army, and later promised blacks, "I will indeed be your Moses, and lead you through the Red Sea of war and bondage to a fairer future of liberty and peace."[13] Thus, when Lincoln was looking for a "War Democrat" to balance the Union party's ticket in 1864 (to replace Vice President Hannibal Hamlin, who wanted to return to the Senate), his eyes almost naturally fell on Andrew Johnson.[14]

As noted earlier, Andrew Johnson was a bundle of contradictions. A man who never joined any religious denomination and was referred to by some of his enemies as an "infidel," in 1855 he defended Roman Catholics against the Know-Nothings and in 1858 opposed the use of federal troops against the Mormons in Utah. An opponent of government spending, he tried to get the federal government to take over and maintain the Hermitage, Andrew Jackson's home. A defender of slavery (until mid-1863), he opposed, at the same time, the Constitution's three-fifths clause.[15] A man who made a large amount of money in real estate, he pioneered a bill that would have given federal land to prospective farmers decades before its ultimate passage (the Homestead Act of 1862). It is little wonder that Radical Republicans had misgauged the new president. Not only was Johnson a wily politician who often told people what they wanted to hear, but he also was as erratic, unpredictable, and inconsistent as almost any other political figure in modern American history.

Your task in this chapter will be to explain the behavior of this immensely complex man with regard to suffrage in the postwar South. If Johnson had made a political career battling against the South's plantation aristocracy and had fought so viciously against the Confederacy, why did he pardon so many former rebels, thus allowing them to vote and hold office? Of the approximately fifteen thousand white southerners who applied for pardons, over seven thousand had been granted by 1866. If Johnson had promised to be a "Moses" to African Americans and had told Massachusetts senator Charles Sumner that "there is no difference between us," why did he not press the states of the former Confederacy—or even states in the North—to approve suffrage for blacks? Who should be allowed to vote in a free society? Who should set voting requirements? How would the United States secure its victory in the American Civil War?

13. For Johnson's 1864 "Moses" speech, see LeRoy P. Graf, ed., *The Papers of Andrew Johnson* (Knoxville: University of Tennessee Press, 1986), Vol. VII, pp. 251–253.
14. For the 1864 election, the Republicans renamed themselves the Union party.

15. See U.S. Constitution, Article I, Section 3.

❧ THE METHOD ❧

Unlike other presidents (James K. Polk, for example), Andrew Johnson did not keep a diary, nor did he write many letters to his friends.[16] Therefore, we have no private letters that can answer the question of Johnson's motivation. Thus, we will have to infer, from Johnson's speeches, interviews, and letters to him, what caused him to take the path that he did.

Begin by reviewing the situation when Johnson became president on April 15, 1865. Union armies occupied parts of the South; principal Confederate officeholders and military leaders were being rounded up and imprisoned; African Americans had been freed and in many cases were abandoning the plantations and heading for southern cities and towns in search of employment. Southern cities like Petersburg, Richmond, Atlanta, and Columbia had been totally or partially destroyed, and the vast majority of white southerners agreed with Georgian Herschel V. Walker when he wrote that the "people are soul-sick and heartily tired of the hateful, hopeless strife" and wanted only to resume their former lives in peace. Indeed, the South was crushed and prostrate; it would have to accept almost any plan for its reconstruction that the federal government demanded.

16. For example, the Thomas Jefferson papers (being published by Princeton University), when finished, may exceed seventy-five volumes. Johnson's papers (published by the University of Tennessee Press) will be completed in sixteen to seventeen volumes. And in Volume VIII of the *Johnson Papers* (which covers May–August 1865), of the 815 items, only 87 are by Johnson, the rest being letters, memorials, petitions, and other items to him.

Recall also, however, that Johnson was a Democrat who was now at the head of a Republican administration. Did his political future lie with the Republicans or the Democrats? Too, Republicans must have realized that a quick restoration of the South (whose white voters were mostly Democrats) to its normal place in the Union could jeopardize their own political position. Could enfranchised blacks provide the foundation of a Republican party in the South? In addition, it was still not clear that Lincoln's assassination had not been part of a massive southern conspiracy. Would northerners want the South to "pay" for Lincoln's death?

Finally, Congress was not in session when Lincoln was assassinated and would not convene in regular session until December 1865. If Johnson wanted to restore all the southern states to their proper places in the Union and if he knew that his own terms were dramatically different from those of Congress, then he would have to hurry. Believing, as did Lincoln, that the president had the authority to do this (under Article IV, Section 4 of the Constitution, guaranteeing each state a republican form of government), Johnson had no time to waste. State governments would have to be reorganized, new state constitutions written, requirements for voting decided on, and state and federal elections held using those suffrage requirements.

As you examine each piece of evidence, make a note of what that piece might be telling you about why Johnson chose to adopt a lenient pol-

CHAPTER 11

THE PROBLEMS OF
RECONSTRUCTION:
ANDREW JOHNSON,
CONGRESS, AND
SOUTHERN
SUFFRAGE

icy of reconstruction—pardoning numerous former Confederates and not insisting (when he certainly had the opportunity) that southern states enfranchise the freedmen. Very few pieces of evidence explicitly state a possible motivation that would explain Johnson's actions. Instead, you will have to use your historical imagination to infer what that motivation might have been.

Very quickly you will see that the evidence points you in many different directions, offering the possibility of not one single motive but several. Use your knowledge of Johnson's background, the man himself, and the situation he faced to conclude which motive was the *most likely,* the most plausible. Determining why certain individuals in the past behaved in the ways they did is the most difficult and hazardous task that historians do. And yet it is something they must do nearly every day in order to make the past understandable to themselves and to others.

In the evidence, spelling and punctuation have been left unaltered from the original text.

ᘓ THE EVIDENCE ᘓ

Sources 1–7 and 9–14 from Paul H. Bergeron, ed., *The Papers of Andrew Johnson* (Knoxville: University of Tennessee Press, 1989–1992), Vol. VIII, pp. 62–63, 119, 129–130, 136–137, 188, 282, 289–290, 365, 378, 516–523, 599–600; Vol. IX, pp. 179–180; Vol. X, pp. 43–47.

1. Johnson's Reply to a Delegation of African American Clergymen, May 11, 1865.

I was the first that stood in a slave community and announced the great fact that the slaves of Tennessee were free upon the same principle as those were who assumed to own them.

I know it is easy to talk and proclaim sentiments upon paper, but it is one thing to have theories and another to reduce them to practice; and I must say here, what I have no doubt is permanently fixed in your minds, and the impression deep, that there is one thing you ought to teach, and they should understand, that in a transition state, passing from bond to free, when the tyrant's rod has been bent and the yoke broken, we find too many—it is best to talk plain—there are, I say, too many in this transition state, passing from bondage to freedom, who feel as if they should have nothing to do, and fall back upon the Government for support; too many incline to become loafers and depend upon the Government to take care of them. They seem to think that with freedom every thing they need is to come like manna from heaven.

Now, I want to impress this upon your minds, that freedom simply means liberty to work and enjoy the product of your own hands. This is the correct definition of freedom, in the most extensive sense of the term. . . .

[*Johnson then told the ministers that they must quickly perform marriage ceremonies for ex-slaves who had not been formally married.*]

It is not necessary for me to give you any assurance of what my future course will be in reference to your condition. Now, when the ordeal is passed, there can be no reason to think that I shall turn back in the great cause in which I have sacrificed much, and perilled all.

I can give you no assurance worth more than my course heretofore, and I shall continue to do all that I can for the elevation and amelioration of your condition; and I trust in God the time may soon come when you shall be gathered together, in a clime and country suited to you, should it be found that the two races cannot get along together.

I trust God will continue to conduct us till the great end shall be accomplished, and the work reach its great consummation. . . .

2. Joseph Noxon[17] to Johnson, May 27, 1865.

Andrew Johnson Prest.

You say you believe in democratic government, or *consent* of loyal people. Yet you *dare not* avow with practical effect the right of the colord man to vote. Are you honest?

You profess to protect loyal men & to punish traitors; yet you *refuse* the franchise to loyal colord people, the *only* means effectual for their protection or advancement. Are you honest?

You know rebels disappointed will wreak revenge on loyal blacks, & yet you refuse the franchise for their protection.

You say you have no right to grant it. You know in the first elections to be held to reorganize a seceded state *you* have the *power*, the *right*, & the *duty* to say who shall vote. Otherwise rebels will re-elect rebels, as witness Virginia.

You know by *prompt* & vigorous action *now*, the question of negro suffrage can be *settled* & *accepted* by the people as an *accomplished fact*. Why not settle it & take it *out* of political controversy.

17. Joseph Noxon was a Tennessee Unionist who was driven out of the state by Confederates for being a scout for the Union army. He was an ally of Johnson.

CHAPTER 11

THE PROBLEMS OF
RECONSTRUCTION:
ANDREW JOHNSON,
CONGRESS, AND
SOUTHERN
SUFFRAGE

Do you believe the *loyal* Union party's success essential to the peace & prosperity of this country? Then dont refuse 850,000 *loyal votes* that are *always sure* for liberty & the Republic.

3. Amnesty Proclamation, May 29, 1865.

To the end, therefore, that the authority of the government of the United States may be restored, and that peace, order, and freedom may be established, I, ANDREW JOHNSON, President of the United States, do proclaim and declare that I hereby grant to all persons who have, directly or indirectly, participated in the existing rebellion, except as hereinafter excepted, amnesty and pardon, with restoration of all rights of property, except as to slaves, and except in cases where legal proceedings, under the laws of the United States providing for the confiscation of property of persons engaged in rebellion, have been instituted; but upon the condition, nevertheless, that every such person shall take and subscribe the following oath, (or affirmation,) and thenceforward keep and maintain said oath inviolate; and which oath shall be registered for permanent preservation, and shall be of the tenor and effect following, to wit:

I, _____ _____, do solemnly swear, (or affirm,) in presence of Almighty God, that I will henceforth faithfully support, protect, and defend the Constitution of the United States, and the union of the States thereunder; and that I will, in like manner, abide by, and faithfully support all laws and proclamations which have been made during the existing rebellion with reference to the emancipation of slaves. So help me God.

The following classes of persons are excepted from the benefits of this proclamation: 1st, all who are or shall have been pretended civil or diplomatic officers or otherwise domestic or foreign agents of the pretended Confederate government; 2d, all who left judicial stations under the United States to aid the rebellion; 3d, all who shall have been military or naval officers of said pretended Confederate government above the rank of colonel in the army or lieutenant in the navy; 4th, all who left seats in the Congress of the United States to aid the rebellion; 5th, all who resigned or tendered resignations of their commissions in the army or navy of the United States to evade duty in resisting the rebellion; 6th, all who have engaged in any way in treating otherwise than lawfully as prisoners of war persons found in the United States service, as officers, soldiers, seamen, or in other capacities; 7th, all persons who have been, or are absentees from the United States for the purpose of aiding the rebellion; 8th, all military and naval officers in the rebel service, who were educated by the government in the Military Academy at West Point or the United States Naval Academy; 9th, all persons who held the pretended offices of governors of States in insurrection against the United States; 10th, all persons who left their homes within the jurisdiction and protection of the United States, and passed beyond the Federal military lines into the pretended Confederate States for the purpose of aiding the rebellion; 11th, all persons who have been engaged in the destruction of the commerce of the United States upon the high seas, and all persons who have made raids into the United States from Canada, or been engaged in destroying the commerce of the United States upon the lakes and rivers that separate the British Provinces from the United States; 12th, all persons who, at the time when they seek to obtain the benefits hereof by taking the oath herein prescribed, are in military, naval, or civil confinement, or custody, or under bonds of the civil, military, or naval authorities, or agents of the United States as prisoners of war, or persons detained for offences of any kind, either before or after conviction; 13th, all persons who have voluntarily participated in said rebellion, and the estimated value of whose taxable property is over twenty thousand dollars; 14th, all persons who have taken the oath of amnesty as prescribed in the President's proclamation of December 8th, A.D. 1863, or an oath of allegiance to the government of the United States since the date of said proclamation, and who have not thenceforward kept and maintained the same inviolate. . . .

4. Proclamation Establishing Government for North Carolina, May 29, 1865.

Whereas the 4th section of the 4th article of the Constitution of the United States declares that the United States shall guarantee to every State in the Union a republican form of government, and shall protect each of them against invasion and domestic violence; and whereas the President of the United States is, by the Constitution, made Commander-in-chief of the army and navy, as well as chief civil executive officer of the United States, and is bound by solemn oath faithfully to execute the office of President of the United States, and to take care that the laws be faithfully executed; and whereas the rebellion, which has been waged by a portion of the people

CHAPTER 11

THE PROBLEMS OF
RECONSTRUCTION:
ANDREW JOHNSON,
CONGRESS, AND
SOUTHERN
SUFFRAGE

of the United States against the properly constituted authorities of the government thereof, in the most violent and revolting form, but whose organized and armed forces have now been almost entirely overcome, has, in its revolutionary progress, deprived the people of the State of North Carolina of all civil government; and whereas it becomes necessary and proper to carry out and enforce the obligations of the United States to the people of North Carolina, in securing them in the enjoyment of a republican form of government:

Now, THEREFORE, in obedience to the high and solemn duties imposed upon me by the Constitution of the United States, and for the purpose of enabling the loyal people of said State to organize a State government, whereby justice may be established, domestic tranquillity insured, and loyal citizens protected in all their rights of life, liberty, and property, I, ANDREW JOHNSON, President of the United States, and commander-in-chief of the army and navy of the United States, do hereby appoint WILLIAM W. HOLDEN provisional governor of the State of North Carolina, whose duty it shall be, at the earliest practicable period, to prescribe such rules and regulations as may be necessary and proper for convening a convention, composed of delegates to be chosen by that portion of the people of said State who are loyal to the United States, and no others, for the purpose of altering or amending the constitution thereof; and with authority to exercise, within the limits of said State, all the powers necessary and proper to enable such loyal people of the State of North Carolina to restore said State to its constitutional relations to the Federal government, and to present such a republican form of State government as will entitle the State to the guarantee of the United States therefor, and its people to protection by the United States against invasion, insurrection, and domestic violence; *provided* that, in any election that may be hereafter held for choosing delegates to any State convention as aforesaid, no person shall be qualified as an elector, or shall be eligible as a member of such convention, unless he shall have previously taken and subscribed the oath of amnesty, as set forth in the President's proclamation of May 29, A.D. 1865, and is a voter qualified as prescribed by the constitution and laws of the State of North Carolina in force immediately before the 20th day of May, A.D. 1861, the date of the so-called ordinance of secession; and the said convention, when convened, or the legislature that may be thereafter assembled, will prescribe the qualification of electors, and the eligibility of persons to hold office under the constitution and laws of the State, a power the people of the several States composing the Federal Union have rightfully exercised from the origin of the government to the present time. . . .

5. James B. Bingham to Johnson, June 6, 1865.

Memphis, Tenn., June 6, 1865.

Dear Governor:[18]

I have only time to congratulate you. Thus far every thing goes right. Your amnesty gives satisfaction to all fair-minded men, and you have struck the true keynote on reconstruction. Your position on the question of negro suffrage is impregnable. It belongs, under the constitution to the States. Wendell Phillips, Greeley & Chase[19] will kick against that in vain. The country will sustain you. I find a great re-action going on in your favor. Fellows who used to curse and damn you begin now to talk sweet about you, and to do you justice. Lincoln never was as popular with Tennesseeans as you are to-day; and I believe what is true of Tennesseeans is equally so of the people of the loyal States.

6. Interview with a Delegation of South Carolina Former Confederates, June 24, 1865.

. . . I will again say to you that slavery is gone. Its status is changed. There is no hope you can entertain of being admitted to representation either in the Senate or House of Representatives till you give evidence that you, too, have accepted and recognized that that institution is gone. That done, the policy adopted is not to restore the supremacy of the Government at the point of the bayonet, but by the action of the people. While this rebellion has emancipated a great many negroes, it has emancipated still more white men. The negro in South Carolina that belonged to a man that owned from one to five hundred slaves, thought himself better than the white man who owned none. He felt the white man's superior. I know the position of the poor white man in the South, compelled to till the barren, sandy, and—poor soil for a subsistence. You cannot deny how he was, in your eyes, of less value than the negro. Some here in the North think they can control and exercise a greater influence over the negro than you can, though his future must materially depend on you. Let us speak plainly on this subject. I, too

18. Bingham, a fellow Tennessean, was addressing Johnson as the former governor of Tennessee.
19. Phillips was the president of the American Anti-Slavery Society, Horace Greeley was the editor of the *New York Tribune* and a noted abolitionist, and Salmon P. Chase was chief justice of the United States and a prominent Radical Republican.

CHAPTER 11

THE PROBLEMS OF
RECONSTRUCTION:
ANDREW JOHNSON,
CONGRESS, AND
SOUTHERN
SUFFRAGE

am a Southern man, have owned slaves, bought slaves, but never sold one. You and I understand this better; we know our friends are mistaken, [here the President rose up and continued emphatically,] and I tell you that I don't want you to have the control of these negro votes against the vote of this poor white man. I repeat our friends here are mistaken, as you and I know as to where the control of negro vote would fall. When they come to talk about the elective franchise, I say let each State judge for itself. I am for free government; for emancipation; and am for emancipating the white man as well as the black man. . . .

7. Duff Green to Johnson, June 25, 1865.[20]

Confidential
To His Ex Andrew Johnson
President U States

You are now in a Situation Calling for the Sympathy and Support of your friends, for no one in your position, with a proper regard for his reputation, can be indifferent to the opinion of his Country men and that opinion will be indicated by the Election in 1868.

That extraordinary efforts will be made to organise an unscrupulous opposition to your administration and to your Election in 1868 you cannot doubt. That Chase or Sherman[21] or both will be opposing Candidates is clearly indicated, and that the vote of the South will control the Election in your favor, if you act wisely is to me now manifest.

The democracy of the north look to the South to reinstate them in power. If you identify yourself with the ultra abolitionists, in thier [sic] warfare on the South, then the democracy will rally on Sherman, and, aided as he will be by his brother's influence in Ohio, he will carry the conservative Whigs and organise the North West & the South against New England. If you so act, towards the South, as to command thier [sic] Confidence and Support you will carry the democratic party and unite the North West & the South in your support and Secure an overwhelming majority.

Do you ask what the South want? They desire to be reinstated as loyal, patriotic members of the Union. They want your proclamation restoring

20. Duff Green (1791–1875) was a journalist, businessman, and politician. He was a member of Andrew Jackson's Kitchen Cabinet, continued to be influential throughout the antebellum period, and supported the Confederacy during the Civil War.
21. Chief Justice Salmon Chase and General William Tecumseh Sherman, both rumored to have been presidential aspirants.

the people of the South to thier [*sic*] rights as loyal citizens and to thier [*sic*] rights of property.

Let the fourth day of July be a day of Jubilee. Throw wide open the prison doors. Send home the Captives to thier [*sic*] anxious friends at the public expense. Recal the Exiles and rest assured that there will be one unanimous loyal grateful response throughout the South and that no one can compete with you for thier [*sic*] confidence or Support. I would make no exceptions among those who are guilty of political offences only. No not one. But if exceptions are made they should be few. I would be glad to see and converse with you but will not obtrude.

Your Sincere freind [*sic*] Duff Green

Source 8 from Beverly Wilson Palmer, ed., *The Selected Letters of Charles Sumner* (Boston: Northeastern University Press, 1990), Vol. II, pp. 312–313.

8. Charles Sumner[22] to Salmon P. Chase,[23] July 1, 1865.

There is madness in the Presdt.—His policy is already dividing the party & drawing the praises of the copperheads. Of course, if he perseveres he will become the temporary head of the latter, to be cast aside at the proper moment.

The people were ready to accept the true principle. Never before were they so ready. Business-men see how clearly their welfare is associated with its establishment.

The Blairs have triumphed.[24] I see their influence, not only here but in other things. When I left Washington Mr Johnson had assured me that on this question "there was no difference between us."

He has appointed Carl Schurtz [Schurz][25] to visit the rebel states & report on the reconstruction policy & has said that, if the present policy did not work well, he was ready to change it. Alas! that the country should be subjected to this uncertainty, where from the beginning our rulers ought to have been clear & positive.

22. Charles Sumner (1811–1874) was a U.S. senator from Massachusetts and a leader of the Radical Republicans in the Senate.
23. Salmon P. Chase (1808–1873) was chief justice of the United States and a Radical Republican.
24. Francis Preston Blair and his son Montgomery Blair, of Maryland, were political intimates of Johnson who believed that southern whites should decide who should vote in the southern states. See Source 14 on page 23.
25. Carl Schurz (1829–1906) was a Union veteran, a journalist, and an advocate of enfranchisement for blacks.

CHAPTER 11

THE PROBLEMS OF
RECONSTRUCTION:
ANDREW JOHNSON,
CONGRESS, AND
SOUTHERN
SUFFRAGE

9. Thaddeus Stevens to Johnson, July 6, 1865.[26]

His Excellency Andrew Johnson
Sir

I am sure you will pardon me for speaking to you with a candor to which men in high places are seldom accustomed. Among all the leading Union men of the North with whom I have had intercourse I do not find one who approves of your policy. They believe that "restoration" as announced by you will destroy our party (which is of but little consequence) and will greatly injure the country. Can you not hold your hand and wait the action of Congress and in the mean time govern them by military rulers? Profuse pardoning also will greatly embarrass Congress if they should wish to make the enemy pay the expenses of the war or a part of it.

10. Francis Preston Blair[27] to Johnson, August 1, 1865.

The rebellion is crushed and with it the Slavery that animated it, but like the Hydra it puts out new heads—from the vines of the old trunk. It sprouts out with the bold front of negro equality. Negro suffrage shouts out on one side with a political aspect and on the other we have the social aspect to emerge in the shape of amalgamation. What can come of this adulturation of our Anglo-Saxon race and Anglo-Saxon Government by Africanization, but the degradation of the free spirit & lofty aspirations which our race inherited from their ancestry and brought to this continent; and turn that whole portion of it engaged as manual Operatives into that class of mongrels which cannot but spring from the unnatural blending of the blacks & whites in one common class of laborers and giving to both an assimilation through that color, which has unhappily marked servitude during all generations from the days of Ham.[28] The result would inevitably be to make a distinction in caste and put a brand on all our race associated in employment with people of color & crisped hair. It would not create equality between those thus associated and those engaged in professional & political

26. Thaddeus Stevens (1792–1868) was a U.S. senator from Pennsylvania and one of the leading Radical Republicans.
27. Francis Preston Blair (1821–1875), a native of Kentucky, was an opponent of slavery, a brigadier general in the Union army, and was opposed to the enfranchisement of the freedmen.
28. A reference to the commonly held belief at the time that Ham, the disgraced and banished son of Noah, was the father of the Negro race. See Genesis 9:21–25.

pursuits. It would hasten the creation of a lower order—a serfdom—a foundation for an Aristocracy crowned with Royalty. . . .

The idea that suffrage will produce equality between the two races at the South is illusory. The black freedmen will find the prejudices of caste increased among the mass of white laborers by the new priviledge. They will become competitors with the superior race in that which touches their pride and it will be found more than was necessary to get under the wing of the master who hires them, for protection. They will be obliged to have white leaders at the polls as they had in the camps of both armies & those who hire them will control their ballot more absolutely than has ever been done by persons occupying similar relations because their safety will depend upon their employers in the exercise of their priviledge in the service of an increased prejudice & more powerful caste. It is absurd to suppose that the rich, educated, intelligent men will not command the suffrages of their negro hirelings if they venture to bring them to the polls to assert equality with the whites. . . .

The result of the contact of races marked by nature to be distinct has induced all the great statesmen of our country to look to colonization & segregation as the means of saving the colored race & giving to them a Government of their own & with it the equality and independence they desire & deserve. The party who oppose this scheme, (yours as well as your predecessors), have no expectation of maintaining equality for the emancipated by suffrage. They assert it for them, some with a view to drive the whites from the Gulf States—others with the design of keeping those States out of the Union. To vote their members of congress out because those States refuse to obey the behests of other States as to the regulation of the right of suffrage, committed to them by the constitution, is to vote a dissolution of the Union—a subversion of the constitution. The pretense of establishing negro equality in a country which is compelled by the fist of the central Government to submit its suffrage to its control, makes the idea of equality with the arbitrary power asserting this superiority, absolutely absurd. If the Representatives of a state in one section are expelled because it does not surrender its constitutional rights, may not a state in another section be expelled because it will not surrender some of its rights at the dictation of a majority in congress? Why not expell the representatives from California & Oregon for refusing the suffrage to the Chinese & the whole group of the North eastern States for refusing it to free negroes? This movement against the south has its motive in the ambition which prompted Mr. Chase to say at the beginning of the rebellion, "Let the Seceding States go, they are not worth fighting for." . . .

CHAPTER 11

THE PROBLEMS OF
RECONSTRUCTION:
ANDREW JOHNSON,
CONGRESS, AND
SOUTHERN
SUFFRAGE

The motions of the coming elections are felt already in the great States of New York Ohio & Pennsylvania. The Democracy which gave such immense votes against Lincoln during a war that commanded even their approval at heart, are now in favor of all the objects you design to accomplish by it. You indeed make it their war by the consequences you bring from it, and those men who now seek to pervert those consequences into a defeat of the restoration of the Union, with equality among the States, deserve to forfeit the favor they gained by giving the war their countenance. The Democrats will nominate candidates pledged to support all your leading policy. Their opponents are already out in Massachusetts and other states with manifestos not only at war with your avowed policy but abhorent to the constitution & tending to make Congress a revolutionary club—a convention of northern representatives bent on subjecting the south to their will and using negro enfranchisement as the means of the disfranchisement of our white brethren of that section, of their equality as citizens and states in the Union. . . .

This is your mission at this moment on entering the new Era of our history and let me entreat you to open the process of the new elections and of the creation of new parties in the approaching Congress with a new Cabinet strongly imbued with your opinions, entirely worthy of your confidence and of a caste calculated to win the confidence of men of all parties, who are willing to embrace the scheme of restoration to which you commit your administration in the nomination of the heads of its Departments.

The Democracy, I learn, north and South will make its nominations for National & State Representatives & for other functionaries of men of the type to which I have Just referred. The Republicans will be divided in their nominations, a portion going for the scheme of the Faneuil Hall manifesto derived from the movement which took the shape of the bill passed & presented to the President at the last congress to defeat his plan of re-Union.[29] If you declare your design to the nation by the creation of a new cabinet to express & to execute it distinctly & patently, the party opposed to it who would go to the people & come into congress as the friends of the administration, but really to defeat its policy, will I believe be reduced to a faction. But if you allow them to proceed under the shadow of a great party name, & under prestige already acquired by them of swaying the Cabinet they will command in Congress as at the last session & through it may

29. On June 21, 1865, Republicans met at Faneuil Hall in Boston and endorsed African American suffrage.

command the country unless overthrown by the Democracy which will take a stand against it and the Rump Cabinet. . . .

If however you were at once to make a new Cabinet drawn from the different sections of the country and representing the various parties in it, yet agreeing to support your plan of reconstruction, on an issue so essential, it would be no matter what party organization returned members, men who gave in this adhesion would become identified with the administration. Their election would be your success and in this epoch of reconstruction would create a new party, embracing the whole Union, adverse to that of Faneuil Hall limited to a northern latitude and exulting in a revolutionary creed. . . .

The vote of the south will be drawn almost as an unit to the side of that party which it finds in opposition to a ministry known to be hostile to its dearest rights in the Union & confederated with the scheme promulgated at Faneuil Hall, which would deprive its *States* of equality *as States,* would create a war of caste & a war of Sections a war of factions breaking up the ancient foundations of the constitution. . . .

11. Johnson to Mississippi Provisional Governor William L. Sharkey, August 15, 1865.

Governor William L. Sharkey,
Jackson, Miss.

I am gratified to see that you have organized your Convention without difficulty. I hope that without delay your Convention will amend your State Constitution abolishing slavery, and denying to all future legislatures the power to legislate that there is property in man—Also that they will adopt the Amendment to the Constitution of the United States abolishing slavery.

If you could extend the elective franchise to all persons of color who can read the constitution of the United States in English and write their names, and to all persons of color who own real estate valued at not less than two-hundred and fifty dollars and pay taxes thereon, you would completely disarm the adversary and set an example the other States will follow.

This you can do with perfect safety, and you thus place the Southern States, in reference to free persons of color, upon the same basis with the Free States. I hope and trust your convention will do this, and as a consequence the Radicals, who are wild upon negro franchise, will be completely

CHAPTER 11

THE PROBLEMS OF
RECONSTRUCTION:
ANDREW JOHNSON,
CONGRESS, AND
SOUTHERN
SUFFRAGE

foiled in their attempts to keep the Southern States from renewing their relations to the Union by not accepting their Senators and Representatives.

12. Johnson's Interview with George L. Stearns, October 3, 1865.

[Johnson]: We must not be in too much of a hurry; it is better to let them [white southerners] reconstruct themselves than to force them to it; for if they go wrong, the power is in our hands and we can check them at any stage, to the end, and oblige them to correct their errors; we must be patient with them. I did not expect to keep out all who were excluded from the amnesty, or even a large number of them, but I intended they should sue for pardon, and so realize the enormity of the crime they had committed.

You could not have broached the subject of equal suffrage, at the North, seven years ago, and we must remember that the changes at the South have been more rapid, and they have been obliged to accept more unpalatable truth than the North has; we must give them time to digest a part, for we cannot expect such large affairs will be comprehended and digested at once. We must give them time to understand their new position.

I have nothing to conceal in these matters, and have no desire or willingness to take indirect courses to obtain what we want.

Our government is a grand and lofty structure; in searching for its foundation we find it rests on the broad basis of popular rights. The elective franchise is not a natural right, but a political right. I am opposed to giving the States too much power, and also to a great consolidation of power in the central government.

If I interfered with the vote in the rebel States, to dictate that the negro shall vote, I might do the same thing for my own purposes in Pennsylvania. Our only safety lies in allowing each State to control the right of voting by its own laws, and we have the power to control the rebel States if they go wrong. If they rebel we have the army, and can control them by it, and, if necessary by legislation also. If the General Government controls the right to vote in the States, it may establish such rules as will restrict the vote to a small number of persons, and thus create a central despotism.

My position here is different from what it would be if I was in Tennessee.

There I should try to introduce negro suffrage gradually; first those who had served in the army; those who could read and write, and perhaps a property qualification for others, say $200 or $250.

It will not do to let the negroes have universal suffrage now. It would breed a war of races.

There was a time in the Southern States when the slaves of large owners looked down upon non-slaveowners because they did not own slaves; the larger the number of slaves their masters owned, the prouder they were, and this has produced hostility between the mass of the whites and the negroes. The outrages are mostly from non-slaveholding whites against the negro, and from the negro upon the non-slaveholding whites.

The negro will vote with the late master whom he does not hate, rather than with the non-slaveholding white, whom he does hate. Universal suffrage would create another war, not against us, but a war of races. . . .

13. Johnson's Interview with an African American Delegation, February 7, 1866.

[THE PRESIDENT.] Now, it is always best to talk about things practically and in a common sense way. Yes, I have said, and I repeat here, that if the colored man in the United States could find no other Moses, or any Moses that would be more able and efficient than myself, I would be his Moses to lead him from bondage to freedom; that I would pass him from a land where he had lived in slavery to a land (if it were in our reach) of freedom. Yes, I would be willing to pass with him through the Red sea to the Land of Promise—to the land of liberty; but I am not willing, under either circumstance, to adopt a policy which I believe will only result in the sacrifice of his life and the shedding of his blood. I think I know what I say. I feel what I say; and I feel well assured that if the policy urged by some be persisted in, it will result in great injury to the white as well as to the colored man. There is a great deal of talk about the sword in one hand accomplishing an end, and the ballot accomplishing another at the ballot-box.

These things all do very well, and sometimes have forcible application. We talk about justice; we talk about right; we say that the white man has been in the wrong in keeping the black man in slavery as long as he has. That is all true. Again, we talk about the Declaration of Independence and equality before the law. You understand all that, and know how to appreciate it. But, now, let us look each other in the face; let us go to the great mass of colored men throughout the slave States; let us take the condition in which they are at the present time—and it is bad enough, we all know—and suppose, by some magic touch you could say to every one, "You shall vote to-morrow," how much would that ameliorate their condition at this time? . . .

CHAPTER 11

THE PROBLEMS OF
RECONSTRUCTION:
ANDREW JOHNSON,
CONGRESS, AND
SOUTHERN
SUFFRAGE

[Here Johnson stated that, in his opinion, the former slave looked down on the nonslaveholding whites and identified more closely with his former master. Frederick Douglass (1817?–1895), an important African American abolitionist editor and speaker and a member of the delegation, disagreed with Johnson. Johnson continued his statement.]

Now, we are talking about where we are going to begin. We have got at the hate that existed between the two races. The query comes up whether these two races, situated as they were before, without preparation, without time for passion and excitement to be appeased, and without time for the slightest improvement, whether the one should be turned loose upon the other, and be thrown together at the ballot-box with this enmity and hate existing between them. The query comes up right there, whether we don't commence a war of races. I think I understand this thing, and especially is this the case when you force it upon a people without their consent.

You have spoken about government. Where is power derived from? We say it is derived from the people. Let us take it so and refer to the District of Columbia by way of illustration. Suppose, for instance, here, in this political community, which, to a certain extent must have government, must have laws, and putting it now upon the broadest basis you can put it—take into consideration the relation which the white has heretofore borne to the colored race—is it proper to force upon this community, without their consent, the elective franchise, without regard to color, making it universal?

Now, where do you begin? Government must have a controlling power; must have a lodgment. For instance, suppose Congress should pass a law authorizing an election to be held at which all over twenty-one years of age, without regard to color, should be allowed to vote, and a majority should decide at such election that the elective franchise should not be universal; what would you do about it? Who would settle it? Do you deny that first great principle of the right of the people to govern themselves? Will you resort to an arbitrary power, and say a majority of the people shall receive a state of things they are opposed to? . . .

Each community is better prepared to determine the depository of its political power than anybody else, and it is for the Legislature, for the people of Ohio to say who shall vote, and not for the Congress of the United States. I might go down here to the ballot-box to-morrow and vote directly for universal suffrage; but if a great majority of the people said no, I should consider it would be tyrannical in me to attempt to force such upon them without their will. It is a fundamental tenet in my creed that the will of the people must be obeyed. Is there anything wrong or unfair in that?

MR. DOUGLASS (smiling). A great deal that is wrong, Mr. President, with all respect.

THE PRESIDENT. It is the people of the States that must for themselves determine this thing. I do not want to be engaged in a work that will commence a war of races. I want to begin the work of preparation, and the States, or the people in each community, if a man demeans himself well, and shows evidence that this new state of affairs will operate, will protect him in all his rights, and give him every possible advantage when they become reconciled socially and politically to this state of things. Then will this new order of things work harmoniously; but forced upon the people before they are prepared for it, it will be resisted, and work inharmoniously. I feel a conviction that driving this matter upon the people, upon the community, will result in the injury of both races, and the ruin of one or the other. God knows I have no desire but the good of the whole human race. I would it were so that all you advocate could be done in the twinkling of an eye; but it is not in the nature of things, and I do not assume or pretend to be wiser than Providence, or stronger than the laws of nature.

Let us now seek to discover the laws governing this thing. There is a great law controlling it; let us endeavor to find out what that law is, and conform our actions to it. All the details will then properly adjust themselves and work out well in the end.

God knows that anything I can do I will do. In the mighty process by which the great end is to be reached, anything I can do to elevate the races, to soften and ameliorate their condition I will do, and to be able to do so is the sincere desire of my heart.

I am glad to have met you, and thank you for the compliment you have paid me.

MR. DOUGLASS. I have to return to you our thanks, Mr. President, for so kindly granting us this interview. We did not come here expecting to argue this question with your Excellency, but simply to state what were our views and wishes in the premises. If we were disposed to argue the question, and you would grant us permission, of course we would endeavor to controvert some of the positions you have assumed. . . .

THE PRESIDENT. I think you will find, so far as the South is concerned, that if you will all inculcate there the idea in connection with the one you urge, that the colored people can live and advance in civilization to

CHAPTER 11

THE PROBLEMS OF
RECONSTRUCTION:
ANDREW JOHNSON,
CONGRESS, AND
SOUTHERN
SUFFRAGE

better advantage elsewhere than crowded right down there in the
South, it would be better for them.[30]

Source 14 from Hans L. Trefousse, *Andrew Johnson, A Biography* (New York:
W. W. Norton, 1989), p. 233.

14. Christopher Memminger to Carl Schurz, April 26, 1871.[31]

I think you are right in saying that if we had originally adopted a different
course as to the Negroes, we would have escaped present difficulties [con-
gressional Reconstruction]. But if you will consider for a moment, you will
see that it was as impossible, as for us to have emancipated them before
the war. The then President [Johnson] held up before us the hope of a
"white man's government," and this led us to set aside Negro suffrage.

---

30. According to one of Johnson's secretaries, after the delegation left his office, Johnson
erupted, "Those d----d sons of b-----s thought they had me in a trap! I know that d----d Douglass;
he's just like any nigger, and he would sooner cut a white man's throat as not." See *The Papers
of Andrew Johnson,* Vol. X, p. 48, n. 3.
31. Memminger (1803–1888) was a former Confederate secretary of the treasury.

Source 15 from Morton Keller, *The Art and Politics of Thomas Nast* (New York: Oxford University Press, 1968), plate 55. Courtesy of the publisher.

15. Thomas Nast Cartoon Concerning Suffrage in the South, August 5, 1865.

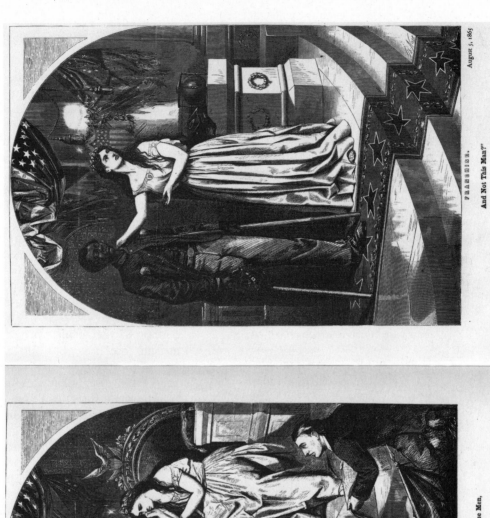

FRANCHISE.
And Not This Man?

August 5, 1865

[55]

PARDON.
Columbia.—"Shall I Trust These Men,

CHAPTER 11

THE PROBLEMS OF
RECONSTRUCTION:
ANDREW JOHNSON,
CONGRESS, AND
SOUTHERN
SUFFRAGE

 QUESTIONS TO CONSIDER

Remember that your task in this chapter is to determine why President Andrew Johnson chose the path he did with regard to who should vote in the postwar South—pardoning thousands of ex-Confederates whom he had specifically excepted from his general amnesty (Source 3) while simultaneously opposing African American suffrage.

Whenever historians find the central question they seek to answer too large or too complicated, they often break that question into smaller questions that they can answer. The central question in this chapter lends itself to such an approach. That question can be divided into two parts:

1. Why did President Johnson restore voting rights (through pardoning) to so many former Confederates whom he previously had excluded?
2. Why did President Johnson resist extending the suffrage to African Americans?

As you can readily see, once having answered these two smaller questions, you will be able to put the two answers together to answer the central question.

Sources 1 and 2 concern African Americans, but in decidedly different ways. Source 1 is Johnson's reply to a delegation of African American clergymen. How do the president's remarks reveal his attitude toward African Americans? What examples can you glean from his remarks that reveal this attitude? By inference, can the source be used to help explain why

Johnson resisted African Americans' voting? See also Source 13, an interview between Johnson and a delegation of African Americans. Here again Johnson reveals his attitude toward African Americans, but there are other possible motives as well. When the president refers to the "shedding of his [the black man's] blood," to what is he referring? How does he see relations between the African Americans and poor whites? Between African Americans and the South's plantation owners? Finally, what bodies did Johnson believe should establish qualifications to vote?

Source 2 also deals with African American suffrage, but again in a quite different way. Joseph Noxon, the letter writer, clearly believes that African American voters could be used to build a Republican party in the postwar South.[32] For this same argument, see also Sources 8 and 9. That Johnson did not take Noxon's advice (to enfranchise black voters to build a Republican party in the South) can be explained either by the fact that he disagreed with the political tactic or by the fact that he had other political maneuvers in mind. See the very important letters to Johnson from Duff Green (Source 7) and Francis Preston Blair (Source 10). What do you think Johnson's political ambitions were? How would his opposing African American suffrage aid those ambi-

32. Remember that the Union party Noxon referred to is the name the Republicans took for the 1864 electoral campaign.

tions? See also Sources 5 and 9. Source 4, Johnson's "Proclamation Establishing Government for North Carolina," says nothing about requiring the states formerly in rebellion to institute African American suffrage. What signal did that send to the white South? See Source 14.

In his interview with the delegation of former Confederates from South Carolina (Source 6), Johnson hints at another possible motive for opposing African American suffrage. Remember that the president had built his political career on the support of the South's yeoman white farmers and on his almost continual political warfare with the planter elite. How did Johnson believe African Americans would vote?

In his interview with George L. Stearns (Source 12), Johnson offers what he believed was a constitutional objection to his institution of black suffrage (see also Sources 5, 9, and 13).

Thus we have not one possible motive that explains Johnson's opposition to African Americans but at least five possible motives (prejudice against blacks, political ambition, desire to avoid race war, fear of how African Americans would vote, and constitutional reservations). How are you to establish which of these was the most important? By examining the evidence more closely (including Sources 11 and 12, two rather insincere statements in support of very limited black suffrage), try to determine when Johnson is being the most genuine and the least duplicitous. Make an effort to determine which of the letter writers (or receivers of letters from him) were closest to Johnson—people around whom he might more readily "let his hair down." Does any single motive stand out or underlie other motives?

As to the pardoning of former Confederates, begin with Source 3, Johnson's Amnesty Proclamation, in which he specifically excludes fourteen classes of people from general amnesty and pardon. What groups are excluded? Why do you suppose Johnson granted pardons to many in these excluded groups? Review the five possible motives regarding opposing African American suffrage. Do any of those possible motives help to explain why Johnson pardoned almost half of all individuals who requested that he do so? See also Sources 7 and 10.[33]

Now put the two questions back together. What motive or motives do you believe best explain President Andrew Johnson's decisions with regard to who should vote in the postwar South and, by implication, what Johnson believed the nature of politics and race relations in the postwar South should be?

---

33. With the exception of Jefferson Davis, ultimately all former Confederates either were pardoned or died before their cases were taken up (as in the case of Robert E. Lee). Davis was "restored to the full rights of citizenship" by joint congressional resolution on October 17, 1978.

CHAPTER 11

THE PROBLEMS OF
RECONSTRUCTION:
ANDREW JOHNSON,
CONGRESS, AND
SOUTHERN
SUFFRAGE

EPILOGUE

President Johnson's efforts to have all the states of the former Confederacy restored to their normal places in the Union before Congress reconvened in December 1865 turned out to be an almost complete disaster. The president's less-than-subtle signals to the South that he favored a mild reconstruction, would not insist on ratification of the Thirteenth Amendment or African American suffrage, and would oppose Radical Republicans' efforts to impose a harsher reconstruction caused the South to believe that it could act with impunity. Only North Carolina admitted that secession had been wrong; South Carolina refused to repudiate its Confederate debt; Mississippi did not ratify the Thirteenth Amendment.[34] When elections were held to send representatives back to the federal Congress, four former Confederate generals, five former colonels, and numerous former Confederate congressmen were elected. In Mississippi, the winning candidate for governor was elected before he had been pardoned. Reorganized southern state legislators passed a series of laws known as "black codes," differing little from the old slave codes. Violence against African Americans was widespread.

Northerners were appalled, sensing that the victory earned with an enormous amount of blood (approximately 360,000 Union dead) appeared to be slipping through their fingers. Union

34. The Mississippi legislature actually did ratify the Thirteenth Amendment—on March 16, 1995.

veterans running for office and editors and cartoonists such as Thomas Nast (Source 15) whipped northern voters into a frenzy of anti-South enthusiasm, and in the congressional elections of 1866 they returned a Congress in which Radical Republicans were strong enough to override Johnson's vetoes and pass a series of Reconstruction acts that were considerably harsher than Johnson's more lenient plans. The South was divided into five military districts in which commanders had power over civil governments, were instructed to register voters (especially African Americans) and to disfranchise disloyal whites, and were to organize state constitutional conventions to draft new state constitutions (which had to be acceptable to Congress). When states had written acceptable constitutions *and* had ratified the Fourteenth Amendment, then they could take their normal places in the Union.

President Johnson's futile efforts to block Radical Reconstruction, along with his attempt to remove Secretary of War Edwin Stanton from his cabinet, led to his impeachment by the House of Representatives. And although he was not removed from the presidency (the Senate failed by one vote to achieve the two-thirds necessary for removal), his effectiveness as a chief executive was completely eroded. Johnson's dream of winning the presidency in his own right in 1868 (whether through a Republican nomination or by fashioning a new political party of disaffected southerners and conservative northerners) completely collapsed. The Democrats, viewing Johnson as a political albatross, ignored him in favor of New York politician and former governor Horatio Seymour. For their part, the Republicans nominated the popular and malleable Ulysses Grant.

Although Radical Reconstruction was never as harsh as white southerners chose to remember it, white southerners nevertheless resisted even the mildest efforts to change their economic, social, and political institutions. Reconstruction state governments accomplished some worthwhile objectives (especially in establishing state-financed systems of public education in the South), but they were opposed by a majority of white southerners. And as northern fervor diminished and general amnesty proclamations restored the suffrage to all but a few former Confederates, gradually white southerners recaptured control of their state governments and (as they put it) "redeemed" their states.[35] The disputed presidential election of 1876 finally put an end to Reconstruction in the South.

Andrew Johnson returned to Tennessee in 1869 with the hope of rebuilding his smashed political career, but the remainder of his life was filled with sadness. His wife, Eliza, had become an invalid and required almost constant care. One of his sons, an alcoholic, committed suicide. He lost his bid to return to the U.S. Senate in 1869, was the subject of some vicious rumors (including alcoholism and marital infidelity), contracted cholera in 1873, and lost well over $70,000 in the financial panic of that year. At last elected to the Senate in 1875, he died of a stroke before taking office. His wife followed him six months later.

Increasingly impatient with the South's poor record regarding African American suffrage, in 1869 Congress passed, and a year later a sufficient number of states ratified, the Fifteenth Amendment to the Constitution, which prohibited denying the vote to individuals "on account of race, color, or previous condition of servitude." Ironically, the last state to ratify the Fifteenth Amendment was Johnson's home state of Tennessee, which did so on April 2, 1997.

---

35. Virginia and Tennessee were "redeemed" in 1869, North Carolina in 1870, Georgia in 1871, Texas in 1873, Alabama and Arkansas in 1874, and Mississippi in 1875. By the election of 1876, only South Carolina, Florida, and Louisiana remained under Radical rule.

TEXT CREDITS

CHAPTER ONE

Source 10: From Miguel Leon-Portilla, ed., *The Broken Spears: The Aztec Account of the Conquest of Mexico.* © 1962, 1990 by Beacon Press. Used by permission of Beacon Press, Boston.

CHAPTER TWO

Source 1: The Threat of Mrs. Anne Hutchinson. Reprinted by permission of the publisher from *The History of the Colony and Province of Massachusetts-Bay, Vol. 2* by Thomas Hutchinson. Cambridge, MA: Harvard University Press. Copyright © 1936 by the President and Fellows of Harvard College.

CHAPTER THREE

Sources 2, 4–6, 12, 15–17: Reprinted from Philip J. Greven, Jr., *Four Generations: Population, Land, and Family in Colonial Andover, Massachusetts.* Copyright © 1970 by Cornell University. Used by permission of the publisher, Cornell University.

Sources 3, 6, 8–10, 14, 17, 19: Excerpts from *The Minutemen and Their World* by Robert A. Gross. Copyright © 1976 by Robert A. Gross. New York: Hill and Wang, a division of Farrar, Strauss & Giroux, Inc.

Sources 7, 11, 13: Data from *The Evolution of American Society, 1700–1815* by James A. Henretta. Copyright © 1973 by D. C. Heath and Company. Reprinted by permission of the publisher.

Sources 18, 20–22: Reprinted from *The Journal of Interdisciplinary History,* VI (1976), 549, 557, 564, with permission of the editors of *The Journal of Interdisciplinary History* and The MIT Press, Cambridge, MA. © 1976 by the Massachusetts Institute of Technology and the editors of *The Journal of Interdisciplinary History.*

CHAPTER FOUR

Source 3: The Trial of Captain Thomas Preston. Reprinted by permission of the publisher from *The Legal Papers of John Adams,* Vol. III by John Adams. Cambridge, MA: Harvard University Press. Copyright © 1965 by the Massachusetts Historical Society.

Sources 4 and 5: from Anthony D. Darling, *Red Coat and Brown Bess,* Historical Arms Series, No. 12 (Bloomfield, Ontario). Courtesy of Museum Restoration Service, © 1970, 1981.

CHAPTER FIVE

Sources 10–11: Adapted from Billy G. Smith, *The "Lower Sort": Philadelphia's Laboring People, 1750–1800.* Copyright © 1990 by Cornell University. Used by permission of the publisher, Cornell University.

Sources 13–14: Excerpts from *Letters of Benjamin Rush,* Vol. II, edited by L. H. Butterfield, American Philosophical Society, 1951, pp. 644–645, 657–658. Reprinted by permission.

CHAPTER SIX

Map 1: Adapted from Grace Steele Woodward, *The Cherokees* (Norman: University of Oklahoma Press, 1963), pp. 206–207. Copyright © 1963 by the University of Oklahoma Press, Norman, Publishing Division of the University of Oklahoma. Reprinted by permission.

Map 2: From Duane H. Kind, ed., *The Cherokee Nation: A Troubled History* (Knoxville: University of Tennessee Press, 1979), p. 50.

CHAPTER EIGHT

Sources 1–16: From *Lay My Burden Down: A Folk History of Slavery* from Federal Writer's Project, by B. A. Botkin. Copyright 1945. Reprinted by permission.

Sources 22–23: Songs from S. Stuckey, "Through the Prism of Folklore," *Massachusetts Review,* 1968, reprinted by permission of the Editors of *Massachusetts Review.*

Source 24: From *Narrative of the Life of Frederick Douglass* by Frederick Douglass, pp. 1–3, 13–15, 36–37, 40–41, 44–46, and 74–75. Copyright 1963 by Doubleday. Reprinted by permission of Doubleday, a division of Bantam, Doubleday, Dell Publishing Group, Inc.

Source 25: Excerpts from *Incidents in the Life of a Slave Girl* by Linda Brent. Edited by Walter Magnes Teller. Introduction and Notes copyright © 1973 by Walter Magnes Teller, reprinted by permission of Harcourt Brace & Company.

CHAPTER TEN

Sources 4, 7, 9, 13: *The Collected Works of Abraham Lincoln,* Roy P. Basler, ed.. Copyright © 1953 by the Abraham Lincoln Association. Reprinted by permission of Rutgers University Press.

Source 20: Selections are reprinted from *The Sable Arm: Negro Troops in the Union Army, 1861–1865,* by Dudley Taylor Cornish, by permission of W. W. Norton & Company, Inc. Copyright © 1966 by W. W. Norton & Company, Inc. Copyright © 1956 by Dudley Taylor Cornish.

Sources 23–26, 29, 32, 34–36: From Robert F. Durden, *The Gray and the Black.* Reprinted by permission of the publisher, Louisiana State University Press.

Sources 27, 33: From *Letters of Warren Akin, Confederate Congressman.* Edited by Bell Irwin Wiley. Reprinted by permission of University of Georgia Press.